I0015309

Getting Started with Kubernetes

Second Edition

Harness the power of Kubernetes to manage Docker
deployments with ease

Jonathan Baier

BIRMINGHAM - MUMBAI

Getting Started with Kubernetes

Second Edition

Copyright © 2017 Packt Publishing

All rights reserved. No part of this book may be reproduced, stored in a retrieval system, or transmitted in any form or by any means, without the prior written permission of the publisher, except in the case of brief quotations embedded in critical articles or reviews.

Every effort has been made in the preparation of this book to ensure the accuracy of the information presented. However, the information contained in this book is sold without warranty, either express or implied. Neither the author, nor Packt Publishing, and its dealers and distributors will be held liable for any damages caused or alleged to be caused directly or indirectly by this book.

Packt Publishing has endeavored to provide trademark information about all of the companies and products mentioned in this book by the appropriate use of capitals. However, Packt Publishing cannot guarantee the accuracy of this information.

First published: December 2015

Second edition: May 2017

Production reference: 1300517

Published by Packt Publishing Ltd.
Livery Place
35 Livery Street
Birmingham
B3 2PB, UK.

ISBN 978-1-78728-336-7

www.packtpub.com

Credits

Author
Jonathan Baier

Reviewer
Jay Payne

Commissioning Editor
Pratik Shah

Acquisition Editor
Prachi Bisht

Content Development Editor
Monika Sangwan

Technical Editor
Devesh Chugh

Copy Editor
Tom Jacob

Project Coordinator
Kinjal Bari

Proofreader
Safis Editing

Indexer
Mariammal Chettiyar

Graphics
Kirk D'Penha

Production Coordinator
Aparna Bhagat

About the Author

Jonathan Baier is an emerging technology leader living in Brooklyn, New York. He has had a passion for technology since an early age. When he was 14 years old, he was so interested in the family computer (an IBM PCjr) that he pored over the several hundred pages of BASIC and DOS manuals. Then, he taught himself to code a very poorly-written version of Tic-Tac-Toe. During his teen years, he started a computer support business. Since then, he has dabbled in entrepreneurship several times throughout his life.

He currently enjoys working for Moody's as Vice President of Global Cloud Engineering. He has over a decade of experience delivering technology strategies and solutions for both public and private sector businesses of all sizes. He has a breadth of experience working with a wide variety of technologies and he enjoys helping organizations and management embrace new technology to transform their businesses.

Working in the areas of architecture, containerization, and cloud security, he has created strategic roadmaps to guide and help mature the overall IT capabilities of various enterprises. Furthermore, he has helped organizations of various sizes build and implement their cloud strategy and solve the many challenges that arise when "designs on paper" meet reality.

Acknowledgement

I'd like to give a tremendous thank you to my wonderful wife, Tomoko, and my playful son, Nikko. You both gave me incredible support and motivation during the writing process for both editions of this book. There were many early morning, long weekend and late night writing sessions that I could not have done without you both. You're smiles move mountains I could not on my own. You are my True north and guiding light in the storm.

I'd also like to give a special thanks to all my colleagues and friends at Cloud Technology Partners. Many of whom provided the encouragement and support for the original inception of this book. I'd like to especially thank Mike Kavis, David Linthicum, Alan Zall, Lisa Noon, Charles Radi and also the amazing CTP marketing team (Brad Young, Shannon Croy, and Nicole Givin) for guiding me along the way!

About the Reviewer

Jay Payne has been a database administrator 5 at Rackspace for over 10 years, working on the design, development, implementation, and operation of storage systems.

Previously, Jay worked on billing and support systems for hosting companies. For the last 20 years, he has primarily focused on the data life cycle from database architecture, administration, operations, reporting, disaster recovery, and compliance. He has domain experience in hosting, finance, billing, and customer support industries.

www.PacktPub.com

For support files and downloads related to your book, please visit www.PacktPub.com.

Did you know that Packt offers eBook versions of every book published, with PDF and ePub files available? You can upgrade to the eBook version at www.PacktPub.com and as a print book customer, you are entitled to a discount on the eBook copy. Get in touch with us at service@packtpub.com for more details.

At www.PacktPub.com, you can also read a collection of free technical articles, sign up for a range of free newsletters and receive exclusive discounts and offers on Packt books and eBooks.

https://www.packtpub.com/mapt

Get the most in-demand software skills with Mapt. Mapt gives you full access to all Packt books and video courses, as well as industry-leading tools to help you plan your personal development and advance your career.

Why subscribe?

- Fully searchable across every book published by Packt
- Copy and paste, print, and bookmark content
- On demand and accessible via a web browser

Customer Feedback

Thanks for purchasing this Packt book. At Packt, quality is at the heart of our editorial process. To help us improve, please leave us an honest review on this book's Amazon page at `https://www.amazon.com/dp/1787283364`.

If you'd like to join our team of regular reviewers, you can e-mail us at `customerreviews@packtpub.com`. We award our regular reviewers with free eBooks and videos in exchange for their valuable feedback. Help us be relentless in improving our products!

Table of Contents

Preface   1

Chapter 1: Introduction to Kubernetes   9

  A brief overview of containers   10
    What is a container?   10
  Why are containers so cool?   13
    The advantages of Continuous Integration/Continuous Deployment   13
    Resource utilization   14
  Microservices and orchestration   14
    Future challenges   15
  The birth of Kubernetes   15
  Our first cluster   16
    Kubernetes UI   22
    Grafana   24
    Command line   26
    Services running on the master   27
    Services running on the minions   30
    Tear down cluster   32
  Working with other providers   32
    Resetting the cluster   36
    Modifying kube-up parameters   37
    Alternatives to kube-up.sh   37
    Starting from scratch   38
      Cluster setup   38
      Installing Kubernetes components (kubelet and kubeadm)   39
      Setting up a Master   40
      Joining nodes   40
      Networking   41
      Joining the cluster   42
  Summary   42
    References   43

Chapter 2: Pods, Services, Replication Controllers, and Labels   45

  The architecture   45
    Master   47
    Node (formerly minions)   47
  Core constructs   48

Pods	48
Pod example	48
Labels	50
The container's afterlife	50
Services	51
Replication controllers and replica sets	52
Our first Kubernetes application	52
More on labels	59
Replica sets	62
Health checks	63
TCP checks	68
Life cycle hooks or graceful shutdown	69
Application scheduling	71
Scheduling example	71
Summary	75
References	75
Chapter 3: Networking, Load Balancers, and Ingress	77
Kubernetes networking	77
Networking options	78
Networking comparisons	79
Docker	79
Docker user-defined networks	79
Weave	80
Flannel	80
Project Calico	81
Canal	81
Balanced design	81
Advanced services	82
External services	84
Internal services	85
Custom load balancing	86
Cross-node proxy	89
Custom ports	90
Multiple ports	91
Ingress	92
Migrations, multicluster, and more	98
Custom addressing	100
Service discovery	101
DNS	101
Multitenancy	102

Limits	103
A note on resource usage	107
Summary	107
References	107
Chapter 4: Updates, Gradual Rollouts, and Autoscaling	109
Example set up	110
Scaling up	111
Smooth updates	112
Testing, releases, and cutovers	114
Application autoscaling	118
Scaling a cluster	121
Autoscaling	121
Scaling up the cluster on GCE	122
Scaling up the cluster on AWS	125
Scaling manually	127
Summary	127
Chapter 5: Deployments, Jobs, and DaemonSets	129
Deployments	129
Scaling	131
Updates and rollouts	132
History and rollbacks	135
Autoscaling	137
Jobs	139
Other types of jobs	141
Parallel jobs	142
Scheduled jobs	142
DaemonSets	143
Node selection	144
Summary	147
References	147
Chapter 6: Storage and Running Stateful Applications	149
Persistent storage	149
Temporary disks	150
Cloud volumes	151
GCE persistent disks	151
AWS Elastic Block Store	157
Other storage options	158
PersistentVolumes and StorageClasses	158
StatefulSets	159

A stateful example   160
Summary   166
References   166
Chapter 7: Continuous Delivery   167
Integrating with continuous delivery pipeline   167
Gulp.js   168
Prerequisites   168
Gulp build example   168
Kubernetes plugin for Jenkins   172
Prerequisites   172
Installing plugins   173
Configuring the Kubernetes plugin   176
Bonus fun   181
Summary   181
Chapter 8: Monitoring and Logging   183
Monitoring operations   183
Built-in monitoring   184
Exploring Heapster   186
Customizing our dashboards   189
FluentD and Google Cloud Logging   194
FluentD   195
Maturing our monitoring operations   196
GCE (StackDriver)   196
Sign-up for GCE monitoring   196
Alerts   197
Beyond system monitoring with Sysdig   198
Sysdig Cloud   198
Detailed views   200
Topology views   200
Metrics   203
Alerting   203
The sysdig command line   205
The csysdig command-line UI   206
Prometheus   208
Summary   209
References   209
Chapter 9: Cluster Federation   211
Introduction to federation   211
Setting up federation   212
Contexts   212

New clusters for federation 213
Initializing the federation control plane 214
Adding clusters to the federation system 215
Federated resources 215
Federated configurations 218
Other federated resources 221
True multi-cloud 222
Summary 222

Chapter 10: Container Security 223

Basics of container security 223
Keeping containers contained 224
Resource exhaustion and orchestration security 224
Image repositories 225
Continuous vulnerability scanning 225
Image signing and verification 226
Kubernetes cluster security 227
Secure API calls 228
Secure node communication 228
Authorization and authentication plugins 229
Admission controllers 229
Pod security policies and context 230
Enabling beta APIs 230
Creating a PodSecurityPolicy 232
Creating a pod with a PodSecurityContext 236
Clean up 237
Additional considerations 237
Securing sensitive application data (secrets) 238
Summary 239
References 239

Chapter 11: Extending Kubernetes with OCP, CoreOS, and Tectonic 241

The importance of standards 241
The Open Container Initiative 242
Cloud Native Computing Foundation 243
Standard container specification 243
CoreOS 245
rkt 247
etcd 247
Kubernetes with CoreOS 247
Tectonic 249
Dashboard highlights 250

Summary	254
References	255
Chapter 12: Towards Production Ready	257
Ready for production	257
Ready, set, go	259
Third-party companies	259
Private registries	260
Google Container Engine	260
Azure Container Service	261
ClusterHQ	261
Portworx	261
Shippable	262
Twistlock	262
AquaSec	262
Mesosphere (Kubernetes on Mesos)	263
Deis	263
OpenShift	263
Where to learn more?	264
Summary	264
Index	265

Preface

This book is a guide to getting started with Kubernetes and overall container management. We will walk you through the features and functions of Kubernetes and show how it fits into an overall operations strategy. You'll learn what hurdles lurk in moving a container off the developer's laptop and managing them at a larger scale. You'll also see how Kubernetes is the perfect tool to help you face these challenges with confidence.

What this book covers

Chapter 1, *Introduction to Kubernetes*, is a brief overview of containers and the how, what, and why of Kubernetes orchestration, exploring how it impacts your business goals and everyday operations.

Chapter 2, *Pods, Services, Replication Controllers, and Labels*, uses a few simple examples to explore core Kubernetes constructs, namely pods, services, replication controllers, replica sets, and labels. Basic operations including health checks and scheduling will also be covered.

Chapter 3, *Networking, Load Balancers, and Ingress*, covers cluster networking for Kubernetes and the Kubernetes proxy. It also takes a deeper dive into services, finishing up, it shows a brief overview of some higher level isolation features for mutli-tenancy.

Chapter 4, *Updates, Gradual Rollouts, and Autoscaling*, is a quick look at how to roll out updates and new features with minimal disruption to uptime. We will also look at scaling for applications and the Kubernetes cluster.

Chapter 5, *Deployments, Jobs, and DaemonSets*, covers both long-running application deployments as well as short-lived jobs. We will also look at using DaemonSets to run containers on all or subsets of nodes in the cluster.

Chapter 6, *Storage and Running Stateful Applications*, covers storage concerns and persistent data across pods and the container life cycle. We will also look at new constructs for working with stateful application in Kubernetes.

Chapter 7, *Continuous Delivery*, explains how to integrate Kubernetes into your continuous delivery pipeline. We will see how to use a k8s cluster with Gulp.js and Jenkins as well.

Chapter 8, *Monitoring and Logging*, teaches how to use and customize built-in and third-party monitoring tools on your Kubernetes cluster. We will look at built-in logging and monitoring, the Google Cloud Monitoring/Logging service, and Sysdig.

Chapter 9, *Cluster Federation*, enables you to try out the new federation capabilities and explains how to use them to manage multiple clusters across cloud providers. We will also cover the federated version of the core constructs from previous chapters.

Chapter 10, *Container Security*, teaches the basics of container security from the container runtime level to the host itself. It also explains how to apply these concepts to running containers and some of the security concerns and practices that relate specifically to running Kubernetes.

Chapter 11, *Extending Kubernetes with OCP, CoreOS, and Tectonic*, discovers how open standards benefit the entire container ecosystem. We'll look at a few of the prominent standards organizations and cover CoreOS and Tectonic, exploring their advantages as a host OS and enterprise platform.

Chapter 12, *Towards Production Ready*, the final chapter, shows some of the helpful tools and third-party projects that are available and where you can go to get more help.

What you need for this book

This book will cover downloading and running the Kubernetes project. You'll need access to a Linux system (VirtualBox will work if you are on Windows) and some familiarity with the command shell.

Additionally, you should have a Google Cloud Platform account. You can sign up for a free trial here:

```
https://cloud.google.com/
```

Also, an AWS account is necessary for a few sections of the book. You can sign up for a free trial here:

```
https://aws.amazon.com/
```

Who this book is for

Whether you're heads down in development, neck deep in operations, or looking forward as an executive, Kubernetes and this book are for you. *Getting Started with Kubernetes* will help you understand how to move your container applications into production with best practices and step by step walk-throughs tied to a real-world operational strategy. You'll learn how Kubernetes fits into your everyday operations, which can help you prepare for production-ready container application stacks.

Having some familiarity with Docker containers, general software developments, and operations at a high-level will be helpful.

Conventions

In this book, you will find a number of text styles that distinguish between different kinds of information. Here are some examples of these styles and an explanation of their meaning.

Code words in text, folder names, filenames, file extensions, and pathnames are shown as follows: "Do a simple `curl` command to the pod IP."

URLs are shown as follows:

```
http://swagger.io/
```

If we wish you to replace a portion of the URL with your own values it will be shown like this:

```
https://<your master ip>/swagger-ui/
```

Resource definition files and other code blocks are set as follows:

```
apiVersion: v1
kind: Pod
metadata:
  name: node-js-pod
spec:
  containers:
  - name: node-js-pod
    image: bitnami/apache:latest
    ports:
    - containerPort: 80
```

When we wish you to replace a portion of the listing with your own value, the relevant lines or items are set in bold between less than and greater than symbols:

```
  subsets:
  - addresses:
    - IP: <X.X.X.X>
    ports:
      - name: http
        port: 80
        protocol: TCP
```

Any command-line input or output is written as follows:

```
$ kubectl get pods
```

New terms and **important words** are shown in bold. Words that you see on the screen, for example, in menus or dialog boxes, appear in the text like this: "Clicking the **Add New** button moves you to the next screen."

There are several areas where the text refers to key-value pairs or to input dialogs on the screen. In these case the **key** or **input label** will be shown in bold and the *value* will be shown in bold italics. For example: "In the box labelled **Timeout** enter *5s*."

Warnings or important notes appear in a box like this.

Tips and tricks appear like this.

Reader feedback

Feedback from our readers is always welcome. Let us know what you think about this book-what you liked or disliked. Reader feedback is important for us as it helps us develop titles that you will really get the most out of.

To send us general feedback, simply e-mail feedback@packtpub.com, and mention the book's title in the subject of your message.

If there is a topic that you have expertise in and you are interested in either writing or contributing to a book, see our author guide at www.packtpub.com/authors.

Customer support

Now that you are the proud owner of a Packt book, we have a number of things to help you to get the most from your purchase.

Downloading the example code

You can download the example code files for this book from your account at `http://www.packtpub.com`. If you purchased this book elsewhere, you can visit `http://www.packtpub.com/support` and register to have the files e-mailed directly to you.

You can download the code files by following these steps:

1. Log in or register to our website using your e-mail address and password.
2. Hover the mouse pointer on the **SUPPORT** tab at the top.
3. Click on **Code Downloads & Errata**.
4. Enter the name of the book in the **Search** box.
5. Select the book for which you're looking to download the code files.
6. Choose from the drop-down menu where you purchased this book from.
7. Click on **Code Download**.

Once the file is downloaded, please make sure that you unzip or extract the folder using the latest version of:

- WinRAR / 7-Zip for Windows
- Zipeg / iZip / UnRarX for Mac
- 7-Zip / PeaZip for Linux

The code bundle for the book is also hosted on GitHub at `https://github.com/PacktPublishing/Getting-Started-with-Kubernetes-Second-Edition`. We also have other code bundles from our rich catalog of books and videos available at `https://github.com/PacktPublishing/`. Check them out!

Downloading the color images of this book

We also provide you with a PDF file that has color images of the screenshots/diagrams used in this book. The color images will help you better understand the changes in the output. You can download this file from

`https://www.packtpub.com/sites/default/files/downloads/GettingStartedwithKub ernetesSecondEdition_ColorImages.pdf`.

Errata

Although we have taken every care to ensure the accuracy of our content, mistakes do happen. If you find a mistake in one of our books-maybe a mistake in the text or the code-we would be grateful if you could report this to us. By doing so, you can save other readers from frustration and help us improve subsequent versions of this book. If you find any errata, please report them by visiting `http://www.packtpub.com/submit-errata`, selecting your book, clicking on the **Errata Submission Form** link, and entering the details of your errata. Once your errata are verified, your submission will be accepted and the errata will be uploaded to our website or added to any list of existing errata under the Errata section of that title.

To view the previously submitted errata, go to `https://www.packtpub.com/books/conten t/support`and enter the name of the book in the search field. The required information will appear under the **Errata** section.

Piracy

Piracy of copyrighted material on the Internet is an ongoing problem across all media. At Packt, we take the protection of our copyright and licenses very seriously. If you come across any illegal copies of our works in any form on the Internet, please provide us with the location address or website name immediately so that we can pursue a remedy.

Please contact us at `copyright@packtpub.com` with a link to the suspected pirated material.

We appreciate your help in protecting our authors and our ability to bring you valuable content.

Questions

If you have a problem with any aspect of this book, you can contact us at `questions@packtpub.com`, and we will do our best to address the problem.

1
Introduction to Kubernetes

In this book, we will help you learn to build and manage Kubernetes clusters. You will be given some of the basic container concepts and the operational context, wherever possible. Throughout the book, you'll be given examples that you can apply as you progress through the book. By the end of the book, you should have a solid foundation and even dabble in some of the more advance topics such as federation and security.

This chapter will give a brief overview of containers and how they work as well as why management and orchestration is important to your business and/or project team. The chapter will also give a brief overview of how Kubernetes orchestration can enhance our container management strategy and how we can get a basic Kubernetes cluster up, running, and ready for container deployments.

This chapter will include the following topics:

- Introducing container operations and management
- Why container management is important?
- The advantages of Kubernetes
- Downloading the latest Kubernetes
- Installing and starting up a new Kubernetes cluster
- The components of a Kubernetes cluster

A brief overview of containers

Over the past three years, **containers** have grown in popularity like wildfire. You would be hard-pressed to attend an IT conference without finding popular sessions on Docker or containers in general.

Docker lies at the heart of the mass adoption and the excitement in the container space. As Malcom McLean revolutionized the physical shipping world in the 1950s by creating a standardized shipping container, which is used today for everything from ice cube trays to automobiles (you can refer to more details about this in point 1 in the *References* section at the end of the chapter), Linux containers are revolutionizing the software development world by making application environments portable and consistent across the infrastructure landscape. As an organization, Docker has taken the existing container technology to a new level by making it easy to implement and replicate across environments and providers.

What is a container?

At the core of container technology are **control groups** (**cgroups**) and namespaces. Additionally, Docker uses union filesystems for added benefits to the container development process.

Cgroups work by allowing the host to share and also limit the resources each process or container can consume. This is important for both, resource utilization and security, as it prevents **denial-of-service attacks** on the host's hardware resources. Several containers can share CPU and memory while staying within the predefined constraints.

Namespaces offer another form of isolation for process interaction within operating systems. Namespaces limit the visibility a process has on other processes, networking, filesystems, and user ID components. Container processes are limited to see only what is in the same namespace. Processes from containers or the host processes are not directly accessible from within this container process. Additionally, Docker gives each container its own networking stack that protects the sockets and interfaces in a similar fashion.

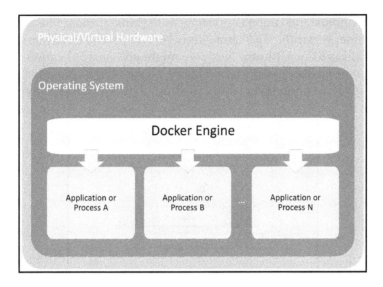

Composition of a container

Union filesystems are also a key advantage of using Docker containers. Containers run from an image. Much like an image in the VM or Cloud world, it represents state at a particular point in time. Container images snapshot the filesystem, but tend to be much smaller than a VM. The container shares the host kernel and generally runs a much smaller set of processes, so the filesystem and boot strap period tend to be much smaller. Though those constraints are not strictly enforced. Second, the union filesystem allows for efficient storage, download, and execution of these images.

The easiest way to understand union filesystems is to think of them like a layer cake with each layer baked independently. The Linux kernel is our base layer; then, we might add an OS such as **Red Hat Linux** or **Ubuntu**. Next, we might add an application such as **Nginx** or **Apache**. Every change creates a new layer. Finally, as you make changes and new layers are added, you'll always have a top layer (think frosting) that is a writable layer.

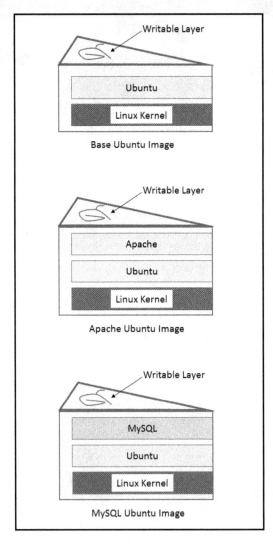

Layered filesystem

What makes this truly efficient is that Docker caches the layers the first time we build them. So, let's say that we have an image with Ubuntu and then add Apache and build the image. Next, we build MySQL with Ubuntu as the base. The second build will be much faster because the Ubuntu layer is already cached. Essentially, our chocolate and vanilla layers, from the preceding *Layered filesystem* figure, are already baked. We simply need to bake the pistachio (MySQL) layer, assemble, and add the icing (the writable layer).

Why are containers so cool?

Containers on their own are not a new technology and have in fact been around for many years. What truly sets Docker apart is the tooling and ease of use they have brought to the community. Modern development practices promote the use of Continuous Integration and Continuous Deployment. These techniques, when done right, can have a profound impact on your software product quality.

The advantages of Continuous Integration/Continuous Deployment

ThoughtWorks defines **Continuous Integration** as a development practice that requires developers to integrate code into a shared repository several times a day. By having a continuous process of building and deploying code, organizations are able to instill quality control and testing as part of the everyday work cycle. The result is that updates and bug fixes happen much faster and the overall quality improves.

However, there has always been a challenge in creating development environments that match that of testing and production. Often inconsistencies in these environments make it difficult to gain the full advantage of continuous delivery.

Using Docker, developers are now able to have truly portable deployments. Containers that are deployed on a developer's laptop are easily deployed on an in-house staging server. They are then easily transferred to the production server running in the cloud. This is because Docker builds containers up with build files that specify parent layers. One advantage of this is that it becomes very easy to ensure OS, package, and application versions are the same across development, staging, and production environments.

Because all the dependencies are packaged into the layer, the same host server can have multiple containers running a variety of OS or package versions. Further, we can have various languages and frameworks on the same host server without the typical dependency clashes we would get in a **virtual machine** (**VM**) with a single operating system.

Resource utilization

The well-defined isolation and layer filesystem also make containers ideal for running systems with a very small footprint and domain-specific purposes. A streamlined deployment and release process means we can deploy quickly and often. As such, many companies have reduced their deployment time from weeks or months to days and hours in some cases. This development life cycle lends itself extremely well to small, targeted teams working on small chunks of a larger application.

Microservices and orchestration

As we break down an application into very specific domains, we need a uniform way to communicate between all the various pieces and domains. Web services have served this purpose for years, but the added isolation and granular focus that containers bring have paved a way for **microservices**.

The definition for microservices can be a bit nebulous, but a definition from Martin Fowler, a respected author and speaker on software development, says this (you can refer to more details about this in point 2 in the *References* section at the end of the chapter):

> *In short, the microservice architectural style is an approach to developing a single application as a suite of small services, each running in its own process and communicating with lightweight mechanisms, often an HTTP resource API. These services are built around business capabilities and independently deployable by fully automated deployment machinery. There is a bare minimum of centralized management of these services, which may be written in different programming languages and use different data storage technologies.*

As the pivot to containerization and as microservices evolve in an organization, they will soon need a strategy to maintain many containers and microservices. Some organizations will have hundreds or even thousands of containers running in the years ahead.

Future challenges

Life cycle processes alone are an important piece of operations and management. How will we automatically recover when a container fails? Which upstream services are affected by such an outage? How will we patch our applications with minimal downtime? How will we scale up our containers and services as our traffic grows?

Networking and processing are also important concerns. Some processes are part of the same service and may benefit from the proximity to the network. Databases, for example, may send large amounts of data to a particular microservice for processing. How will we place containers near each other in our cluster? Is there common data that needs to be accessed? How will new services be discovered and made available to other systems?

Resource utilization is also a key. The small footprint of containers means that we can optimize our infrastructure for greater utilization. Extending the savings started in the elastic cloud will take us even further toward minimizing wasted hardware. How will we schedule workloads most efficiently? How will we ensure that our important applications always have the right resources? How can we run less important workloads on spare capacity?

Finally, portability is a key factor in moving many organizations to containerization. Docker makes it very easy to deploy a standard container across various operating systems, cloud providers, and on-premise hardware or even developer laptops. However, we still need tooling to move containers around. How will we move containers between different nodes on our cluster? How will we roll out updates with minimal disruption? What process do we use to perform blue-green deployments or canary releases?

Whether you are starting to build out individual microservices and separating concerns into isolated containers or if you simply want to take full advantage of the portability and immutability in your application development, the need for management and orchestration becomes clear. This is where orchestration tools such as Kubernetes offer the biggest value.

The birth of Kubernetes

Kubernetes (K8s) is an open source project that was released by Google in June, 2014. Google released the project as part of an effort to share their own infrastructure and technology advantage with the community at large.

Google launches 2 billion containers a week in their infrastructure and has been using container technology for over a decade. Originally, they were building a system named **Borg**, now called **Omega**, to schedule their vast quantities of workloads across their ever-expanding data center footprint. They took many of the lessons they learned over the years and rewrote their existing data center management tool for wide adoption by the rest of the world. The result was the Kubernetes open-source project (you can refer to more details about this in point 3 in the *References* section at the end of the chapter).

Since its initial release in 2014, K8s has undergone rapid development with contributions all across the open-source community, including Red Hat, VMware, and Canonical. The 1.0 release of Kubernetes went live in July, 2015. Since then, it's been a fast-paced evolution of the project with wide support from one of the largest open-source communities on GitHub today. We'll be covering version 1.5 throughout the book. K8s gives organizations a tool to deal with some of the major operations and management concerns. We will explore how Kubernetes helps deal with resource utilization, high availability, updates, patching, networking, service discovery, monitoring, and logging.

Our first cluster

Kubernetes is supported on a variety of platforms and OSes. For the examples in this book, I used an Ubuntu 16.04 Linux VirtualBox for my client and **Google Compute Engine** (**GCE**) with Debian for the cluster itself. We will also take a brief look at a cluster running on **Amazon Web Services** (**AWS**) with Ubuntu.

To save some money, both GCP and AWS offer free tiers and trial offers for their cloud infrastructure. It's worth using these free trials for your Kubernetes learning, if possible.

Most of the concepts and examples in this book should work on any installation of a Kubernetes cluster. To get more information on other platform setups, refer to the Kubernetes getting started page on the following GitHub link:
http://kubernetes.io/docs/getting-started-guides/

First, let's make sure that our environment is properly set up before we install Kubernetes. Start by updating packages:

```
$ sudo apt-get update
```

Install Python and curl if they are not present:

```
$ sudo apt-get install python
$ sudo apt-get install curl
```

Install the **gcloud** SDK:

```
$ curl https://sdk.cloud.google.com | bash
```

We will need to start a new shell before `gcloud` is on our path.

Configure your **Google Cloud Platform** (**GCP**) account information. This should automatically open a browser from where we can log in to our Google Cloud account and authorize the SDK:

```
$ gcloud auth login
```

If you have problems with login or want to use another browser, you can optionally use the `--no-launch-browser` command. Copy and paste the URL to the machine and/or browser of your choice. Log in with your Google Cloud credentials and click **Allow** on the permissions page. Finally, you should receive an authorization code that you can copy and paste back into the shell where the prompt is waiting.

A default project should be set, but we can verify this with the following command:

```
$ gcloud config list project
```

We can modify this and set a new default project with this command. Make sure to use **project ID** and not **project name**, as follows:

```
$ gcloud config set project <PROJECT ID>
```

We can find our project ID in the console at the following URL:
`https://console.developers.google.com/project`
Alternatively, we can list active projects:
`$ gcloud alpha projects list`

Now that we have our environment set up, installing the latest Kubernetes version is done in a single step, as follows:

```
$ curl -sS https://get.k8s.io | bash
```

It may take a minute or two to download Kubernetes depending on your connection speed. Earlier versions would automatically call the `kube-up.sh` script and start building our cluster. In version 1.5, we will need to call the `kube-up.sh` script ourselves to launch the cluster. By default, it will use the Google Cloud and GCE:

```
$ kubernetes/cluster/kube-up.sh
```

After you run the `kube-up.sh` script, we will see quite a few lines roll past. Let's take a look at them one section at a time:

```
... Starting cluster in us-central1-b using provider gce
... calling verify-prereqs

All components are up to date.

All components are up to date.

All components are up to date.
```

GCE prerequisite check

 If your `gcloud` components are not up to date, you may be prompted to update them.

The preceding image, *GCE prerequisite check*, shows the checks for prerequisites as well as making sure that all components are up to date. This is specific to each provider. In the case of GCE, it will verify that the SDK is installed and that all components are up to date. If not, you will see a prompt at this point to install or update:

```
... calling kube-up
Your active configuration is: [default]

Project: dynamic-nomad-152102
Zone: us-central1-b
gs://kubernetes-staging-549d6b8d9c/kubernetes-devel/
+++ Staging server tars to Google Storage: gs://kubernetes-staging-549d6b8d9c/kub
ernetes-devel
+++ kubernetes-server-linux-amd64.tar.gz uploaded (sha1 = 5df19e3745bbc8c7d1a5bf6
d61d9e1b0d189db64)
+++ kubernetes-salt.tar.gz uploaded (sha1 = 95e855d893e4549b935aed8736f3a2372ae7c
cd3)
+++ kubernetes-manifests.tar.gz uploaded (sha1 = e9c52530a14612c91f45e017743925a0
dba6dcc8)
INSTANCE_GROUPS=
NODE_NAMES=
```

Upload cluster packages

Now the script is turning up the cluster. Again, this is specific to the provider. For GCE, it first checks to make sure that the SDK is configured for a default **project** and **zone**. If they are set, you'll see those in the output.

Next, it uploads the server binaries to Google Cloud storage, as seen in the **Creating gs:...** lines:

```
Looking for already existing resources
Starting master and configuring firewalls
Created [https://www.googleapis.com/compute/v1/projects/dynamic-nomad-152102/zon
es/us-central1-b/disks/kubernetes-master-pd].
NAME                   ZONE           SIZE_GB  TYPE    STATUS
kubernetes-master-pd   us-central1-b  20       pd-ssd  READY

New disks are unformatted. You must format and mount a disk before it
can be used. You can find instructions on how to do this at:

https://cloud.google.com/compute/docs/disks/add-persistent-disk#formatting

Created [https://www.googleapis.com/compute/v1/projects/dynamic-nomad-152102/glo
bal/firewalls/kubernetes-master-https].
NAME                    NETWORK  SRC_RANGES  RULES    SRC_TAGS  TARGET_TAGS
kubernetes-master-https default  0.0.0.0/0   tcp:443            kubernetes-mast
er
Created [https://www.googleapis.com/compute/v1/projects/dynamic-nomad-152102/reg
ions/us-central1/addresses/kubernetes-master-ip].
Generating certs for alternate-names: IP:23.251.158.223,IP:10.0.0.1,DNS:kubernet
es,DNS:kubernetes.default,DNS:kubernetes.default.svc,DNS:kubernetes.default.svc.
cluster.local,DNS:kubernetes-master
```

Master creation

It then checks for any pieces of a cluster already running. Then, we finally start creating the cluster. In the output in the preceding figure *Master creation*, we see it creating the **master** server, IP address, and appropriate firewall configurations for the cluster:

```
+++ Logging using Fluentd to gcp
WARNING: You have selected a disk size of under [200GB]. This may result in poor
 I/O performance. For more information, see: https://developers.google.com/compu
te/docs/disks#pdperformance.
Created [https://www.googleapis.com/compute/v1/projects/dynamic-nomad-152102/glo
bal/firewalls/kubernetes-minion-all].
NAME                     NETWORK   SRC_RANGES      RULES                SRC_TAG
S   TARGET_TAGS
kubernetes-minion-all   default   10.244.0.0/14  tcp,udp,icmp,esp,ah,sctp
    kubernetes-minion
Created [https://www.googleapis.com/compute/v1/projects/dynamic-nomad-152102/zon
es/us-central1-b/instances/kubernetes-master].
NAME                ZONE           MACHINE_TYPE    PREEMPTIBLE   INTERNAL_IP  EXTER
NAL_IP     STATUS
kubernetes-master  us-central1-b  n1-standard-1                 10.128.0.2   23.25
1.158.223  RUNNING
Creating minions.
Attempt 1 to create kubernetes-minion-template
WARNING: You have selected a disk size of under [200GB]. This may result in poor
 I/O performance. For more information, see: https://developers.google.com/compu
te/docs/disks#pdperformance.
Created [https://www.googleapis.com/compute/v1/projects/dynamic-nomad-152102/glo
bal/instanceTemplates/kubernetes-minion-template].
NAME                        MACHINE_TYPE    PREEMPTIBLE   CREATION_TIMESTAMP
kubernetes-minion-template  n1-standard-2                 2016-12-10T04:25:37.527-
08:00
Created [https://www.googleapis.com/compute/v1/projects/dynamic-nomad-152102/zon
es/us-central1-b/instanceGroupManagers/kubernetes-minion-group].
NAME                    LOCATION       SCOPE  BASE_INSTANCE_NAME       SIZE  TA
RGET_SIZE  INSTANCE_TEMPLATE          AUTOSCALED
kubernetes-minion-group  us-central1-b  zone   kubernetes-minion-group  0     3
            kubernetes-minion-template  no
Waiting for group to become stable, current operations: creating: 3
Waiting for group to become stable, current operations: creating: 3
Waiting for group to become stable, current operations: creating: 1
Group is stable
```

Minion creation

Finally, it creates the **minions** or **nodes** for our cluster. This is where our container workloads will actually run. It will continually loop and wait while all the minions start up. By default, the cluster will have four nodes (minions), but K8s supports having more than 1000 (and soon beyond). We will come back to scaling the nodes later on in the book.

```
INSTANCE_GROUPS=kubernetes-minion-group
NODE_NAMES=kubernetes-minion-group-41wq kubernetes-minion-group-7vh1 kubernetes-
minion-group-oyos
Trying to find master named 'kubernetes-master'
Looking for address 'kubernetes-master-ip'
Using master: kubernetes-master (external IP: 23.251.158.223)
Waiting up to 300 seconds for cluster initialization.

  This will continually check to see if the API for kubernetes is reachable.
  This may time out if there was some uncaught error during start up.

.................Kubernetes cluster created.
cluster "dynamic-nomad-152102_kubernetes" set.
user "dynamic-nomad-152102_kubernetes" set.
context "dynamic-nomad-152102_kubernetes" set.
switched to context "dynamic-nomad-152102_kubernetes".
user "dynamic-nomad-152102_kubernetes-basic-auth" set.
Wrote config for dynamic-nomad-152102_kubernetes to /home/grizz/.kube/config

Kubernetes cluster is running.  The master is running at:

  https://23.251.158.223

The user name and password to use is located in /home/grizz/.kube/config.
```

Cluster completion

Now that everything is created, the cluster is initialized and started. Assuming that everything goes well, we will get an IP address for the master. Also, note that configuration along with the cluster management credentials are stored in home/<Username>/.kube/config:

```
... calling validate-cluster
Waiting for 4 ready nodes. 1 ready nodes, 1 registered. Retrying.
Waiting for 4 ready nodes. 1 ready nodes, 4 registered. Retrying.
Waiting for 4 ready nodes. 1 ready nodes, 4 registered. Retrying.
Waiting for 4 ready nodes. 3 ready nodes, 4 registered. Retrying.
Found 4 node(s).
NAME                              STATUS                    AGE
kubernetes-master                 Ready,SchedulingDisabled  1m
kubernetes-minion-group-41wq      Ready                     53s
kubernetes-minion-group-7vh1      Ready                     1m
kubernetes-minion-group-oyos      Ready                     52s
Validate output:
NAME                 STATUS    MESSAGE              ERROR
controller-manager   Healthy   ok
scheduler            Healthy   ok
etcd-0               Healthy   {"health": "true"}
etcd-1               Healthy   {"health": "true"}
Cluster validation succeeded
```

Cluster validation

Then, the script will validate the cluster. At this point, we are no longer running provider-specific code. The validation script will query the cluster via the `kubectl.sh` script. This is the central script for managing our cluster. In this case, it checks the number of minions found, registered, and in a ready state. It loops through giving the cluster up to 10 minutes to finish initialization.

After a successful startup, a summary of the minions and the cluster component health is printed on the screen:

```
Done, listing cluster services:

Kubernetes master is running at https://23.251.158.223
GLBCDefaultBackend is running at https://23.251.158.223/api/v1/proxy/namespaces/k
ube-system/services/default-http-backend
Heapster is running at https://23.251.158.223/api/v1/proxy/namespaces/kube-system
/services/heapster
KubeDNS is running at https://23.251.158.223/api/v1/proxy/namespaces/kube-system/
services/kube-dns
kubernetes-dashboard is running at https://23.251.158.223/api/v1/proxy/namespaces
/kube-system/services/kubernetes-dashboard
Grafana is running at https://23.251.158.223/api/v1/proxy/namespaces/kube-system/
services/monitoring-grafana
InfluxDB is running at https://23.251.158.223/api/v1/proxy/namespaces/kube-system
/services/monitoring-influxdb

To further debug and diagnose cluster problems, use 'kubectl cluster-info dump'.
```

Cluster summary

Finally, a `kubectl cluster-info` command is run, which outputs the URL for the master services including DNS, UI, and monitoring. Let's take a look at some of these components.

Kubernetes UI

Open a browser and run the following code:

```
https://<your master ip>/ui/
```

The certificate is self-signed by default, so you'll need to ignore the warnings in your browser before proceeding. After this, we will see a login dialog. This is where we use the credentials listed during the K8s installation. We can find them at any time by simply using the `config` command:

```
$ kubectl config view
```

Now that we have credentials for login, use those, and we should see a dashboard like the following image:

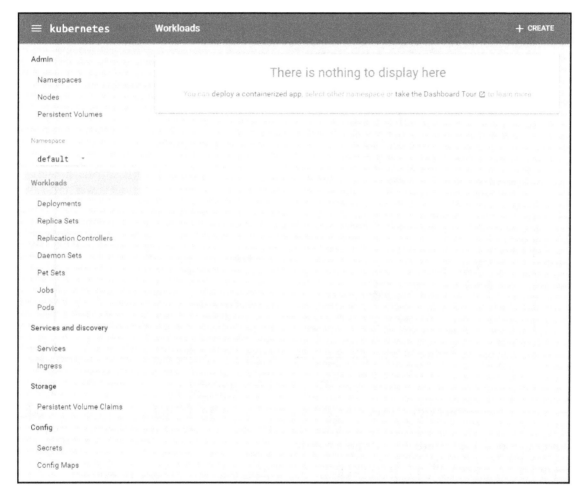

Kubernetes UI dashboard

The main dashboard takes us to a page with not much display at first. There is a link to deploy a containerized app that will take you to a GUI for deployment. This GUI can be a very easy way to get started deploying apps without worrying about the YAML syntax for Kubernetes. However, as your use of containers matures, it's good practice to use the YAML definitions that are checked in to source control.

If you click on the **Nodes** link on the left-hand side menu, you will see some metrics on the current cluster nodes:

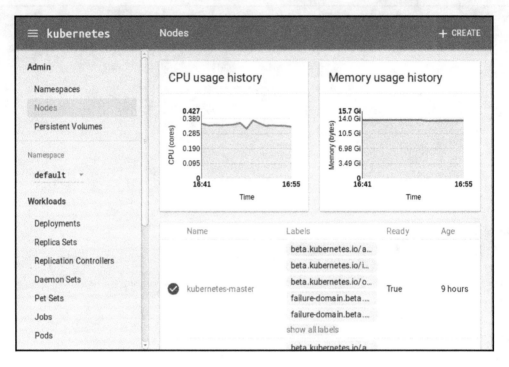

Kubernetes Node Dashboard

At the top, we see an aggregate of the CPU and memory usages followed by a listing of our cluster nodes. Clicking on one of the nodes will take us to a page with detailed information about that node, its health, and various metrics.

The Kubernetes UI has a lot of other views that will become more useful as we start launching real applications and adding configurations to the cluster.

Grafana

Another service installed by default is **Grafana**. This tool will give us a dashboard to view metrics on the cluster nodes. We can access it using the following syntax in a browser: `https://<your master ip>/api/v1/proxy/namespaces/kube-system/services/monitoring-grafana`

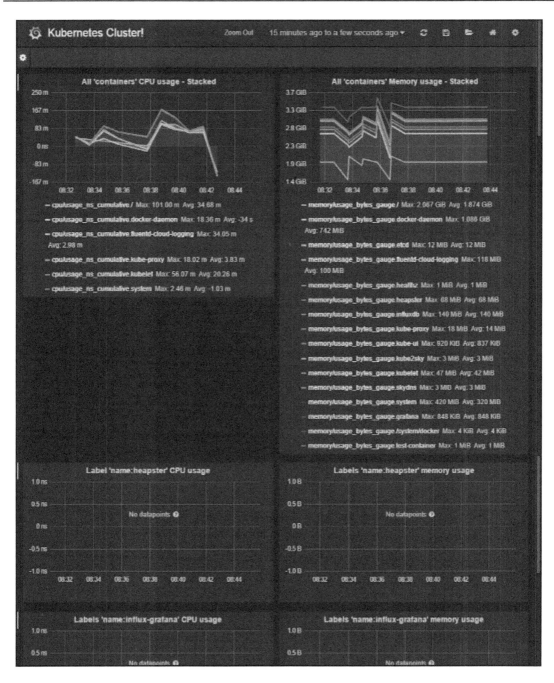

Kubernetes Grafana dashboard

From the main page, click on the **Home** dropdown and select **Cluster**. Here, Kubernetes is actually running a number of services. **Heapster** is used to collect the resource usage on the **pods** and **nodes** and stores the information in **InfluxDB**. The results, such as CPU and memory usage, are what we see in the Grafana UI. We will explore this in depth in Chapter 8, *Monitoring and Logging*.

Command line

The kubectl script has commands to explore our cluster and the workloads running on it. You can find it in the /kubernetes/client/bin folder. We will be using this command throughout the book, so let's take a second to set up our environment. We can do so by putting the binaries folder on our PATH, in the following manner:

```
$ export PATH=$PATH:/<Path where you downloaded K8s>/kubernetes/client/bin
$ chmod +x /<Path where you downloaded K8s>/kubernetes/client/bin
```

 You may choose to download the kubernetes folder outside your home folder, so modify the preceding command as appropriate.
It is also a good idea to make the changes permanent by adding the export command to the end of your .bashrc file in your home directory.

Now that we have kubectl on our path, we can start working with it. It has quite a few commands. Since we have not spun up any applications yet, most of these commands will not be very interesting. However, we can explore with two commands right away.

First, we have already seen the cluster-info command during initialization, but we can run it again at any time with the following command:

```
$ kubectl cluster-info
```

Another useful command is get. It can be used to see currently running **services**, **pods**, **replication controllers**, and a lot more. Here are the three examples that are useful right out of the gate:

- List the nodes in our cluster:

```
$ kubectl get nodes
```

- List cluster events:

```
$ kubectl get events
```

- Finally, we can see any services that are running in the cluster, as follows:

```
$ kubectl get services
```

To start with, we will only see one service, named `kubernetes`. This service is the core API server for the cluster.

Services running on the master

Let's dig a little bit deeper into our new cluster and its core services. By default, machines are named with the `kubernetes-` prefix. We can modify this using `$KUBE_GCE_INSTANCE_PREFIX` before a cluster is spun up. For the cluster we just started, the master should be named `kubernetes-master`. We can use the `gcloud` command-line utility to SSH into the machine. The following command will start an SSH session with the master node. Be sure to substitute your project ID and zone to match your environment. Also, note that you can launch SSH from the Google Cloud console using the following syntax:

```
$ gcloud compute ssh --zone "<your gce zone>" "kubernetes-master"
```

If you have trouble with SSH via the Google Cloud CLI, you can use the Console which has a built-in SSH client. Simply go to the **VM instances** page and you'll see an **SSH** option as a column in the kubernetes-master listing. Alternatively, the VM instance details page has the SSH option at the top.

Once we are logged in, we should get a standard shell prompt. Let's run the `docker` command that filters for `Image` and `Status`:

```
$ sudo docker ps --format 'table {{.Image}}t{{.Status}}'
```

```
IMAGE                                                                         STATUS
gcr.io/google_containers/node-problem-detector:v0.1                           Up 13 hours
gcr.io/google_containers/pause-amd64:3.0                                      Up 13 hours
gcr.io/google_containers/fluentd-gcp:1.21                                     Up 13 hours
gcr.io/google_containers/kube-apiserver:fa481b6112db7dcce46bfc8cfbf149a2      Up 13 hours
gcr.io/google_containers/etcd:2.2.1                                           Up 13 hours
gcr.io/google_containers/etcd:2.2.1                                           Up 13 hours
gcr.io/google_containers/rescheduler:v0.2.1                                   Up 13 hours
gcr.io/google_containers/glbc:0.8.0                                           Up 13 hours
gcr.io/google-containers/kube-addon-manager:v5.1                              Up 13 hours
gcr.io/google_containers/etcd-empty-dir-cleanup:0.0.1                         Up 13 hours
gcr.io/google_containers/kube-controller-manager:9b1fc8f7afac597ccb49e34778214c49  Up 13 hours
gcr.io/google_containers/kube-scheduler:67b73a442b6a6f362a086ea4ab8dc1cd      Up 13 hours
gcr.io/google_containers/pause-amd64:3.0                                      Up 13 hours
gcr.io/google_containers/pause-amd64:3.0                                      Up 13 hours
gcr.io/google_containers/pause-amd64:3.0                                      Up 13 hours
gcr.io/google_containers/pause-amd64:3.0                                      Up 13 hours
gcr.io/google_containers/pause-amd64:3.0                                      Up 13 hours
gcr.io/google_containers/pause-amd64:3.0                                      Up 13 hours
gcr.io/google_containers/pause-amd64:3.0                                      Up 13 hours
gcr.io/google_containers/pause-amd64:3.0                                      Up 13 hours
gcr.io/google_containers/pause-amd64:3.0                                      Up 13 hours
```

Master container listing

Even though we have not deployed any applications on Kubernetes yet, we note that there are several containers already running. The following is a brief description of each container:

- `fluentd-gcp`: This container collects and sends the cluster logs file to the Google Cloud Logging service.
- `node-problem-detector`: This container is a daemon that runs on every node and currently detects issues at the hardware and kernel layer.
- `rescheduler`: This is another add-on container that makes sure critical components are always running. In cases of low resources availability, it may even remove less critical pods to make room.

- `glbc`: This is another Kubernetes add-on container that provides Google Cloud Layer 7 load balancing using the new *Ingress* capability.
- `kube-addon-manager`: This component is core to the extension of Kubernetes through various add-ons. It also periodically applies any changes to the `/etc/kubernetes/addons` directory.
- `etcd-empty-dir-cleanup`: A utility to cleanup empty keys in etcd.
- `kube-controller-manager`: This is a controller manager that controls a variety of cluster functions, ensuring accurate and up-to-date replication is one of its vital roles. Additionally, it monitors, manages, and discovers new nodes. Finally, it manages and updates service endpoints.
- `kube-apiserver`: This container runs the API server. As we explored in the Swagger interface, this RESTful API allows us to create, query, update, and remove various components of our Kubernetes cluster.
- `kube-scheduler`: This scheduler takes unscheduled pods and binds them to nodes based on the current scheduling algorithm.
- `etcd`: This runs the **etcd** software built by CoreOS, and it is a distributed and consistent key-value store. This is where the Kubernetes cluster state is stored, updated, and retrieved by various components of K8s.
- `pause`: This container is often referred to as the pod infrastructure container and is used to set up and hold the networking namespace and resource limits for each pod.

I omitted the amd64 for many of these names to make this more generic. The purpose of the pods remains the same.

To exit the SSH session, simply type `exit` at the prompt.

In the next chapter, we will also show how a few of these services work together in the first image, *Kubernetes core architecture*.

Services running on the minions

We could SSH to one of the minions, but since Kubernetes schedules workloads across the cluster, we would not see all the containers on a single minion. However, we can look at the pods running on all the minions using the `kubectl` command:

```
$ kubectl get pods
```

Since we have not started any applications on the cluster yet, we don't see any pods. However, there are actually several system pods running pieces of the Kubernetes infrastructure. We can see these pods by specifying the `kube-system` namespace. We will explore namespaces and their significance later, but for now, the `--namespace=kube-system` command can be used to look at these K8s system resources, as follows:

```
$ kubectl get pods --namespace=kube-system
```

We should see something similar to the following:

```
etcd-empty-dir-cleanup-kubernetes-master
etcd-server-events-kubernetes-master
etcd-server-kubernetes-master
fluentd-cloud-logging-kubernetes-master
fluentd-cloud-logging-kubernetes-minion-group-xxxx
heapster-v1.2.0-xxxx
kube-addon-manager-kubernetes-master
kube-apiserver-kubernetes-master
kube-controller-manager-kubernetes-master
kube-dns-xxxx
kube-dns-autoscaler-xxxx
kube-proxy-kubernetes-minion-group-xxxx
kube-scheduler-kubernetes-master
kubernetes-dashboard-xxxx
17-default-backend-xxxx
17-lb-controller-v0.8.0-kubernetes-master
monitoring-influxdb-grafana-xxxx
node-problem-detector-v0.1-xxxx
rescheduler-v0.2.1-kubernetes-master
```

The first six lines should look familiar. Some of these are the services we saw running on the master and will see pieces of these on the nodes. There are a few additional services we have not seen yet. The `kube-dns` option provides the DNS and service discovery plumbing, `kubernetes-dashboard-xxxx` is the user interface for Kubernetes, `l7-default-backend-xxxx` provides the default load balancing backend for the new Layer-7 load balancing capability, and `heapster-v1.2.0-xxxx` and `monitoring-influx-grafana` provide the **Heapster** database and user interface to monitor resource usage across the cluster. Finally, `kube-proxy-kubernetes-minion-group-xxxx` is the proxy which directs traffic to the proper backing services and pods running on our cluster.

If we did SSH into a random minion, we would see several containers that run across a few of these pods. A sample might look like this image:

```
IMAGE                                                               STATUS
gcr.io/google_containers/exechealthz-amd64:1.2                      Up 13 hours
gcr.io/google_containers/kube-dnsmasq-amd64:1.4                     Up 13 hours
gcr.io/google_containers/heapster_grafana:v3.1.1                    Up 13 hours
gcr.io/google_containers/kubedns-amd64:1.8                          Up 13 hours
gcr.io/google_containers/heapster_influxdb:v0.7                     Up 13 hours
gcr.io/google_containers/defaultbackend:1.0                         Up 13 hours
gcr.io/google_containers/pause-amd64:3.0                            Up 13 hours
gcr.io/google_containers/pause-amd64:3.0                            Up 13 hours
gcr.io/google_containers/pause-amd64:3.0                            Up 13 hours
gcr.io/google_containers/fluentd-gcp:1.25                           Up 13 hours
gcr.io/google_containers/node-problem-detector:v0.1                 Up 13 hours
gcr.io/google_containers/kube-proxy:b87ffd2bf726a72a00bbc021970cb855 Up 13 hours
gcr.io/google_containers/pause-amd64:3.0                            Up 13 hours
gcr.io/google_containers/pause-amd64:3.0                            Up 13 hours
gcr.io/google_containers/pause-amd64:3.0                            Up 13 hours
```

Minion container listing

Again, we saw a similar line up of services on the master. The services we did not see on the master include the following:

- `kubedns`: This container monitors the service and endpoint resources in Kubernetes and synchronizes any changes to DNS lookups.
- `kube-dnsmasq`: This is another container that provides DNS caching.
- `dnsmasq-metrics`: This provides metric reporting for DNS services in cluster.
- `l7-defaultbackend`: This is the default backend for handling the GCE L7 load balancer and *Ingress*.

- `kube-proxy`: This is the network and service proxy for your cluster. This component makes sure service traffic is directed to wherever your workloads are running on the cluster. We will explore this in more depth later in the book.
- `heapster`: This container is for monitoring and analytics.
- `addon-resizer`: This cluster utility is for scaling containers.
- `heapster_grafana`: This does resource usage and monitoring.
- `heapster_influxdb`: This time-series database is for Heapster data.
- `cluster-proportional-autoscaler`: This cluster utility is for scaling containers in proportion to the cluster size.
- `exechealthz`: This performs health checks on the pods.

 Again, I have omitted the amd64 for many of these names to make this more generic. The purpose of the pods remains the same.

Tear down cluster

Alright, this is our first cluster on GCE, but let's explore some other providers. To keep things simple, we need to remove the one we just created on GCE. We can tear down the cluster with one simple command:

```
$ kube-down.sh
```

Working with other providers

By default, Kubernetes uses the GCE provider for Google Cloud. We can override this default by setting the KUBERNETES_PROVIDER environment variable. The following providers are supported with values listed in this table:

Provider	KUBERNETES_PROVIDER value	Type
Google Compute Engine	gce	Public cloud
Google Container Engine	gke	Public cloud
Amazon Web Services	aws	Public cloud

Microsoft Azure	`azure`	Public cloud
Hashicorp Vagrant	`vagrant`	Virtual development environment
VMware vSphere	`vsphere`	Private cloud/on-premise virtualization
Libvirt running CoreOS	`libvirt-coreos`	Virtualization management tool
Canonical Juju (folks behind Ubuntu)	`juju`	OS service orchestration tool

Kubernetes providers

Let's try setting up the cluster on AWS. As a prerequisite, we need to have AWS **Command Line Interface** (**CLI**) installed and configured for our account. The AWS CLI installation and configuration documentation can be found at the following links:

- Installation documentation:
  `http://docs.aws.amazon.com/cli/latest/userguide/installing.html#instal l-bundle-other-os`
- Configuration documentation:
  `http://docs.aws.amazon.com/cli/latest/userguide/cli-chap-getting-start ed.html`

Then, it is a simple environment variable setting, as follows:

```
$ export KUBERNETES_PROVIDER=aws
```

Again, we can use the `kube-up.sh` command to spin up the cluster, as follows:

```
$ kube-up.sh
```

As with GCE, the setup activity will take a few minutes. It will stage files in **S3** and create the appropriate instances, **Virtual Private Cloud** (**VPC**), security groups, and so on in our AWS account. Then, the Kubernetes cluster will be set up and started. Once everything is finished and started, we should see the cluster validation at the end of the output:

```
... calling validate-cluster
Waiting for 4 ready nodes. 0 ready nodes, 2 registered. Retrying.
Waiting for 4 ready nodes. 2 ready nodes, 2 registered. Retrying.
Waiting for 4 ready nodes. 2 ready nodes, 4 registered. Retrying.
Waiting for 4 ready nodes. 2 ready nodes, 4 registered. Retrying.
Found 4 node(s).
NAME                                            STATUS   AGE
ip-172-20-0-129.us-west-2.compute.internal      Ready    37s
ip-172-20-0-130.us-west-2.compute.internal      Ready    1m
ip-172-20-0-131.us-west-2.compute.internal      Ready    1m
ip-172-20-0-132.us-west-2.compute.internal      Ready    34s
Validate output:
NAME                 STATUS    MESSAGE              ERROR
controller-manager   Healthy   ok
scheduler            Healthy   ok
etcd-0               Healthy   {"health": "true"}
etcd-1               Healthy   {"health": "true"}
Cluster validation succeeded
Done, listing cluster services:

Kubernetes master is running at https://35.161.9.65
Elasticsearch is running at https://35.161.9.65/api/v1/proxy/namespaces/kube-system/serv
ices/elasticsearch-logging
Heapster is running at https://35.161.9.65/api/v1/proxy/namespaces/kube-system/services/
heapster
Kibana is running at https://35.161.9.65/api/v1/proxy/namespaces/kube-system/services/ki
bana-logging
KubeDNS is running at https://35.161.9.65/api/v1/proxy/namespaces/kube-system/services/k
ube-dns
kubernetes-dashboard is running at https://35.161.9.65/api/v1/proxy/namespaces/kube-syst
em/services/kubernetes-dashboard
Grafana is running at https://35.161.9.65/api/v1/proxy/namespaces/kube-system/services/m
onitoring-grafana
InfluxDB is running at https://35.161.9.65/api/v1/proxy/namespaces/kube-system/services/
monitoring-influxdb

To further debug and diagnose cluster problems, use 'kubectl cluster-info dump'.
```

AWS cluster validation

Note that the region where the cluster is spun up is determined by the KUBE_AWS_ZONE environment variable. By default, this is set to us-west-2a (the region is derived from this Availability Zone). Even if you have a region set in your AWS CLI, it will use the region defined in KUBE_AWS_ZONE.

Once again, we will SSH into master. This time, we can use the native SSH client. We'll find the key files in `/home/<username>/.ssh`:

```
$ ssh -v -i /home/<username>/.ssh/kube_aws_rsa ubuntu@<Your master IP>
```

We'll use `sudo docker ps --format 'table {{.Image}}t{{.Status}}'` to explore the running containers. We should see something like the following:

```
IMAGE                                                                              STATUS
gcr.io/google_containers/kube-apiserver:fa481b6112db7dcce46bfc8cfbf149a2           Up 47 minutes
gcr.io/google_containers/kube-scheduler:67b73a442b6a6f362a086ea4ab8dc1cd           Up 47 minutes
gcr.io/google_containers/kube-controller-manager:9b1fc8f7afac597ccb49e34778214c49  Up 47 minutes
gcr.io/google_containers/etcd:2.2.1                                                Up 47 minutes
gcr.io/google_containers/etcd:2.2.1                                                Up 47 minutes
gcr.io/google-containers/kube-addon-manager:v5.1                                   Up 47 minutes
gcr.io/google_containers/pause-amd64:3.0                                           Up 47 minutes
gcr.io/google_containers/pause-amd64:3.0                                           Up 47 minutes
gcr.io/google_containers/pause-amd64:3.0                                           Up 48 minutes
gcr.io/google_containers/pause-amd64:3.0                                           Up 48 minutes
gcr.io/google_containers/pause-amd64:3.0                                           Up 48 minutes
gcr.io/google_containers/pause-amd64:3.0                                           Up 48 minutes
```

Master container listing (AWS)

We see some of the same containers as our GCE cluster had. However, there are several missing. We see the core Kubernetes components, but the `fluentd-gcp` service is missing as well as some of the newer utilities such as `node-problem-detector`, `rescheduler`, `glbc`, `kube-addon-manager`, and `etcd-empty-dir-cleanup`. This reflects some of the subtle differences in the `kube-up` script between various Public Cloud providers. This is ultimately decided by the efforts of the large Kubernetes open-source community, but GCP often has many of the latest features first.

On the AWS provider, **Elasticsearch** and **Kibana** are set up for us. We can find the Kibana UI using the following syntax as URL:

```
https://<your master ip>/api/v1/proxy/namespaces/kube-
system/services/kibana-logging
```

As in the case of the UI, you will be prompted for admin credentials, which can be obtained using the `config` command, as shown here:

```
$ kubectl config view
```

On the first visit, you'll need to set up your index. You can leave the defaults and choose **@timestamp** for the Time-field name. Then, click on **Create** and you'll be taken to the index settings page. From there, click on the **Discover** tab at the top and you can explore the log dashboards:

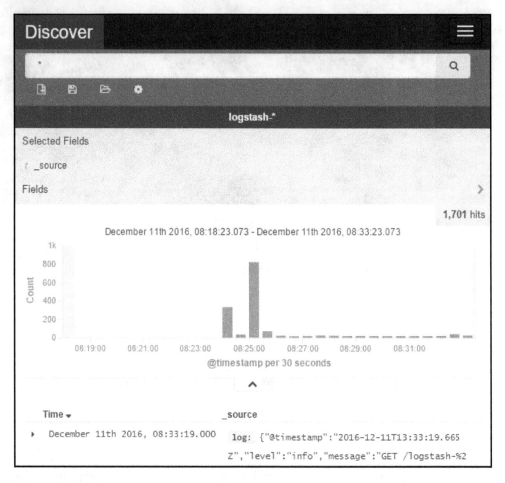

Kubernetes Kibana dashboard

Resetting the cluster

You just had a little taste of running the cluster on AWS. For the remainder of the book, I will be basing my examples on a GCE cluster. For the best experience following along, you can get back to a GCE cluster easily.

Simply tear down the AWS cluster, as follows:

```
$ kube-down.sh
```

Then, create a GCE cluster again using the following:

```
$ export KUBERNETES_PROVIDER=gce
$ kube-up.sh
```

Modifying kube-up parameters

It's worth getting to know the parameters used for the `kube-up.sh` script. Each provider under the `kubernetes/cluster/` folder has its own `su` folder which containers a `config-default.sh` script.

For example, `kubernetes/cluster/aws/config-default.sh` has the default settings for using `kube-up.sh` with AWS. At the start of this script, you will see many of these values defined as well as environment variables that can be used to overrides the defaults.

In the following example, the `ZONE` variable is set for the script and it uses the value from the environment variable named `KUBE_AWS_ZONE`. If this variable is not set, it will use the default `us-west-2a`:

```
ZONE=${KUBE_AWS_ZONE:-us-west-2a}
```

Understanding these parameters will help you get a lot more mileage out of your `kube-up.sh` script.

Alternatives to kube-up.sh

The `kube-up.sh` script is still a pretty handy way to get started using Kubernetes on your platform of choice. However, it's not without flaws and can sometimes run aground when conditions are not just so.

Luckily, since K8's inception, a number of alternative methods for creating clusters have emerged. Two such GitHub projects are *KOPs* and *kube-aws*. While the later is tied to AWS, they both provide an alternative method to easily spinning up your new cluster:

- `https://github.com/kubernetes/kops`
- `https://github.com/coreos/kube-aws`

Additionally, a number of managed services have arisen including **Google Container Engine (GKE)** and Microsoft **Azure Container Service (ACS)**, which provide an automated install and some managed cluster operations. We will look at a brief demo of these in Chapter 12, *Towards Production Ready*.

Starting from scratch

Finally, there is the option to start from scratch. Luckily, starting in 1.4, the Kubernetes team has put a major focus in easing the cluster setup process. To that end they have introduced kubeadm for Ubuntu 16.04, CentOS 7, and HypriotOS v1.0.1+.

Let's take a quick look at spinning up a cluster on AWS from scratch using the kubeadm tool.

Cluster setup

We will need to provision our cluster master and nodes beforehand. For the moment, we are limited to the operating systems and version listed earlier. Additionally, it is recommended that you have at least 1 GB of RAM and all the nodes must have network connectivity to one another.

For this walk through, we will need one t2.medium (master node) and three t2.mirco (nodes) sized instances on AWS. These instance have burstable CPU and come with the minimum 1 GB of RAM needed. We will need to create one master and three worker nodes.

We will also need to create some security groups for the cluster. The following ports are needed for the master:

Type	Protocol	Port range	Source
All Traffic	All	All	{This SG ID (Master SG)}
All Traffic	All	All	{Node SG ID}
SSH	TCP	22	{Your Local Machine's IP}
HTTTPS	TCP	443	{Range allowed to access K8s API and UI}

Master Security Group Rules

The next table shows the ports node security groups:

Type	Protocol	Port range	Source
All Traffic	All	All	{Master SG ID}
All Traffic	All	All	{This SG ID (Node SG)}
SSH	TCP	22	{Your Local Machine's IP}

Node Security Group Rules

Once you have these SGs, go ahead and spin up four instances (one t2.medium and three t2.mircos) using Ubuntu 16.04. If you are new to AWS, refer to the documentation on spinning up EC2 instances at the following URL:

```
http://docs.aws.amazon.com/AWSEC2/latest/UserGuide/LaunchingAndUsingInstances.html
```

Be sure to identify the t2.medium instance as the master and associate the master security group. Name the other three as nodes and associate the node security group with those.

 These steps are adapted from the walk-through in the manual. For more information or to work with an alternative to Ubuntu refer to `https://kub ernetes.io/docs/getting-started-guides/kubeadm/`.

Installing Kubernetes components (kubelet and kubeadm)

Next we will need to SSH into all four of the instances and install the Kubernetes components.

As root, perform the following steps on all four instances:

1. Update packages and install the `apt-transport-https` package so we can download from sources that use HTTPS:

```
$ apt-get update
$ apt-get install -y apt-transport-https
```

2. Install the Google Cloud public key:

```
$ curl -s https://packages.cloud.google.com/apt/doc/apt-key.gpg |
apt-key add -
```

3. Next, create a source list for the Kubernetes package downloads with your favorite editor:

```
$ vi /etc/apt/sources.list.d/kubernetes.list
```

4. Use the following as contents for this file and save:

```
deb http://apt.kubernetes.io/ kubernetes-xenial main
```

Listing 1-1. `/etc/apt/sources.list.d/kubernetes.list`

5. Update your sources once more:

```
$ apt-get update
```

6. Install Docker and the core Kubernetes components:

```
$ apt-get install -y docker.io
$ apt-get install -y kubelet kubeadm kubectl kubernetes-cni
```

Setting up a Master

On the instance you have previously chosen as *master*, we will run master initialization. Again, as root run the following command:

```
$ kubeadm init
```

Note that initialization can only be run once, so if you run into problems you'll `kubeadm reset`.

Joining nodes

After a successful initialization, you will get a join command that can be used by the nodes. Copy this down for the join process later on. It should look similar to this:

```
$ kubeadm join --token=<some token> <master ip address>
```

The token is used to authenticate cluster nodes, so make sure to store it somewhere securely for future use.

Networking

Our cluster will need a networking layer for the pods to communicate on. Note that kubeadm requires a CNI compatible network fabric. The list of plugins currently available can be found here:

```
http://kubernetes.io/docs/admin/addons/
```

For our example, we will use calico. We will need to create the calico components on our cluster using the following `yaml`. For convenience you can download it here:

```
http://docs.projectcalico.org/v1.6/getting-started/kubernetes/installation/hosted/kubeadm/calico.yaml
```

Once you have this file on your *master*, create the components with the following command:

```
$ kubectl apply -f calico.yaml
```

Give this a minute to run setup and then list the `kube-system` nodes to check:

```
$ kubectl get pods --namespace=kube-system
```

You should get a listing similar to the following one with three new calico pods and one completed job that is not shown:

```
NAME                                        READY   STATUS    RESTARTS   AGE
calico-etcd-7ckip                           1/1     Running   0          43s
calico-node-em917                           2/2     Running   0          43s
calico-policy-controller-i43ct              1/1     Running   0          43s
dummy-2088944543-efrgw                      1/1     Running   0          2m
etcd-ip-172-30-0-26                         1/1     Running   0          1m
kube-apiserver-ip-172-30-0-26               1/1     Running   0          2m
kube-controller-manager-ip-172-30-0-26      1/1     Running   0          2m
kube-discovery-1150918428-1kntn             1/1     Running   0          2m
kube-dns-654381707-6u52r                    2/3     Running   0          1m
kube-proxy-00wu7                            1/1     Running   0          1m
kube-scheduler-ip-172-30-0-26               1/1     Running   0          1m
  info: 1 completed object(s) was(were) not shown in pods list. Pass --show-all
to see all objects.
```

Calico setup

Joining the cluster

Now we need to run the `join` command we copied earlier, on each of our node instances:

```
$ kubeadm join --token=<some token> <master ip address>
```

Once you've finished that, you should be able to see all nodes from the master by running this command:

```
$ kubectl get nodes
```

If all went well, this will show three nodes and one master, as shown here:

```
NAME              STATUS          AGE
ip-172-30-0-22    Ready           6m
ip-172-30-0-26    Ready,master    8m
ip-172-30-0-28    Ready           6m
ip-172-30-0-8     Ready           6m
```

Calico setup

Summary

We took a very brief look at how containers work and how they lend themselves to the new architecture patterns in microservices. You should now have a better understanding of how these two forces will require a variety of operations and management tasks and how Kubernetes offers strong features to address these challenges. We created two different clusters on both GCE and AWS and explored the startup script as well as some of the built-in features of Kubernetes. Finally, we looked at the alternatives to the kube-up script and tried the new kubeadm tool on AWS with Ubuntu 16.04.

In the next chapter, we will explore the core concept and abstractions K8s provides to manage containers and full application stacks. We will also look at basic scheduling, service discovery, and health checking.

References

1. Malcom McLean entry on PBS website: `https://www.pbs.org/wgbh/theymadeamerica/whomade/mclean_hi.html`
2. Martin Fowler on microservices: `http://martinfowler.com/articles/microservices.html`
3. Kubernetes GitHub project page: `https://github.com/kubernetes/kubernetes`
4. `https://www.thoughtworks.com/continuous-integration`
5. `https://docs.docker.com/`
6. `http://kubernetes.io/docs/getting-started-guides/kubeadm/`

2
Pods, Services, Replication Controllers, and Labels

This chapter will cover the core Kubernetes constructs, namely **pods**, **services**, **replication controllers**, **replica sets**, and **labels**. A few simple application examples will be included to demonstrate each construct. The chapter will also cover basic operations for your cluster. Finally, **health checks** and **scheduling** will be introduced with a few examples.

This chapter will discuss the following topics:

- Kubernetes overall architecture
- Introduction to core Kubernetes constructs, namely pods, services, replication controllers, replica sets, and labels
- Understanding how labels can ease management of a Kubernetes cluster
- Understanding how to monitor services and container health
- Understanding how to set up scheduling constraints based on available cluster resources

The architecture

Although, **Docker** brings a helpful layer of abstraction and tooling around container management, Kubernetes brings similar assistance to orchestrating containers at scale and managing full application stacks.

K8s moves up the stack giving us constructs to deal with management at the application or service level. This gives us automation and tooling to ensure high availability, application stack, and service-wide portability. K8s also allows finer control of resource usage, such as CPU, memory, and disk space across our infrastructure.

Kubernetes provides this higher level of orchestration management by giving us key constructs to combine multiple containers, endpoints, and data into full application stacks and services. K8s also provides the tooling to manage the when, where, and how many of the stack and its components:

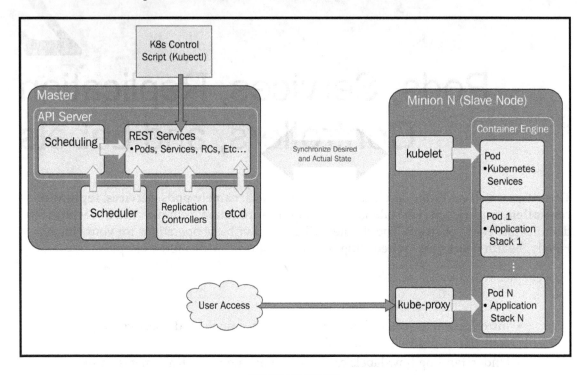

Kubernetes core architecture

In the preceding figure, we see the core architecture of Kubernetes. Most administrative interactions are done via the `kubectl` script and/or RESTful service calls to the API.

Note the ideas of the desired state and actual state carefully. This is the key to how Kubernetes manages the cluster and its workloads. All the pieces of K8s are constantly working to monitor the current actual state and synchronize it with the desired state defined by the administrators via the API server or `kubectl` script. There will be times when these states do not match up, but the system is always working to reconcile the two.

Master

Essentially, **master** is the brain of our cluster. Here, we have the core API server, which maintains RESTful web services for querying and defining our desired cluster and workload state. It's important to note that the control pane only accesses the master to initiate changes and not the nodes directly.

Additionally, the master includes the **scheduler**, which works with the API server to schedule workloads in the form of pods on the actual minion nodes. These pods include the various containers that make up our application stacks. By default, the basic Kubernetes scheduler spreads pods across the cluster and uses different nodes for matching pod replicas. Kubernetes also allows specifying necessary resources for each container, so scheduling can be altered by these additional factors.

The replication controller/replica set works with the API server to ensure that the correct number of pod replicas are running at any given time. This is exemplary of the desired state concept. If our replication controller/replica set is defining three replicas and our actual state is two copies of the pod running, then the scheduler will be invoked to add a third pod somewhere on our cluster. The same is true if there are too many pods running in the cluster at any given time. In this way, K8s is always pushing toward that desired state.

Finally, we have **etcd** running as a distributed configuration store. The Kubernetes state is stored here and etcd allows values to be watched for changes. Think of this as the brain's shared memory.

Node (formerly minions)

In each node, we have a couple of components. The **kubelet** interacts with the API server to update the state and to start new workloads that have been invoked by the scheduler.

Kube-proxy provides basic load balancing and directs the traffic destined for specific services to the proper pod on the backend. Refer to the *Services* section later in this chapter.

Finally, we have some default pods, which run various infrastructure services for the node. As we explored briefly in the previous chapter, the pods include services for **Domain Name System (DNS)**, logging, and pod health checks. The default pod will run alongside our scheduled pods on every node.

In v1.0, **minion** was renamed to **node**, but there are still remnants of the term minion in some of the machine naming scripts and documentation that exists on the Web. For clarity, I've added the term minion in addition to node in a few places throughout the book.

Core constructs

Now, let's dive a little deeper and explore some of the core abstractions Kubernetes provides. These abstractions will make it easier to think about our applications and ease the burden of life cycle management, high availability, and scheduling.

Pods

Pods allow you to keep related containers close in terms of the network and hardware infrastructure. Data can live near the application, so processing can be done without incurring a high latency from network traversal. Similarly, common data can be stored on volumes that are shared between a number of containers. Pods essentially allow you to logically group containers and pieces of our application stacks together.

While pods may run one or more containers inside, the pod itself may be one of many that is running on a Kubernetes node (minion). As we'll see, pods give us a logical group of containers that we can then replicate, schedule, and balance service endpoints across.

Pod example

Let's take a quick look at a pod in action. We will spin up a **Node.js** application on the cluster. You'll need a GCE cluster running for this; if you don't already have one started, refer to the *Our first cluster* section in `Chapter 1`, *Introduction to Kubernetes*.

Now, let's make a directory for our definitions. In this example, I will create a folder in the `/book-examples` subfolder under our home directory:

```
$ mkdir book-examples
$ cd book-examples
$ mkdir 02_example
$ cd 02_example
```

Downloading the example code

You can download the example code files from your account at
`http://www.packtpub.com` for all the Packt Publishing books you have
purchased. If you purchased this book elsewhere, you can visit
`http://www.packtpub.com/support` and register to have the files e-mailed
directly to you.

Use your favorite editor to create the following file:

```
apiVersion: v1
kind: Pod
metadata:
  name: node-js-pod
spec:
  containers:
  - name: node-js-pod
    image: bitnami/apache:latest
    ports:
    - containerPort: 80
```

Listing 2-1: `nodejs-pod.yaml`

This file creates a pod named `node-js-pod` with the latest `bitnami/apache` container
running on port `80`. We can check this using the following command:

```
$ kubectl create -f nodejs-pod.yaml
```

The output is as follows:

```
pod "node-js-pod" created
```

This gives us a pod running the specified container. We can see more information on the
pod by running the following command:

```
$ kubectl describe pods/node-js-pod
```

You'll see a good deal of information, such as the pod's status, IP address, and even relevant
log events. You'll note the pod IP address is a private IP address, so we cannot access it
directly from our local machine. Not to worry, as the `kubectl exec` command mirrors
Docker's `exec` functionality. Once the pod shows to be in a running state, we can use this
feature to run a command inside a pod:

```
$ kubectl exec node-js-pod -- curl <private ip address>
```

By default, this runs a command in the first container it finds, but you can select a specific one using the -c argument.

After running the command, you should see some HTML code. We'll have a prettier view later in the chapter, but for now, we can see that our pod is indeed running as expected.

Labels

Labels give us another level of categorization, which becomes very helpful in terms of everyday operations and management. Similar to tags, labels can be used as the basis of service discovery as well as a useful grouping tool for day-to-day operations and management tasks.

Labels are just simple key-value pairs. You will see them on pods, replication controllers, replica sets, services, and so on. The label acts as a selector and tells Kubernetes which resources to work with for a variety of operations. Think of it as a filtering option.

We will take a look at labels more in depth later in this chapter, but first, we will explore the remaining three constructs—services, replication controllers, and replica sets.

The container's afterlife

As Werner Vogels, CTO of AWS, famously said *everything fails all the time;* containers and pods can and will crash, become corrupted, or maybe even just get accidentally shut off by a clumsy admin poking around on one of the nodes. Strong policy and security practices like enforcing least privilege curtail some of these incidents, but involuntary workload slaughter happens and is simply a fact of operations.

Luckily, Kubernetes provides two very valuable constructs to keep this somber affair all tidied up behind the curtains. Services and replication controllers/replica sets give us the ability to keep our applications running with little interruption and graceful recovery.

Services

Services allow us to abstract access away from the consumers of our applications. Using a reliable endpoint, users and other programs can access pods running on your cluster seamlessly.

K8s achieves this by making sure that every node in the cluster runs a proxy named **kube-proxy**. As the name suggests, the job of **kube-proxy** is to proxy communication from a service endpoint back to the corresponding pod that is running the actual application.

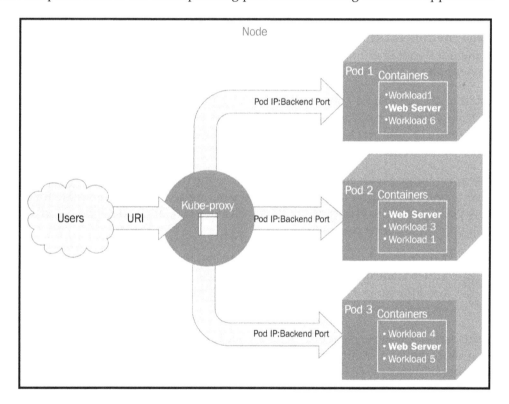

The kube-proxy architecture

Membership of the service load balancing pool is determined by the use of selectors and labels. Pods with matching labels are added to the list of candidates where the service forwards traffic. A virtual IP address and port are used as the entry points for the service, and the traffic is then forwarded to a random pod on a target port defined by either K8s or your definition file.

Updates to service definitions are monitored and coordinated from the K8s cluster master and propagated to the **kube-proxy daemons** running on each node.

> At the moment, kube-proxy is running on the node host itself. There are plans to containerize this and the kubelet by default in the future.

Replication controllers and replica sets

Replication controllers (**RCs**), as the name suggests, manage the number of nodes that a pod and included container images run on. They ensure that an instance of an image is being run with the specific number of copies.

As you start to operationalize your containers and pods, you'll need a way to roll out updates, scale the number of copies running (both up and down), or simply ensure that at least one instance of your stack is always running. RCs create a high-level mechanism to make sure that things are operating correctly across the entire application and cluster.

RCs are simply charged with ensuring that you have the desired scale for your application. You define the number of pod replicas you want running and give it a template for how to create new pods. Just like services, we will use selectors and labels to define a pod's membership in a replication controller.

> Kubernetes doesn't require the strict behavior of the replication controller, which is ideal for long-running processes. In fact, **job controllers** can be used for short lived workloads which allow jobs to be run to a completion state and are well suited for batch work.

Replica sets, are a new type, currently in Beta, that represent an improved version of replication controllers. Currently, the main difference consists of being able to use the new set-based label selectors as we will see in the following examples.

Our first Kubernetes application

Before we move on, let's take a look at these three concepts in action. Kubernetes ships with a number of examples installed, but we will create a new example from scratch to illustrate some of the concepts.

We already created a pod definition file, but as you learned, there are many advantages to running our pods via replication controllers. Again, using the book-examples/02_example folder we made earlier, we will create some definition files and start a cluster of Node.js servers using a replication controller approach. Additionally, we'll add a public face to it with a load-balanced service.

Use your favorite editor to create the following file:

```
apiVersion: v1
kind: ReplicationController
metadata:
  name: node-js
  labels:
    name: node-js
spec:
  replicas: 3
  selector:
    name: node-js
  template:
    metadata:
      labels:
        name: node-js
    spec:
      containers:
      - name: node-js
        image: jonbaier/node-express-info:latest
        ports:
        - containerPort: 80
```

Listing 2-2: `nodejs-controller.yaml`

This is the first resource definition file for our cluster, so let's take a closer look. You'll note that it has four first-level elements (`kind`, `apiVersion`, `metadata`, and `spec`). These are common among all top-level Kubernetes resource definitions:

- `Kind`: This tells K8s the type of resource we are creating. In this case, the type is `ReplicationController`. The `kubectl` script uses a single `create` command for all types of resources. The benefit here is that you can easily create a number of resources of various types without the need for specifying individual parameters for each type. However, it requires that the definition files can identify what it is they are specifying.
- `apiVersion`: This simply tells Kubernetes which version of the schema we are using.

- Metadata: This is where we will give the resource a name and also specify labels that will be used to search and select resources for a given operation. The metadata element also allows you to create annotations, which are for the non-identifying information that might be useful for client tools and libraries.
- Finally, we have spec, which will vary based on the kind or type of resource we are creating. In this case, it's ReplicationController, which ensures the desired number of pods are running. The replicas element defines the desired number of pods, the selector element tells the controller which pods to watch, and finally, the template element defines a template to launch a new pod. The template section contains the same pieces we saw in our pod definition earlier. An important thing to note is that the selector values need to match the labels values specified in the pod template. Remember that this matching is used to select the pods being managed.

Now, let's take a look at the service definition:

```
apiVersion: v1
kind: Service
metadata:
  name: node-js
  labels:
    name: node-js
spec:
  type: LoadBalancer
  ports:
  - port: 80
  selector:
    name: node-js
```

Listing 2-3: nodejs-rc-service.yaml

The YAML here is similar to ReplicationController. The main difference is seen in the service spec element. Here, we define the Service type, listening port, and selector, which tell the Service proxy which pods can answer the service.

Kubernetes supports both YAML and JSON formats for definition files.

Create the Node.js express replication controller:

```
$ kubectl create -f nodejs-controller.yaml
```

The output is as follows:

```
replicationcontroller "node-js" created
```

This gives us a replication controller that ensures that three copies of the container are always running:

```
$ kubectl create -f nodejs-rc-service.yaml
```

The output is as follows:

```
service "node-js" created
```

On GCE, this will create an external load balancer and forwarding rules, but you may need to add additional firewall rules. In my case, the firewall was already open for port 80. However, you may need to open this port, especially if you deploy a service with ports other than 80 and 443.

Alright, now we have a running service, which means that we can access the Node.js servers from a reliable URL. Let's take a look at our running services:

```
$ kubectl get services
```

The following screenshot is the result of the preceding command:

```
NAME         CLUSTER-IP      EXTERNAL-IP     PORT(S)        AGE
kubernetes   10.0.0.1        <none>          443/TCP        11m
node-js      10.0.200.192    35.184.181.18   80:30874/TCP   4m
```

Services listing

In the preceding image (*Services listing*), we should note that the `node-js` service is running, and in the **IP(S)** column, we should have both a private and a public (`130.211.186.84` in the screenshot) IP address. If you don't see the external IP, you may need to wait a minute for the IP to be allocated from GCE. Let's see if we can connect by opening up the public address in a browser:

Host: node-js-u26fd
Running OS: linux
Uptime: 525274
Network Information: 10.244.1.17, fe80::42:aff:fef4:111
DNS Servers: 10.0.0.10,169.254.169.254,10.240.0.1

Container info application

You should see something like the figure *Container info application* . If we visit multiple times, you should note that the container name changes. Essentially, the service load balancer is rotating between available pods on the backend.

> Browsers usually cache web pages, so to really see the container name change, you may need to clear your cache or use a proxy like this one:
> `https://hide.me/en/proxy`

Let's try playing chaos monkey a bit and kill off a few containers to see what Kubernetes does. In order to do this, we need to see where the pods are actually running. First, let's list our pods:

```
$ kubectl get pods
```

The following screenshot is the result of the preceding command:

NAME	READY	STATUS	RESTARTS	AGE
node-js-1fxoy	1/1	Running	0	1d
node-js-m4w4a	1/1	Running	0	1d
node-js-sjc03	1/1	Running	0	1d

Currently running pods

Now, let's get some more details on one of the pods running a `node-js` container. You can do this with the `describe` command with one of the pod names listed in the last command:

```
$ kubectl describe pod/node-js-sjc03
```

The following screenshot is the result of the preceding command:

```
Name:                           node-js-sjc03
Namespace:                      default
Image(s):                       petegoo/node-express-sample:latest
Node:                           kubernetes-minion-aqdf/10.240.142.178
Labels:                         name=node-js
Status:                         Running
Reason:
Message:
IP:                             10.244.0.10
Replication Controllers:        node-js (3/3 replicas created)
Containers:
  node-js:
    Image:          petegoo/node-express-sample:latest
    Limits:
      cpu:                  100m
    State:              Running
      Started:          Tue, 28 Jul 2015 16:57:33 -0400
    Ready:              True
    Restart Count:      0
Conditions:
  Type            Status
  Ready           True
No events.
```

Pod description

You should see the preceding output. The information we need is the `Node:` section. Let's use the node name to **SSH** (short for **Secure Shell**) into the (minion) node running this workload:

```
$ gcloud compute --project "<Your project ID>" ssh --zone "<your gce zone>"
"<Node from
pod describe>"
```

Once SSHed into the node, if we run a `sudo docker ps` command, we should see at least two containers: one running the `pause` image and one running the actual `node-express-info` image. You may see more if the K8s scheduled more than one replica on this node. Let's grab the container ID of the `jonbaier/node-express-info` image (not `gcr.io/google_containers/pause`) and kill it off to see what happens. Save this container ID somewhere for later:

```
$ sudo docker ps --filter="name=node-js"
$ sudo docker stop <node-express container id>
$ sudo docker rm <container id>
$ sudo docker ps --filter="name=node-js"
```

Unless you are really quick you'll probably note that there is still a `node-express-info` container running, but look closely and you'll note that the `container id` is different and the creation time stamp shows only a few seconds ago. If you go back to the service URL, it is functioning as normal. Go ahead and exit the SSH session for now.

Here, we are already seeing Kubernetes playing the role of on-call operations ensuring that our application is always running.

Let's see if we can find any evidence of the outage. Go to the **Events** page in the Kubernetes UI. You can find it by navigating to the **Nodes** page on the main K8s dashboard. Select a node from the list (the same one that we SSHed into) and scroll down to **Events** on the node details page.

You will see a screen similar to the following screenshot:

≡ **kubernetes**	Nodes > gke-cluster-1-default-pool-3185750f-q6sx					+ CREATE
Admin	**Events**					
Namespaces						
Nodes	Message	Source	Sub-object	Count	First seen	Last seen
Persistent Volumes	Starting kubelet.	kubelet gke-cluster-1-default-pool-3185750f-q6sx	-	1	22/12/16 21:42 UTC	22/12/16 21:42 UTC
Namespace						
default ▼	Node gke-cluster-1-default-pool-3185750f-q6sx status is now: NodeHasSufficientDisk	kubelet gke-cluster-1-default-pool-3185750f-q6sx	-	17	22/12/16 21:42 UTC	22/12/16 21:44 UTC
Workloads						
Deployments						
Replica Sets	Node gke-cluster-1-default-pool-3185750f-q6sx status is now: NodeHasSufficientMemory	kubelet gke-cluster-1-default-pool-3185750f-q6sx	-	17	22/12/16 21:42 UTC	22/12/16 21:44 UTC
Replication Controllers						
Daemon Sets						
Pet Sets						
Jobs	Node gke-cluster-1-default-pool-3185750f-q6sx status is now: NodeHasNoDiskPressure	kubelet gke-cluster-1-default-pool-3185750f-q6sx	-	17	22/12/16 21:42 UTC	22/12/16 21:44 UTC
Pods						
Services and discovery						
Services						

Kubernetes UI event page

You should see three recent events. First, Kubernetes pulls the image. Second, it creates a new container with the pulled image. Finally, it starts that container again. You'll note that, from the time stamps, this all happens in less than a second. Time taken may vary based on the cluster size and image pulls, but the recovery is very quick.

More on labels

As mentioned previously, labels are just simple key-value pairs. They are available on pods, replication controllers, replica sets, services, and more. If you recall our service YAML, in *Listing 2-3*: `nodejs-rc-service.yaml`, there was a `selector` attribute. The `selector` attribute tells Kubernetes which labels to use in finding pods to forward traffic for that service.

K8s allows users to work with labels directly on replication controllers, replica sets, and services. Let's modify our replicas and services to include a few more labels. Once again, use your favorite editor and create these two files, as follows:

```
apiVersion: v1
kind: ReplicationController
metadata:
  name: node-js-labels
  labels:
    name: node-js-labels
    app: node-js-express
    deployment: test
spec:
  replicas: 3
  selector:
    name: node-js-labels
    app: node-js-express
    deployment: test
  template:
    metadata:
      labels:
        name: node-js-labels
        app: node-js-express
        deployment: test
    spec:
      containers:
      - name: node-js-labels
        image: jonbaier/node-express-info:latest
        ports:
        - containerPort: 80
```

Listing 2-4: `nodejs-labels-controller.yaml`

```
apiVersion: v1
kind: Service
metadata:
  name: node-js-labels
  labels:
    name: node-js-labels
    app: node-js-express
    deployment: test
spec:
  type: LoadBalancer
  ports:
  - port: 80
  selector:
    name: node-js-labels
    app: node-js-express
    deployment: test
```

Listing 2-5: `nodejs-labels-service.yaml`

Create the replication controller and service as follows:

```
$ kubectl create -f nodejs-labels-controller.yaml
$ kubectl create -f nodejs-labels-service.yaml
```

Let's take a look at how we can use labels in everyday management. The following table shows us the options to select labels:

Operators	Description	Example
= or ==	You can use either style to select keys with values equal to the string on the right	`name = apache`
!=	Select keys with values that do not equal the string on the right	`Environment != test`
in	Select resources whose labels have keys with values in this set	`tier in (web, app)`
notin	Select resources whose labels have keys with values not in this set	`tier notin (lb, app)`
<Key name>	Use a key name only to select resources whose labels contain this key	`tier`

Label selectors

Let's try looking for replicas with `test` deployments:

```
$ kubectl get rc -l deployment=test
```

The following screenshot is the result of the preceding command:

NAME	DESIRED	CURRENT	READY	AGE
node-js-labels	3	3	3	46s

Replication controller listing

You'll notice that it only returns the replication controller we just started. How about services with a label named `component`? Use the following command:

```
$ kubectl get services -l component
```

The following screenshot is the result of the preceding command:

NAME	CLUSTER-IP	EXTERNAL-IP	PORT(S)	AGE
kubernetes	10.0.0.1	<none>	443/TCP	5d

Listing of services with a label named component

Here, we see the core Kubernetes service only. Finally, let's just get the `node-js` servers we started in this chapter. See the following command:

```
$ kubectl get services -l "name in (node-js,node-js-labels)"
```

The following screenshot is the result of the preceding command:

NAME	CLUSTER-IP	EXTERNAL-IP	PORT(S)	AGE
node-js	10.0.13.62	104.197.124.230	80:30798/TCP	14h
node-js-labels	10.0.207.25	104.154.54.104	80:31315/TCP	1m

Listing of services with a label name and a value of node-js or node-js-labels

Additionally, we can perform management tasks across a number of pods and services. For example, we can kill all replication controllers that are part of the `demo` deployment (if we had any running), as follows:

```
$ kubectl delete rc -l deployment=demo
```

Otherwise, kill all services that are part of a `production` or `test` deployment (again, if we had any running), as follows:

```
$ kubectl delete service -l "deployment in (test, production)"
```

It's important to note that, while label selection is quite helpful in day-to-day management tasks, it does require proper deployment hygiene on our part. We need to make sure that we have a tagging standard and that it is actively followed in the resource definition files for everything we run on Kubernetes.

While we used service definition YAML files to create our services thus far, you can actually create them using a `kubectl` command only. To try this out, first run the `get pods` command and get one of the `node-js` pod names. Next, use the following `expose` command to create a service endpoint for just that pod:

```
$ kubectl expose pods node-js-gxkix --port=80 --name=testing-vip --create-external-load-balancer=true
```

This will create a service named `testing-vip` and also a public `vip` (load balancer IP) that can be used to access this pod over port `80`.

There are number of other optional parameters that can be used. These can be found with the following command:

```
kubectl expose --help
```

Replica sets

As discussed earlier, replica sets are the new and improved version of replication controllers. They take advantage of set-based label selection, but they are still considered beta at time of this writing.

Here is an example of a `ReplicaSet` based on and similar to the `ReplicationController` in *listing 2-4*:

```
apiVersion: extensions/v1beta1
kind: ReplicaSet
metadata:
  name: node-js-rs
spec:
  replicas: 3
  selector:
    matchLabels:
      app: node-js-express
      deployment: test
    matchExpressions:
      - {key: name, operator: In, values: [node-js-rs]}
```

```
template:
  metadata:
    labels:
      name: node-js-rs
      app: node-js-express
      deployment: test
  spec:
    containers:
    - name: node-js-rs
      image: jonbaier/node-express-info:latest
      ports:
      - containerPort: 80
```

Listing 2-6: `nodejs-labels-replicaset.yaml`

Health checks

Kubernetes provides two layers of health checking. First, in the form of HTTP or TCP checks, K8s can attempt to connect to a particular endpoint and give a status of healthy on a successful connection. Second, application-specific health checks can be performed using command-line scripts.

Let's take a look at a few health checks in action. First, we'll create a new controller with a health check:

```
apiVersion: v1
kind: ReplicationController
metadata:
  name: node-js
  labels:
    name: node-js
spec:
  replicas: 3
  selector:
    name: node-js
  template:
    metadata:
      labels:
        name: node-js
    spec:
      containers:
      - name: node-js
        image: jonbaier/node-express-info:latest
        ports:
        - containerPort: 80
```

```
livenessProbe:
  # An HTTP health check
  httpGet:
    path: /status/
    port: 80
  initialDelaySeconds: 30
  timeoutSeconds: 1
```

Listing 2-7: `nodejs-health-controller.yaml`

Note the addition of the `livenessprobe` element. This is our core health check element. From here, we can specify `httpGet`, `tcpScoket`, or `exec`. In this example, we use `httpGet` to perform a simple check for a URI on our container. The probe will check the path and port specified and restart the pod if it doesn't successfully return.

 Status codes between 200 and 399 are all considered healthy by the probe.

Finally, `initialDelaySeconds` gives us the flexibility to delay health checks until the pod has finished initializing. The `timeoutSeconds` value is simply the timeout value for the probe.

Let's use our new health check-enabled controller to replace the old `node-js` RC. We can do this using the `replace` command, which will replace the replication controller definition:

```
$ kubectl replace -f nodejs-health-controller.yaml
```

Replacing the RC on its own won't replace our containers because it still has three healthy pods from our first run. Let's kill off those pods and let the updated `ReplicationController` replace them with containers that have health checks:

```
$ kubectl delete pods -l name=node-js
```

Now, after waiting a minute or two, we can list the pods in an RC and grab one of the pod IDs to inspect a bit deeper with the `describe` command:

```
$ kubectl describe rc/node-js
```

The following screenshot is the result of the preceding command:

```
Name:            node-js
Namespace:       default
Image(s):        jonbaier/node-express-info:latest
Selector:        name=node-js
Labels:          name=node-js
Replicas:        3 current / 3 desired
Pods Status:     3 Running / 0 Waiting / 0 Succeeded / 0 Failed
No volumes.
Events:
  FirstSeen      LastSeen        Count    From                            SubobjectPath    Type
  Reason                         Message
  ---------      --------        -----    ----                            -------------    ------
  --      ------                 -------
  42s            42s             1        {replication-controller }                        Normal
SuccessfulCreate                Created pod: node-js-7esbp
  42s            42s             1        {replication-controller }                        Normal
SuccessfulCreate                Created pod: node-js-istu0
  42s            42s             1        {replication-controller }                        Normal
SuccessfulCreate                Created pod: node-js-im7jw
```

Description of node-js replication controller

Now, use the following command for one of the pods:

```
$ kubectl describe pods/node-js-7esbp
```

The following screenshot is the result of the preceding command:

```
Name:                node-js-7esbp
Namespace:           default
Node:                kubernetes-minion-group-k0rn/10.128.0.3
Start Time:          Mon, 02 Jan 2017 13:54:22 -0500
Labels:              name=node-js
Status:              Running
IP:                  10.244.1.18
Controllers:         ReplicationController/node-js
Containers:
  node-js:
    Container ID:     docker://ce35e1fba7c3464cc89607ebd335250a7b52bebd5e03683e3f6313f
35fe68244
    Image:            jonbaier/node-express-info:latest
    Image ID:         docker://sha256:6a276384568844d1840049552f79c69311c3132d3a2b884a
3e9c4e51087a436b
    Port:             80/TCP
    Requests:
      cpu:            100m
    State:            Waiting
      Reason:         CrashLoopBackOff
    Last State:       Terminated
      Reason:         Error
      Exit Code:      137
      Started:        Mon, 02 Jan 2017 14:13:42 -0500
      Finished:       Mon, 02 Jan 2017 14:14:42 -0500
    Ready:            False
    Restart Count:    9
    Liveness:         http-get http://:80/status/ delay=30s timeout=1s period=10s #suc
cess=1 #failure=3
    Volume Mounts:
      /var/run/secrets/kubernetes.io/serviceaccount from default-token-7z353 (ro)
    Environment Variables:        <none>
Conditions:
  Type           Status
  Initialized    True
  Ready          False
  PodScheduled   True
Volumes:
  default-token-7z353:
    Type:         Secret (a volume populated by a Secret)
    SecretName:   default-token-7z353
QoS Class:        Burstable
Tolerations:      <none>
Events:
  FirstSeen    LastSeen      Count    From           Reason         Message                      Subobjec
tPath
                             Type
  ---------    --------      -----    ----           ----           -------                      --------
  -----                      --------
  22m          22m           1        {default-scheduler }                                              N
ormal        Scheduled     Successfully assigned node-js-7esbp to kubernetes-minion
-group-k0rn
  21m          21m           1        {kubelet kubernetes-minion-group-k0rn}  spec.con
tainers{node-js}           Normal    Created        Created container with docker id
4b2b5587a119; Security:[seccomp=unconfined]
  21m          21m           1        {kubelet kubernetes-minion-group-k0rn}  spec.con
tainers{node-js}           Normal    Started        Started container with docker id
4b2b5587a119
  20m          20m           1        {kubelet kubernetes-minion-group-k0rn}  spec.con
tainers{node-js}           Normal    Killing        Killing container with docker id
4b2b5587a119: pod "node-js-7esbp_default(df9e1d36-d11c-11e6-9141-42010a800002)" contain
er "node-js" is unhealthy, it will be killed and re-created.
  20m          20m           1        {kubelet kubernetes-minion-group-k0rn}  spec.con
tainers{node-js}           Normal    Created        Created container with docker id
53e4c1ec9e20; Security:[seccomp=unconfined]
  20m          20m           1        {kubelet kubernetes-minion-group-k0rn}  spec.con
tainers{node-js}           Normal    Started        Started container with docker id
53e4c1ec9e20
```

Description of node-js-1m3cs pod

At the top, we will see the overall pod details. Depending on your timing, under `State`, it will either show `Running` or `Waiting` with a `CrashLoopBackOff` reason and some error information. A bit below that we can see information on our `Liveness` probe and we will likely see a failure count above `0`. Further down we have the pod events. Again, depending on your timing, you are likely to have a number of events for the pod. Within a minute or two, you'll note a pattern of killing, started, and created events repeating over and over again. You should also see a note in the `Killing` entry that the container is unhealthy. This is our health check failing because we don't have a page responding at `/status`.

You may note that if you open a browser to the service load balancer address, it still responds with a page. You can find the load balancer IP with a `kubectl get services` command.

This is happening for a number of reasons. First, the health check is simply failing because `/status` doesn't exist, but the page where the service is pointed is still functioning normally in between restarts. Second, the `livenessProbe` is only charged with restarting the container on a health check fail. There is a separate `readinessProbe` that will remove a container from the pool of pods answering service endpoints.

Let's modify the health check for a page that does exist in our container, so we have a proper health check. We'll also add a readiness check and point it to the nonexistent status page. Open the `nodejs-health-controller.yaml` file and modify the `spec` section to match *Listing 2-8* and save it as `nodejs-health-controller-2.yaml`:

```
apiVersion: v1
kind: ReplicationController
metadata:
  name: node-js
  labels:
    name: node-js
spec:
  replicas: 3
  selector:
    name: node-js
  template:
    metadata:
      labels:
        name: node-js
    spec:
      containers:
      - name: node-js
        image: jonbaier/node-express-info:latest
        ports:
        - containerPort: 80
        livenessProbe:
```

```
        # An HTTP health check
      httpGet:
        path: /
        port: 80
      initialDelaySeconds: 30
      timeoutSeconds: 1
    readinessProbe:
      # An HTTP health check
      httpGet:
        path: /status/
        port: 80
      initialDelaySeconds: 30
      timeoutSeconds: 1
```

Listing 2-8: `nodejs-health-controller-2.yaml`

This time, we will delete the old RC, which will kill the pods with it, and create a new RC with our updated YAML file:

```
$ kubectl delete rc -l name=node-js
$ kubectl create -f nodejs-health-controller-2.yaml
```

Now, when we describe one of the pods, we only see the creation of the pod and the container. However, you'll note that the service load balancer IP no longer works. If we run the describe command on one of the new nodes we'll note a Readiness probe failed error message, but the pod itself continues running. If we change the readiness probe path to path: /, we will again be able to fulfill requests from the main service. Open up `nodejs-health-controller-2.yaml` in an editor and make that update now. Then, once again remove and recreate the replication controller:

```
$ kubectl delete rc -l name=node-js
$ kubectl create -f nodejs-health-controller-2.yaml
```

Now the load balancer IP should work once again. Keep these pods around as we will use them again in Chapter 3, *Networking, Load Balancers, and Ingress*.

TCP checks

Kubernetes also supports health checks via simple TCP socket checks and also with custom command-line scripts. The following snippets are examples of what both use cases look like in the YAML file:

```
livenessProbe:
  exec:
    command:
```

```
-/usr/bin/health/checkHttpServce.sh
initialDelaySeconds:90
timeoutSeconds: 1
```

Listing 2-9: Health check using command-line script

```
livenessProbe:
  tcpSocket:
    port: 80
  initialDelaySeconds: 15
  timeoutSeconds: 1
```

Listing 2-10: Health check using simple TCP Socket connection

Life cycle hooks or graceful shutdown

As you run into failures in real-life scenarios, you may find that you want to take additional action before containers are shutdown or right after they are started. Kubernetes actually provides life cycle hooks for just this kind of use case.

The following example controller definition defines both a `postStart` action and a `preStop` action to take place before Kubernetes moves the container into the next stage of its life cycle (you can refer to more details about this in point 1 in the *References* section at the end of the chapter):

```
apiVersion: v1
kind: ReplicationController
metadata:
  name: apache-hook
  labels:
    name: apache-hook
spec:
  replicas: 3
  selector:
    name: apache-hook
  template:
    metadata:
      labels:
        name: apache-hook
    spec:
      containers:
      - name: apache-hook
        image: bitnami/apache:latest
        ports:
        - containerPort: 80
        lifecycle:
```

```
postStart:
  httpGet:
    path: http://my.registration-server.com/register/
    port: 80
preStop:
  exec:
    command: ["/usr/local/bin/apachectl","-k","graceful-
    stop"]
```

Listing 2-11: `apache-hooks-controller.yaml`

You'll note for the `postStart` hook, we define an `httpGet` action, but for the `preStop` hook, I define an `exec` action. Just as with our health checks, the `httpGet` action attempts to make an HTTP call to the specific endpoint and port combination, while the `exec` action runs a local command in the container.

The `httpGet` and `exec` actions are both supported for the `postStart` and `preStop` hooks. In the case of `preStop`, a parameter named `reason` will be sent to the handler as a parameter. See the following table for valid values:

Reason parameter	Failure Description
Delete	Delete command issued via `kubectl` or the API
Health	Health check fails
Dependency	Dependency failure such as a disk mount failure or a default infrastructure pod crash

Valid preStop reasons (refer to point 1 in *References* section)

It's important to note that hook calls are delivered at least once. Therefore, any logic in the action should gracefully handle multiple calls. Another important note is that `postStart` runs before a pod enters its ready state. If the hook itself fails, the pod will be considered unhealthy.

Application scheduling

Now that we understand how to run containers in pods and even recover from failure, it may be useful to understand how new containers are scheduled on our cluster nodes.

As mentioned earlier, the default behavior for the Kubernetes scheduler is to spread container replicas across the nodes in our cluster. In the absence of all other constraints, the scheduler will place new pods on nodes with the least number of other pods belonging to matching services or replication controllers.

Additionally, the scheduler provides the ability to add constraints based on resources available to the node. Today, this includes minimum CPU and memory allocations. In terms of Docker, these use the **CPU-shares** and **memory limit flags** under the covers.

When additional constraints are defined, Kubernetes will check a node for available resources. If a node does not meet all the constraints, it will move to the next. If no nodes can be found that meet the criteria, then we will see a scheduling error in the logs.

The Kubernetes roadmap also has plans to support networking and storage. Because scheduling is such an important piece of overall operations and management for containers, we should expect to see many additions in this area as the project grows.

Scheduling example

Let's take a look at a quick example of setting some resource limits. If we look at our K8s dashboard, we can get a quick snapshot of the current state of resource usage on our cluster using `https://<your master ip>/api/v1/proxy/namespaces/kube-system/services/kubernetes-dashboard` and clicking on **Nodes** on the left-hand side menu.

We will see a dashboard as shown in the following screenshot:

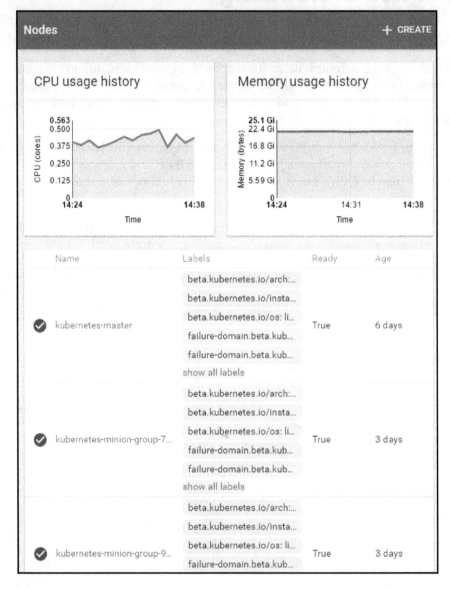

Kube Node dashboard

This view shows the aggregate CPU and memory across the whole cluster, nodes, and master. In this case, we have fairly low CPU utilization, but a decent chunk of memory in use.

Let's see what happens when I try to spin up a few more pods, but this time, we will request `512 Mi` for memory and `1500 m` for the CPU. We'll use `1500 m` to specify 1.5 CPUs; since each node only has 1 CPU, this should result in failure. Here's an example of RC definition:

```
apiVersion: v1
kind: ReplicationController
metadata:
  name: node-js-constraints
  labels:
    name: node-js-constraints
spec:
  replicas: 3
  selector:
    name: node-js-constraints
  template:
    metadata:
      labels:
        name: node-js-constraints
    spec:
      containers:
      - name: node-js-constraints
        image: jonbaier/node-express-info:latest
        ports:
        - containerPort: 80
        resources:
          limits:
            memory: "512Mi"
            cpu: "1500m"
```

Listing 2-12: `nodejs-constraints-controller.yaml`

To open the preceding file, use the following command:

> `$ kubectl create -f nodejs-constraints-controller.yaml`

The replication controller completes successfully, but if we run a `get pods` command, we'll note the `node-js-constraints` pods are stuck in a pending state. If we look a little closer with the `describe pods/<pod-id>` command, we'll note a scheduling error (for `pod-id` use one of the pod names from the first command):

> `$ kubectl get pods`
> `$ kubectl describe pods/<pod-id>`

The following screenshot is the result of the preceding command:

```
Name:            node-js-constraints-n9dlx
Namespace:       default
Node:            /
Labels:          name=node-js-constraints
Status:          Pending
IP:
Controllers:     ReplicationController/node-js-constraints
Containers:
  node-js-constraints:
    Image:       jonbaier/node-express-info:latest
    Port:        80/TCP
    Limits:
      cpu:       1500m
      memory:    512Mi
    Requests:
      cpu:       1500m
      memory:    512Mi
    Volume Mounts:
      /var/run/secrets/kubernetes.io/serviceaccount from default-token-7z353 (ro)
    Environment Variables:       <none>
Conditions:
  Type           Status
  PodScheduled   False
Volumes:
  default-token-7z353:
    Type:        Secret (a volume populated by a Secret)
    SecretName:  default-token-7z353
QoS Class:       Guaranteed
Tolerations:     <none>
Events:
  FirstSeen      LastSeen          Count   From                           SubobjectPath      Type    R
eason                     Message
  ---------      ---------         -----   ----                           --------------     --------
  1m             1m                3       {default-scheduler }                              WarningF
ailedScheduling pod (node-js-constraints-n9dlx) failed to fit in any node
fit failure on node (kubernetes-minion-group-9zf7): Insufficient cpu
fit failure on node (kubernetes-minion-group-k0rn): Insufficient cpu
fit failure on node (kubernetes-minion-group-7th4): Insufficient cpu

  1m             1m                3       {default-scheduler }                    Warning FailedScheduling   p
od (node-js-constraints-n9dlx) failed to fit in any node
fit failure on node (kubernetes-minion-group-7th4): Insufficient cpu
fit failure on node (kubernetes-minion-group-9zf7): Insufficient cpu
fit failure on node (kubernetes-minion-group-k0rn): Insufficient cpu

  1m             41s               2       {default-scheduler }                    Warning FailedScheduling   p
od (node-js-constraints-n9dlx) failed to fit in any node
fit failure on node (kubernetes-minion-group-k0rn): Insufficient cpu
fit failure on node (kubernetes-minion-group-7th4): Insufficient cpu
fit failure on node (kubernetes-minion-group-9zf7): Insufficient cpu
```

Pod description

Note, in the bottom events section, that the `WarningFailedScheduling pod` error listed in `Events` is accompanied by `fit failure on node....Insufficient cpu` after the error. As you can see, Kubernetes could not find a fit in the cluster that met all the constraints we defined.

If we now modify our CPU constraint down to `500 m`, and then recreate our replication controller, we should have all three pods running within a few moments.

Summary

We took a look at the overall architecture for Kubernetes, as well as the core constructs, provided to build your services and application stacks. You should have a better understanding of how these abstractions make it easier to manage the life cycle of your stack and/or services as a whole and not just the individual components. Additionally, we took a first-hand look at how to manage some simple day-to-day tasks using pods, services, and replication controllers. We also looked at how to use Kubernetes to automatically respond to outages via health checks. Finally, we explored the Kubernetes scheduler and some of the constraints users can specify to influence scheduling placement.

In the next chapter, we will dive into the networking layer of Kubernetes. We'll see how networking is done and also look at the core Kubernetes proxy that is used for traffic routing. We will also look at service discovery and the logical namespace groupings.

References

1. https://github.com/GoogleCloudPlatform/kubernetes/blob/release-1.0/doc s/user-guide/container-environment.md#container-hooks

3
Networking, Load Balancers, and Ingress

In this chapter, we will be covering how the Kubernetes cluster handles networking and how it differs from other approaches. We will be describing the three requirements for Kubernetes networking solutions and exploring why these are key to ease of operations. Further, we will take a deeper dive into services and how the Kubernetes proxy works on each node. Finishing up, we will see a brief overview of some higher level isolation features for multitenancy.

This chapter will discuss the following:

- Kubernetes networking
- Advanced services concepts
- Service discovery
- DNS
- Namespace limits and quotas

Kubernetes networking

Networking is a vital concern for production-level operations. At a service level, we need a reliable way for our application components to find and communicate with each other. Introducing containers and clustering into the mix makes things more complex as we now have multiple networking namespaces to bear in mind. Communication and discovery now becomes a feat that must traverse container IP space, host networking, and sometimes even multiple data center network topologies.

Kubernetes benefits here from getting its ancestry from the clustering tools used by Google for the past decade. Networking is one area where Google has outpaced the competition with one of the largest networks on the planet. Earlier, Google built its own hardware switches and **Software-defined Networking** (**SDN**) to give them more control, redundancy, and efficiency in their day-to-day network operations (you can refer to more details about this in point 1 in the *References* section at the end of the chapter). Many of the lessons learned from running and networking two billion containers per week have been distilled into Kubernetes and informed how K8s networking is done.

Networking in Kubernetes requires that each pod has its own IP address. Implementation details may vary based on the underlying infrastructure provider. However, all implementations must adhere to some basic rules. First and second, Kubernetes does not allow the use of **Network Address Translation** (**NAT**) for container-to-container or for container-to-node (minion) traffic. Further, the internal container IP address must match the IP address that is used to communicate with it.

These rules keep much of the complexity out of our networking stack and ease the design of the applications. Further, they eliminate the need to redesign network communication in legacy applications that are migrated from existing infrastructure. Finally, in greenfield applications, they allows for greater scale in handling hundreds, or even thousands of services and application communication.

K8s achieves this pod-wide IP magic using a **placeholder**. Remember that the `pause` container, we saw in Chapter 1, *Introduction to Kubernetes*, under the *Services running on the master* section, is often referred to as a **pod infrastructure container**, and it has the important job of reserving the network resources for our application containers that will be started later on. Essentially, the `pause` container holds the networking namespace and IP address for the entire pod and can be used by all the containers running within. The `pause` container joins first and holds the namespace while the subsequent containers in the pod join it when they start up.

Networking options

Kubernetes provides a wide range of networking options. There are solutions that work with the native networking layers in AWS and GCP. There are various overlay plugins, some of which are discussed in the next section. Finally, there is support for **Container Networking Interface** (**CNI**) plugins. CNI is meant to be a common plugin architecture for containers. It's currently supported by several orchestration tools such as Kubernetes, Mesos, and CloudFoundry. Find out more information at:

`https://github.com/containernetworking/cni.`

Always refer to the Kubernetes documentation for the latest and full list of supported networking options.

Networking comparisons

To get a better understanding of networking in containers, it can be instructive to look at other approaches to container networking. The following approaches do not make an exhaustive list, but should give a taste of the options available.

Docker

The **Docker Engine** creates three types of networks by default. These are **bridged**, **host**, and **none**.

The bridged network is the default choice unless otherwise specified. In this mode, the container has its own networking namespace and is then bridged via virtual interfaces to the host (or node in the case of K8s) network. In the bridged network, two containers can use the same IP range because they are completely isolated. Therefore, service communication requires some additional port mapping through the host side of network interfaces.

Docker also supports a host network, which allows the containers to use the host network stack. Performance is greatly benefited since it removes a level of network virtualization; however, you lose the security of having an isolated network namespace. Additionally, port usage must be managed more carefully since all containers share an IP.

Finally, Docker supports a none network, which creates a container with no external interface. Only a loopback device is shown if you inspect the network interfaces.

In all these scenarios, we are still on a single machine, and outside of a host mode, the container IP space is not available, outside that machine. Connecting containers across two machines then requires **NAT** and **port mapping** for communication.

Docker user-defined networks

In order to address the cross-machine communication issue and allow greater flexibility, Docker also supports user-defined networks via network plugins. These networks exist independent of the containers themselves. In this way, containers can join the same existing **networks**. Through the new plugin architecture, various drivers can be provided for different network use cases.

The first of these is the **bridge** driver, which allows creation of networks somewhat similar to the default bridge network.

The second is the **overlay** driver. In order to coordinate across multiple hosts, they must all agree on the available networks and their topologies. The overlay driver uses a distributed key-value store to synchronize the network creation across multiple hosts.

Docker also supports a **Macvlan** driver, which uses the interface and sub-interfaces on the host. Macvlan offers a more efficient network virtualization and isolation as it bypasses the Linux bridge.

 The plugin mechanism will allow a wide range of networking possibilities in Docker. In fact, many of the third-party options such as Weave have already created their own Docker network plugins.

Weave

Weave provides an overlay network for Docker containers. It can be used as a plugin with the new Docker network plugin interface, and it is also compatible with Kubernetes through a CNI plugin. Like many overlay networks, many criticize the performance impact of the encapsulation overhead. Note that they have recently added a preview release with **Virtual Extensible LAN** (**VXLAN**) encapsulation support, which greatly improves performance. For more information, visit `http://blog.weave.works/2015/06/12/weave-fast-datapath/`.

Flannel

Flannel comes from CoreOS and is an etcd-backed overlay. Flannel gives a full subnet to each host/node enabling a similar pattern to the Kubernetes practice of a routable IP per pod or group of containers. Flannel includes an in-kernel VXLAN encapsulation mode for better performance and has an experimental multi-network mode similar to the overlay Docker plugin. For more information, visit `https://github.com/coreos/flannel`.

Project Calico

Project Calico is a layer 3-based networking model that uses the built-in routing functions of the Linux kernel. Routes are propagated to virtual routers on each host via **Border Gateway Protocol** (**BGP**). Calico can be used for anything from small-scale deploys to large Internet-scale installations. Because it works at a lower level on the network stack, there is no need for additional NAT, tunneling, or overlays. It can interact directly with the underlying network infrastructure. Additionally, it has a support for network-level ACLs to provide additional isolation and security. For more information visit the following URL:
`http://www.projectcalico.org/`.

Canal

Canal merges both Calico for network policy and Flannel for overlay into one solution. It supports both Calico and Flannel type overlays and uses the Calico policy enforcement logic. Users can choose from overlay and non-overlay options with this setup as it combines the features of the preceding two projects. For more information visit the following URL:

`https://github.com/tigera/canal`

Balanced design

It's important to point out the balance Kubernetes is trying to achieve by placing the IP at the pod level. Using unique IP addresses at the host level is problematic as the number of containers grow. Ports must be used to expose services on specific containers and allow external communication. In addition to this, the complexity of running multiple services that may or may not know about each other (and their custom ports) and managing the port space becomes a big issue.

However, assigning an IP address to each container can be overkill. In cases of sizable scale, overlay networks and NATs are needed in order to address each container. Overlay networks add latency, and IP addresses would be taken up by backend services as well since they need to communicate with their frontend counterparts.

Here, we really see an advantage in the abstractions that Kubernetes provides at the application and service level. If I have a web server and a database, we can keep them on the same pod and use a single IP address. The web server and database can use the local interface and standard ports to communicate, and no custom setup is required. Further, services on the backend are not needlessly exposed to other application stacks running elsewhere in the cluster (but possibly on the same host). Since the pod sees the same IP address that the applications running within it see, service discovery does not require any additional translation.

If you need the flexibility of an overlay network, you can still use an overlay at the pod level. Weave, Flannel, and Project Calico can be used with Kubernetes as well as a plethora of other plugins and overlays available now.

This is also very helpful in the context of scheduling the workloads. It is a key to have a simple and standard structure for the scheduler to match constraints and understand where space exists on the cluster's network at any given time. This is a dynamic environment with a variety of applications and tasks running, so any additional complexity here will have rippling effects.

There are also implications for service discovery. New services coming online must determine and register an IP address on which the rest of the world, or at least cluster, can reach them. If NAT is used, the services will need an additional mechanism to learn their externally facing IP.

Advanced services

Let's explore the IP strategy as it relates to services and communication between containers. If you recall, in the *Services* section, Chapter 2, *Pods, Services, Replication Controllers, and Labels*, you learned that Kubernetes is using kube-proxy to determine the proper pod IP address and port serving each request. Behind the scenes, kube-proxy is actually using virtual IPs and iptables to make all this magic work.

Kube-proxy now has two modes—*userspace* and *iptables*. As of now, 1.2 iptables is the default mode. In both modes, kube-proxy is running on every host. Its first duty is to monitor the API from the Kubernetes master. Any updates to services will trigger an update to iptables from kube-proxy. For example, when a new service is created, a virtual IP address is chosen and a rule in iptables is set, which will direct its traffic to kube-proxy via a random port. Thus, we now have a way to capture service-destined traffic on this node. Since kube-proxy is running on all nodes, we have cluster-wide resolution for the service **VIP** (short for **virtual IP**). Additionally, DNS records can point to this VIP as well.

In the userspace mode, we have a hook created in iptables, but the proxying of traffic is still handled by kube-proxy. The iptables rule is only sending traffic to the service entry in kube-proxy at this point. Once kube-proxy receives the traffic for a particular service, it must then forward it to a pod in the service's pool of candidates. It does this using a random port that was selected during service creation. Refer to the following figure for an overview of the flow:

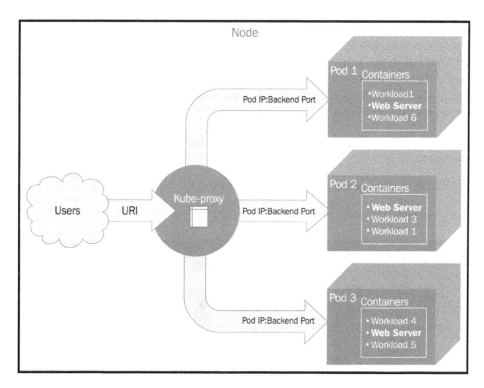

Kube-proxy communication

It is also possible to always forward traffic from the same client IP to the same backend pod/container using the `sessionAffinity` element in your service definition.

In the iptables mode, the pods are coded directly in the iptable rules. This removes the dependency on kube-proxy for actually proxying the traffic. The request will go straight to iptables and then on to the pod. This is faster and removes a possible point of failure. Readiness probe, as we discussed in the *Health Check* section, `Chapter 2`, *Pods, Services, Replication Controllers, and Labels*, is your friend here as this mode also loses the ability to retry pods.

External services

In the previous chapter, we saw a few service examples. For testing and demonstration purposes, we wanted all the services to be externally accessible. This was configured by the `type: LoadBalancer` element in our service definition. The `LoadBalancer` type creates an external load balancer on the cloud provider. We should note that support for external load balancers varies by provider, as does the implementation. In our case, we are using GCE, so integration is pretty smooth. The only additional setup needed is to open firewall rules for the external service ports.

Let's dig a little deeper and do a `describe` command on one of the services from the *More on labels* section in `Chapter 2`, *Pods, Services, Replication Controllers, and Labels*:

```
$ kubectl describe service/node-js-labels
```

The following screenshot is the result of the preceding command:

```
Name:                   node-js-labels
Namespace:              default
Labels:                 app=node-js-express,deployment=test,name=node-js-labels
Selector:               app=node-js-express,name=node-js-labels
Type:                   LoadBalancer
IP:                     10.0.115.200
LoadBalancer Ingress:   146.148.56.25
Port:                   <unnamed>        80/TCP
NodePort:               <unnamed>        30237/TCP
Endpoints:              10.244.0.29:80,10.244.2.34:80,10.244.2.35:80
Session Affinity:       None
No events.
```

Service description

In the output, in the preceding figure, you'll note several key elements. Our `Namespace:` is set to `default`, `Type:` is `LoadBalancer`, and we have the external IP listed under `LoadBalancer Ingress:`. Further, we see `Endpoints:`, which shows us the IPs of the pods available to answer service requests.

Internal services

Let's explore the other types of services we can deploy. First, by default, services are only internally facing. You can specify a type of `clusterIP` to achieve this, but, if no type is defined, `clusterIP` is the assumed type. Let's take a look at an example; note the lack of the `type` element:

```
apiVersion: v1
kind: Service
metadata:
  name: node-js-internal
  labels:
    name: node-js-internal
spec:
  ports:
  - port: 80
  selector:
    name: node-js
```

Listing 3-1: `nodejs-service-internal.yaml`

Use this listing to create the service definition file. You'll need a healthy version of the `node-js` RC (*Listing 2-7*: `nodejs-health-controller-2.yaml`). As you can see, the selector matches on the pods named `node-js` that our RC launched in the previous chapter. We will create the service and then list the currently running services with a filter:

```
$ kubectl create -f nodejs-service-internal.yaml
$ kubectl get services -l name=node-js-internal
```

The following screenshot is the result of the preceding command:

NAME	LABELS	SELECTOR	IP(S)	PORT(S)
node-js-internal	name=node-js-internal	name=node-js	10.0.5.134	80/TCP

Internal service listing

As you can see, we have a new service, but only one IP. Further, the IP address is not externally accessible. We won't be able to test the service from a web browser this time. However, we can use the handy `kubectl exec` command and attempt to connect from one of the other pods. You will need `node-js-pod` (*Listing 2-1*: `nodejs-pod.yaml`) running. Then, you can execute the following command:

```
$ kubectl exec node-js-pod -- curl <node-js-internal IP>
```

This allows us to run a `docker exec` command as if we had a shell in the `node-js-pod` container. It then hits the internal service URL, which forwards to any pods with the `node-js` label.

If all is well, you should get the raw HTML output back. So, you successfully created an internal-only service. This can be useful for backend services that you want to make available to other containers running in your cluster, but not open to the world at large.

Custom load balancing

A third type of service that K8s allows is the `NodePort` type. This type allows us to expose a service through the host or node (minion) on a specific port. In this way, we can use the IP address of any node (minion) and access our service on the assigned node port. Kubernetes will assign a node port by default in the range of `3000-32767`, but you can also specify your own custom port. In the example in *Listing 3-2*: `nodejs-service-nodeport.yaml`, we choose port `30001`, as follows:

```yaml
apiVersion: v1
kind: Service
metadata:
  name: node-js-nodeport
  labels:
    name: node-js-nodeport
spec:
  ports:
  - port: 80
    nodePort: 30001
  selector:
    name: node-js
  type: NodePort
```

Listing 3-2: `nodejs-service-nodeport.yaml`

Once again, create this YAML definition file and create your service, as follows:

```
$ kubectl create -f nodejs-service-nodeport.yaml
```

The output should have a message like this:

```
You have exposed your service on an external port on all nodes in your
cluster.  If you want to expose this service to the external internet,
you may
need to set up firewall rules for the service port(s) (tcp:30001) to se
rve traffic.

See http://releases.k8s.io/HEAD/docs/user-guide/services-firewalls.md f
or more details.
services/node-js-nodeport
```

New GCP firewall rule

You'll note a message about opening firewall ports. Similar to the external load balancer type, `NodePort` is exposing your service externally using ports on the nodes. This could be useful if, for example, you want to use your own load balancer in front of the nodes. Let's make sure that we open those ports on GCP before we test our new service.

From the GCE VM instance console, click on the details for any of your nodes (minions). Then click on the network, which is usually default unless otherwise specified during creation. In **Firewall rules**, we can add a rule by clicking on **Add firewall rule**.

Create a rule like the one shown in the following figure (`tcp:30001` on `0.0.0.0/0` IP range):

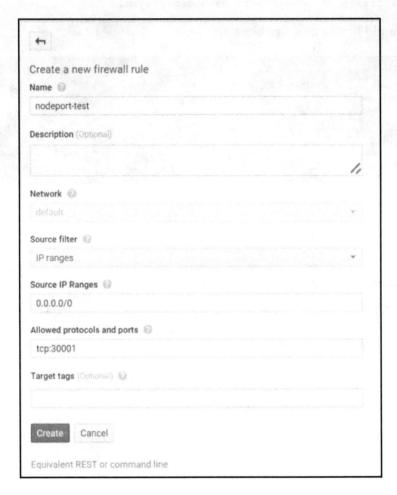

Create New GCP firewall rule

We can now test our new service, by opening a browser and using an IP address of any node (minion) in your cluster. The format to test the new service is as follows:

```
http://<Minoion IP Address>:<NodePort>/
```

Finally, the latest version has added an `ExternalName` type, which maps a CNAME to the service.

Cross-node proxy

Remember that kube-proxy is running on all the nodes, so, even if the pod is not running there, the traffic will be given a proxy to the appropriate host. Refer to the *Cross-node traffic* figure for a visual on how the traffic flows. A user makes a request to an external IP or URL. The request is serviced by **Node** in this case. However, the pod does not happen to run on this node. This is not a problem because the pod IP addresses are routable. So, **Kube-proxy** or **iptables** simply passes traffic onto the pod IP for this service. The network routing then completes on **Node 2**, where the requested application lives:

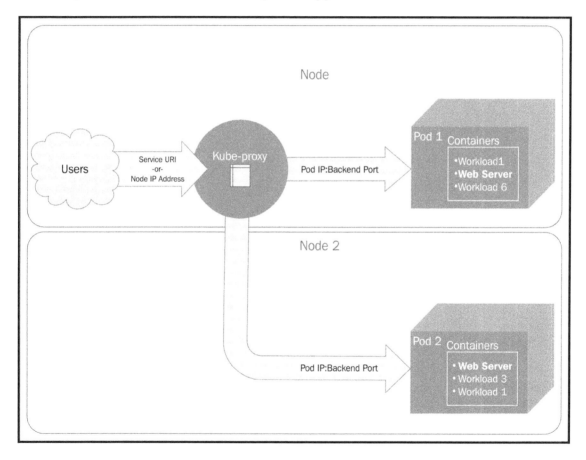

Cross-node traffic

Custom ports

Services also allow you to map your traffic to different ports; then the containers and pods expose themselves. We will create a service that exposes port 90 and forwards traffic to port 80 on the pods. We will call the `node-js-90` pod to reflect the custom port number. Create the following two definition files:

```yaml
apiVersion: v1
kind: ReplicationController
metadata:
  name: node-js-90
  labels:
    name: node-js-90
spec:
  replicas: 3
  selector:
    name: node-js-90
  template:
    metadata:
      labels:
        name: node-js-90
    spec:
      containers:
      - name: node-js-90
        image: jonbaier/node-express-info:latest
        ports:
        - containerPort: 80
```

Listing 3-3: `nodejs-customPort-controller.yaml`

```yaml
apiVersion: v1
kind: Service
metadata:
  name: node-js-90
  labels:
    name: node-js-90
spec:
  type: LoadBalancer
  ports:
  - port: 90
    targetPort: 80
  selector:
    name: node-js-90
```

Listing 3-4: `nodejs-customPort-service.yaml`

You'll note that in the service definition, we have a `targetPort` element. This element tells the service the port to use for pods/containers in the pool. As we saw in previous examples, if you do not specify `targetPort`, it assumes that it's the same port as the service. This port is still used as the service port, but, in this case, we are going to expose the service on port 90 while the containers serve content on port 80.

Create this RC and service and open the appropriate firewall rules, as we did in the last example. It may take a moment for the external load balancer IP to propagate to the `get service` command. Once it does, you should be able to open and see our familiar web application in a browser using the following format:

```
http://<external service IP>:90/
```

Multiple ports

Another custom port use case is that of multiple ports. Many applications expose multiple ports, such as HTTP on port 80 and port 8888 for web servers. The following example shows our app responding on both ports. Once again, we'll also need to add a firewall rule for this port, as we did for *Listing 3-2*: `nodejs-service-nodeport.yaml` previously:

```yaml
apiVersion: v1
kind: ReplicationController
metadata:
  name: node-js-multi
  labels:
    name: node-js-multi
spec:
  replicas: 3
  selector:
    name: node-js-multi
  template:
    metadata:
      labels:
        name: node-js-multi
    spec:
      containers:
      - name: node-js-multi
        image: jonbaier/node-express-multi:latest
        ports:
        - containerPort: 80
        - containerPort: 8888
```

Listing 3-5: `nodejs-multi-controller.yaml`

```
apiVersion: v1
kind: Service
metadata:
  name: node-js-multi
  labels:
    name: node-js-multi
spec:
  type: LoadBalancer
  ports:
  - name: http
    protocol: TCP
    port: 80
  - name: fake-admin-http
    protocol: TCP
    port: 8888
  selector:
    name: node-js-multi
```

Listing 3-6: `nodejs-multi-service.yaml`

The application and container itself must be listening on both ports for this to work. In this example, port `8888` is used to represent a fake admin interface.

If, for example, you want to listen on port `443`, you would need a proper SSL socket listening on the server.

Ingress

We discussed previously how Kubernetes uses the service abstract as a means to proxy traffic to backing pod distributed throughout our cluster. While this is helpful in both scaling and pod recovery, there are more advanced routing scenarios that are not addressed by this design.

To that end, Kubernetes has added an Ingress resource, which allows for custom proxying and load balancing to a back service. Think of it as an extra layer or hop in the routing path before traffic hits our service. Just as an application has a service and backing pods, the Ingress resource needs both an Ingress entry point and an Ingress controller that perform the custom logic. The entry point defines the routes and the controller actually handles the routing. For our examples, we will use the default GCE backend.

Some limitations to be aware of when using the Ingress API can be found here:
`https://github.com/kubernetes/contrib/blob/master/ingress/controllers/gce/BETA_LIMITATIONS.md`

As you may recall, in `Chapter 1`, *Introduction to Kubernetes*, we saw that a GCE cluster comes with a default back which provides Layer 7 load balancing capability. We can see this controller running if we look at the `kube-system` namespace:

```
$ kubectl get rc --namespace=kube-system
```

We should see an RC listed with the `l7-default-backend-v1.0` name, as shown here:

NAME	DESIRED	CURRENT	READY	AGE
kube-dns-v20	1	1	1	8d
kubernetes-dashboard-v1.4.0	1	1	1	8d
l7-default-backend-v1.0	1	1	1	8d
monitoring-influxdb-grafana-v4	1	1	1	8d

GCE Layer 7 Ingress controller

This provides the Ingress controller piece that actually routes the traffic defined in our Ingress entry points. Let's create some resources for an Ingress.

First, we will create a few new replication controllers with my `httpwhalesay` image. This is a remix of the original whalesay that was displayed in a browser. The following listing shows the YAML. Notice the three dashes that let us combine several resources into one YAML file:

```
apiVersion: v1
kind: ReplicationController
metadata:
  name: whale-ingress-a
spec:
  replicas: 1
  template:
    metadata:
      labels:
        app: whale-ingress-a
    spec:
      containers:
      - name: sayhey
        image: jonbaier/httpwhalesay:0.1
        command: ["node", "index.js", "Whale Type A, Here."]
        ports:
        - containerPort: 80
```

```
---
apiVersion: v1
kind: ReplicationController
metadata:
  name: whale-ingress-b
spec:
  replicas: 1
  template:
    metadata:
      labels:
        app: whale-ingress-b
    spec:
      containers:
      - name: sayhey
        image: jonbaier/httpwhalesay:0.1
        command: ["node", "index.js", "Hey man, It's Whale B, Just
        Chillin'."]
        ports:
        - containerPort: 80
```

Listing 3-7. `whale-rcs.yaml`

Notice that we are creating pods with the same container, but different start up parameters.
Take note of these parameters for later. We will also create `Service` endpoints for each of
these RCs:

```
apiVersion: v1
kind: Service
metadata:
  name: whale-svc-a
  labels:
    app: whale-ingress-a
spec:
  type: NodePort
  ports:
  - port: 80
    nodePort: 30301
    protocol: TCP
    name: http
  selector:
    app: whale-ingress-a
---
apiVersion: v1
kind: Service
metadata:
  name: whale-svc-b
  labels:
    app: whale-ingress-b
```

```
spec:
  type: NodePort
  ports:
  - port: 80
    nodePort: 30284
    protocol: TCP
    name: http
  selector:
    app: whale-ingress-b
---
apiVersion: v1
kind: Service
metadata:
 name: whale-svc-default
 labels:
   app: whale-ingress-a
spec:
  type: NodePort
  ports:
  - port: 80
    nodePort: 30302
    protocol: TCP
    name: http
  selector:
    app: whale-ingress-a
```

Listing 3-8. `whale-svcs.yaml`

Again create these with the `kubectl create -f` command, as follows:

```
$ kubectl create -f whale-rcs.yaml
$ kubectl create -f whale-svcs.yaml
```

We should see messages about the RCs and Services successful creation. Next, we need to define the Ingress entry point. We will use `http://a.whale.hey` and `http://b.whale.hey` as our demo entry points:

```
apiVersion: extensions/v1beta1
kind: Ingress
metadata:
  name: whale-ingress
spec:
  rules:
  - host: a.whale.hey
    http:
      paths:
      - path: /
        backend:
```

```
            serviceName: whale-svc-a
            servicePort: 80
  - host: b.whale.hey
    http:
      paths:
      - path: /
        backend:
            serviceName: whale-svc-b
            servicePort: 80
```

Listing 3-9. `whale-ingress.yaml`

Again, use `kubectl create -f` to create this Ingress. Once this is successfully created, we will need to wait a few moments for GCE to give the Ingress a static IP address. Use the following command to watch the Ingress resource:

```
$ kubectl get ingress
```

Once the Ingress has an IP, we should see an entry in ADDRESS like the one shown here:

NAME	HOSTS	ADDRESS	PORTS	AGE
whale-ingress	a.whale.hey,b.whale.hey	130.211.24.177	80	3h

Ingress Description

Since this is not a registered domain name, we will need to specify the resolution in the `curl` command, like this:

```
$ curl --resolve a.whale.hey:80:130.211.24.177 http://a.whale.hey/
```

This should display the following:

Whalesay A

We can also try the second URL and we will get our second RC:

```
$ curl --resolve b.whale.hey:80:130.211.24.177 http://b.whale.hey/
```

Whalesay B

We notice that the images are almost the same, except that the words from each whale reflect the startup parameters from each RC we started earlier. Thus our two Ingress points are directing traffic to different backends.

> In this example, we used the default GCE backend for an Ingress controller. Kubernetes allows us to build our own and Nginx actually has a few versions available as well.

Migrations, multicluster, and more

As you've seen so far, Kubernetes offers a high level of flexibility and customization to create a service abstraction around your containers running in the cluster. However, there may be times where you want to point to something outside your cluster.

An example of this would be working with legacy systems or even applications running on another cluster. In the case of the former, this is a perfectly good strategy in order to migrate to Kubernetes and containers in general. We can begin to manage the service endpoints in Kubernetes while stitching the stack together using the K8s orchestration concepts. Additionally, we can even start bringing over pieces of the stack, as the frontend, one at a time as the organization refactors applications for microservices and/or containerization.

To allow access to non-pod-based applications, the services construct allows you to use endpoints that are outside the cluster. Kubernetes is actually creating an endpoint resource every time you create a service that uses selectors. The `endpoints` object keeps track of the pod IPs in the load balancing pool. You can see this by running a `get endpoints` command, as follows:

```
$ kubectl get endpoints
```

You should see something similar to this:

```
NAME            ENDPOINTS
http-pd         10.244.2.29:80,10.244.2.30:80,10.244.3.16:80
kubernetes      10.240.0.2:443
node-js         10.244.0.12:80,10.244.2.24:80,10.244.3.13:80
```

You'll note an entry for all the services we currently have running on our cluster. For most services, the endpoints are just the IP of each pod running in an RC. As I mentioned, Kubernetes does this automatically based on the selector. As we scale the replicas in a controller with matching labels, Kubernetes will update the endpoints automatically.

If we want to create a service for something that is not a pod and therefore has no labels to select, we can easily do this with both a service and endpoint definition, as follows:

```
apiVersion: v1
kind: Service
metadata:
  name: custom-service
spec:
  type: LoadBalancer
  ports:
  - name: http
    protocol: TCP
    port: 80
```

Listing 3-10: `nodejs-custom-service.yaml`

```
apiVersion: v1
kind: Endpoints
metadata:
  name: custom-service
subsets:
- addresses:
  - ip: <X.X.X.X>
  ports:
    - name: http
      port: 80
      protocol: TCP
```

Listing 3-11: `nodejs-custom-endpoint.yaml`

In the preceding example, you'll need to replace <X.X.X.X> with a real IP address, where the new service can point to. In my case, I used the public load balancer IP from the `node-js-multi` service we created earlier in *listing 3-6*. Go ahead and create these resources now.

If we now run a `get endpoints` command, we will see this IP address at port 80 associated with the `custom-service` endpoint. Further, if we look at the service details, we will see the IP listed in the Endpoints section:

```
$ kubectl describe service/custom-service
```

We can test out this new service by opening the `custom-service` external IP from a browser.

Custom addressing

Another option to customize services is with the `clusterIP` element. In our examples so far, we've not specified an IP address, which means that it chooses the internal address of the service for us. However, we can add this element and choose the IP address in advance with something like `clusterip: 10.0.125.105`.

There may be times when you don't want to load balance and would rather have DNS with *A* records for each pod. For example, software that needs to replicate data evenly to all nodes may rely on *A* records to distribute data. In this case, we can use an example like the following one and set `clusterip` to `None`. Kubernetes will not assign an IP address and instead only assign *A* records in DNS for each of the pods. If you are using DNS, the service should be available at `node-js-none` or `node-js-none.default.cluster.local` from within the cluster. We have the following code:

```
apiVersion: v1
kind: Service
metadata:
  name: node-js-none
  labels:
    name: node-js-none
spec:
  clusterIP: None
  ports:
  - port: 80
  selector:
    name: node-js
```

Listing 3-12: `nodejs-headless-service.yaml`

Test it out after you create this service with the trusty `exec` command:

```
$ kubectl exec node-js-pod -- curl node-js-none
```

Service discovery

As we discussed earlier, the Kubernetes master keeps track of all service definitions and updates. Discovery can occur in one of three ways. The first two methods use Linux environment variables. There is support for the Docker link style of environment variables, but Kubernetes also has its own naming convention. Here is an example of what our `node-js` service example might look like using K8s environment variables (note IPs will vary):

```
NODE_JS_PORT_80_TCP=tcp://10.0.103.215:80
NODE_JS_PORT=tcp://10.0.103.215:80
NODE_JS_PORT_80_TCP_PROTO=tcp
NODE_JS_PORT_80_TCP_PORT=80
NODE_JS_SERVICE_HOST=10.0.103.215
NODE_JS_PORT_80_TCP_ADDR=10.0.103.215
NODE_JS_SERVICE_PORT=80
```

Listing 3-13: Service environment variables

Another option for discovery is through DNS. While environment variables can be useful when DNS is not available, it has drawbacks. The system only creates variables at creation time, so services that come online later will not be discovered or would require some additional tooling to update all the system environments.

DNS

DNS solves the issues seen with environment variables by allowing us to reference the services by their name. As services restart, scale out, or appear anew, the DNS entries will be updating and ensuring that the service name always points to the latest infrastructure. DNS is set up by default in most of the supported providers.

If DNS is supported by your provider, but not set up, you can configure the following variables in your default provider config when you create your Kubernetes cluster:
```
ENABLE_CLUSTER_DNS="${KUBE_ENABLE_CLUSTER_DNS:-true}"
DNS_SERVER_IP="10.0.0.10"
DNS_DOMAIN="cluster.local"
DNS_REPLICAS=1
```

With DNS active, services can be accessed in one of two forms—either the service name itself, `<service-name>` or a fully qualified name that includes the namespace, `<service-name>.<namespace-name>.cluster.local`. In our examples, it would look similar to `node-js-90` or `node-js-90.default.cluster.local`.

Multitenancy

Kubernetes also has an additional construct for isolation at the cluster level. In most cases, you can run Kubernetes and never worry about namespaces; everything will run in the default namespace if not specified. However, in cases where you run multitenancy communities or want broad-scale segregation and isolation of the cluster resources, namespaces can be used to this end.

To start, Kubernetes has two namespaces—`default` and `kube-system`. The `kube-system` namespace is used for all the system-level containers we saw in Chapter 1, *Introduction to Kubernetes*, in the *Services running on the minions* section. The UI, logging, DNS, and so on are all run in `kube-system`. Everything else the user creates runs in the default namespace. However, our resource definition files can optionally specify a custom namespace. For the sake of experimenting, let's take a look at how to build a new namespace.

First, we'll need to create a namespace definition file like the one in this listing:

```
apiVersion: v1
kind: Namespace
metadata:
  name: test
```

Listing 3-14: `test-ns.yaml`

We can go ahead and create this file with our handy `create` command:

```
$ kubectl create -f test-ns.yaml
```

Now we can create resources that use the `test` namespace. The following is an example of a pod using this new namespace:

```
apiVersion: v1
kind: Pod
metadata:
  name: utility
  namespace: test
spec:
  containers:
  - image: debian:latest
    command:
      - sleep
      - "3600"
    name: utility
```

Listing 3-15: `ns-pod.yaml`

While the pod can still access services in other namespaces, it will need to use the long DNS form of `<service-name>.<namespace-name>.cluster.local`. For example, if you were to run a command from inside the container in *Listing 3-15*: `ns-pod.yaml`, you could use `node-js.default.cluster.local` to access the Node.js example from `Chapter 2`, *Pods, Services, Replication Controllers, and Labels*.

Here is a note about resource utilization. At some point in this book, you may run out of space on your cluster to create new Kubernetes resources. The timing will vary based on cluster size, but it's good to keep this in mind and do some clean-up from time to time. Use the following commands to remove old examples:

```
$ kubectl delete pod <pod name>
$ kubectl delete svc <service name>
$ kubectl delete rc <replication controller name>
$ kubectl delete rs <replicaset name>
```

Limits

Let's inspect our new namespace a bit more. Run the `describe` command as follows:

```
$ kubectl describe namespace/test
```

The following screenshot is the result of the preceding command:

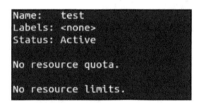

Namespace describe

Kubernetes allows you to both limit the resources used by individual pods or containers and the resources used by the overall namespace using quotas. You'll note that there are no resource **limits** or **quotas** currently set on the `test` namespace.

Suppose we want to limit the footprint of this new namespace; we can set quotas such as the following:

```
apiVersion: v1
kind: ResourceQuota
metadata:
  name: test-quotas
```

```
    namespace: test
spec:
  hard:
    pods: 3
    services: 1
    replicationcontrollers: 1
```

Listing 3-16: `quota.yaml`

 In reality, namespaces would be for larger application communities and would probably never have quotas this low. I am using this in order to ease illustration of the capability in the example.

Here, we will create a quota of 3 pods, 1 RC, and 1 service for the test namespace. As you probably guessed, this is executed once again by our trusty `create` command:

$ kubectl create -f quota.yaml

Now that we have that in place, let's use `describe` on the namespace, as follows:

$ kubectl describe namespace/test

The following screenshot is the result of the preceding command:

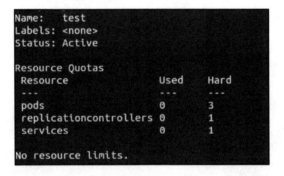

Namespace describe after quota is set

You'll note that we now have some values listed in the quota section and the limits section is still blank. We also have a `Used` column, which lets us know how close to the limits we are at the moment. Let's try to spin up a few pods using the following definition:

```
apiVersion: v1
kind: ReplicationController
metadata:
  name: busybox-ns
  namespace: test
  labels:
    name: busybox-ns
spec:
  replicas: 4
  selector:
    name: busybox-ns
  template:
    metadata:
      labels:
        name: busybox-ns
    spec:
      containers:
      - name: busybox-ns
        image: busybox
        command:
          - sleep
          - "3600"
```

Listing 3-17: `busybox-ns.yaml`

You'll note that we are creating four replicas of this basic pod. After using `create` to build this RC, run the `describe` command on the `test` namespace once more. You'll notice that the `Used` values for pods and RCs are at their max. However, we asked for four replicas and only see three pods in use.

Let's see what's happening with our RC. You might attempt to do that with the command here:

```
kubectl describe rc/busybox-ns
```

However, if you try, you'll be discouraged to see a `not found` message from the server. This is because we created this RC in a new namespace and `kubectl` assumes the default namespace if not specified. This means that we need to specify `--namepsace=test` with every command when we wish to access resources in the `test` namespace.

We can also set the current namespace by working with the context settings. First, we need to find our current context, which is found with the following command:

```
$ kubectl config view | grep current-context
```

Next, we can take that context and set the namespace variable like the following:

```
$ kubectl config set-context <Current Context> --namespace=test
```

Now you can run the kubectl command without the need to specify the namespace. Just remember to switch back when you want to look at the resources running in your default namespace.

Run the command with the namespace specified. If you've set your current namespace as demonstrated in the tip box, you can leave off the --namespace argument:

```
$ kubectl describe rc/busybox-ns --namespace=test
```

The following screenshot is the result of the preceding command:

```
Name:            busybox-ns
Namespace:       test
Image(s):        busybox
Selector:        name=busybox-ns
Labels:          name=busybox-ns
Replicas:        3 current / 4 desired
Pods Status:     3 Running / 0 Waiting / 0 Succeeded / 0 Failed
Events:
  FirstSeen                        LastSeen                         Count   F
rom                      SubobjectPath    Reason                    Message
  Mon, 17 Aug 2015 16:29:43 -0400    Mon, 17 Aug 2015 16:29:43 -0400 1       {
replication-controller }                  successfulCreate          Created p
od: busybox-ns-spfrn
  Mon, 17 Aug 2015 16:29:43 -0400    Mon, 17 Aug 2015 16:29:43 -0400 1       {
replication-controller }                  successfulCreate          Created p
od: busybox-ns-xjf6q
  Mon, 17 Aug 2015 16:29:43 -0400    Mon, 17 Aug 2015 16:29:43 -0400 1       {
replication-controller }                  successfulCreate          Created p
od: busybox-ns-zeuuy
  Mon, 17 Aug 2015 16:29:44 -0400    Mon, 17 Aug 2015 16:33:01 -0400 18      {
replication-controller }                  failedCreate              Error cre
ating: Pod "busybox-ns-" is forbidden: Limited to 3 pods
```

Namespace quotas

As you can see in the preceding image, the first three pods were successfully created, but our final one fails with the `Limited to 3 pods` error.

This is an easy way to set limits for resources partitioned out at a community scale. It's worth noting that you can also set quotas for CPU, memory, persistent volumes, and secrets. Additionally, limits work in a similar way to quota, but they set the limit for each pod or container within the namespace.

A note on resource usage

As most of the examples in this book utilize GCP or AWS, it can be costly to keep everything running. It's also easy to run out of resources using the default cluster size, especially if you keep every example running. Therefore, you may want to delete older pods, replication controllers, replica sets, and services periodically. You can also destroy the cluster and recreate using `Chapter 1`, *Introduction to Kubernetes* as a way to lower your cloud provider bill.

Summary

We took a deeper look into networking and services in Kubernetes. You should now understand how networking communications are designed in K8s and feel comfortable accessing your services internally and externally. We saw how kube-proxy balances traffic both locally and across the cluster. Additionally, we explored the new Ingress resources that allow us finer control of incoming traffic. We also looked briefly at how DNS and service discovery is achieved in Kubernetes. We finished off with quick look at namespace and isolation for multitenancy.

References

1. http://www.wired.com/2015/06/google-reveals-secret-gear-connects-online-empire/

4
Updates, Gradual Rollouts, and Autoscaling

This chapter will expand upon the core concepts, which show you how to roll out updates and test new features of your application with minimal disruption to up-time. It will cover the basics of doing application updates, gradual rollouts, and A/B testing. In addition, we will look at scaling the Kubernetes cluster itself.

This chapter will discuss the following topics:

- Application scaling
- Rolling updates
- A/B testing
- Application autoscaling
- Scaling up your cluster

Since version 1.2, Kubernetes has released a Deployments API. Deployments are the recommended way to deal with scaling and application updates going forward. However, it is still considered beta at the time of writing this book, while rolling updates has been stable for several versions. We will explore rolling updates in this chapter as an introduction to the scaling concept and then dive into the preferred method of using deployments in the next chapter.

Example set up

Before we start exploring the various capabilities built into Kubernetes for scaling and updates, we will need a new example environment. We are going to use a variation of our previous container image with a blue background (refer to the *v0.1 and v0.2 (side by side)* image, later in this chapter, for a comparison). We have the following code:

```yaml
apiVersion: v1
kind: ReplicationController
metadata:
  name: node-js-scale
  labels:
    name: node-js-scale
spec:
  replicas: 1
  selector:
    name: node-js-scale
  template:
    metadata:
      labels:
        name: node-js-scale
    spec:
      containers:
      - name: node-js-scale
        image: jonbaier/pod-scaling:0.1
        ports:
        - containerPort: 80
```

Listing 4-1: `pod-scaling-controller.yaml`

```yaml
apiVersion: v1
kind: Service
metadata:
  name: node-js-scale
  labels:
    name: node-js-scale
spec:
  type: LoadBalancer
  sessionAffinity: ClientIP
  ports:
  - port: 80
  selector:
    name: node-js-scale
```

Listing 4-2: `pod-scaling-service.yaml`

Create these services with the following commands:

```
$ kubectl create -f pod-scaling-controller.yaml
$ kubectl create -f pod-scaling-service.yaml
```

 The public IP address for the service may take a moment to create.

Scaling up

Over time, as you run your applications in the Kubernetes cluster, you will find that some applications need more resources, whereas others can manage with fewer resources. Instead of removing the entire RC (and associated pods), we want a more seamless way to scale our application up and down.

Thankfully, Kubernetes includes a `scale` command, which is suited specifically for this purpose. The `scale` command works both with Replication Controllers and the new Deployments abstraction. For now, we will explore the usage with Replication Controllers. In our new example, we have only one replica running. You can check this with a `get pods` command:

```
$ kubectl get pods -l name=node-js-scale
```

Let's try scaling that up to three with the following command:

```
$ kubectl scale --replicas=3 rc/node-js-scale
```

If all goes well, you'll simply see the **scaled** word on the output of your terminal window.

 Optionally, you can specify the `--current-replicas` flag as a verification step. The scaling will only occur if the actual number of replicas currently running matches this count.

After listing our pods once again, we should now see three pods running with a name similar to `node-js-scale-`**XXXXX**, where the X characters are a random string.

You can also use the `scale` command to reduce the number of replicas. In either case, the `scale` command adds or removes the necessary pod replicas, and the service automatically updates and balances across new or remaining replicas.

Smooth updates

The scaling of our application up and down as our resource demands change is useful for many production scenarios, but what about simple application updates? Any production system will have code updates, patches, and feature additions. These could be occurring monthly, weekly, or even daily. Making sure that we have a reliable way to push out these changes without interruption to our users is a paramount consideration.

Once again, we benefit from the years of experience the Kubernetes system is built on. There is a built-in support for rolling updates with the 1.0 version. The `rolling-update` command allows us to update entire RCs or just the underlying Docker image used by each replica. We can also specify an update interval, which will allow us to update one pod at a time and wait until proceeding to the next.

Let's take our scaling example and perform a rolling update to the 0.2 version of our container image. We will use an update interval of 2 minutes, so we can watch the process as it happens in the following way:

```
$ kubectl rolling-update node-js-scale --image=jonbaier/pod-scaling:0.2 --update-period="2m"
```

You should see some text about creating a new RC named `node-js-scale-XXXXX`, where the X characters will be a random string of numbers and letters. In addition, you will see the beginning of a loop that is starting one replica of the new version and removing one from the existing RC. This process will continue until the new RC has the full count of replicas running.

If we want to follow along in real time, we can open another terminal window and use the `get pods` command, along with a label filter, to see what's happening:

```
$ kubectl get pods -l name=node-js-scale
```

This command will filter for pods with `node-js-scale` in the name. If you run this after issuing the `rolling-update` command, you should see several pods running as it creates new versions and removes the old ones one by one.

The full output of the previous `rolling-update` command should look something like the screenshot below:

```
Creating node-js-scale-10ea08ff9a118ac6a93f85547ed2d8f6
At beginning of loop: node-js-scale replicas: 2, node-js-scale-10ea08ff9a118ac6a
93f85547ed2d8f6 replicas: 1
Updating node-js-scale replicas: 2, node-js-scale-10ea08ff9a118ac6a93f85547ed2d8
f6 replicas: 1
At end of loop: node-js-scale replicas: 2, node-js-scale-10ea08ff9a118ac6a93f855
47ed2d8f6 replicas: 1
At beginning of loop: node-js-scale replicas: 1, node-js-scale-10ea08ff9a118ac6a
93f85547ed2d8f6 replicas: 2
Updating node-js-scale replicas: 1, node-js-scale-10ea08ff9a118ac6a93f85547ed2d8
f6 replicas: 2
At end of loop: node-js-scale replicas: 1, node-js-scale-10ea08ff9a118ac6a93f855
47ed2d8f6 replicas: 2
At beginning of loop: node-js-scale replicas: 0, node-js-scale-10ea08ff9a118ac6a
93f85547ed2d8f6 replicas: 3
Updating node-js-scale replicas: 0, node-js-scale-10ea08ff9a118ac6a93f85547ed2d8
f6 replicas: 3
At end of loop: node-js-scale replicas: 0, node-js-scale-10ea08ff9a118ac6a93f855
47ed2d8f6 replicas: 3
Update succeeded. Deleting old controller: node-js-scale
Renaming node-js-scale-10ea08ff9a118ac6a93f85547ed2d8f6 to node-js-scale
node-js-scale
```

The scaling output

As we can see here, Kubernetes is first creating a new RC named `node-js-scale-10ea08ff9a118ac6a93f85547ed28f6`. K8s then loops through one by one, creating a new pod in the new controller and removing one from the old. This continues until the new controller has the full replica count and the old one is at zero. After this, the old controller is deleted and the new one is renamed with the original controller name.

If you run a `get pods` command now, you'll notice that the pods still all have a longer name. Alternatively, we could have specified the name of a new controller in the command, and Kubernetes will create a new RC and pods using that name. Once again, the controller of the old name simply disappears after updating is completed. I recommend that you specify a new name for the updated controller to avoid confusion in your pod naming down the line. The same `update` command with this method will look like this:

```
$ kubectl rolling-update node-js-scale node-js-scale-v2.0 --
image=jonbaier/pod-scaling:0.2 --update-period="2m"
```

Using the static external IP address from the service we created in the first section, we can open the service in a browser. We should see our standard container information page. However, you'll notice that the title now says **Pod Scaling v0.2** and the background is light yellow:

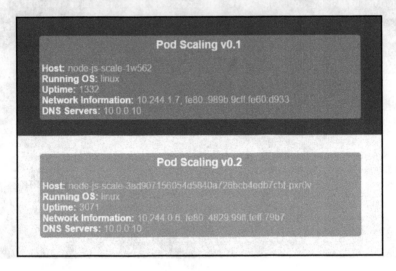

v0.1 and v0.2 (side by side)

It's worth noting that, during the entire update process, we've only been looking at pods and RCs. We didn't do anything with our service, but the service is still running fine and now directing to the new version of our pods. This is because our service is using label selectors for membership. Because both our old and new replicas use the same labels, the service has no problem using the new pods to service requests. The updates are done on the pods one by one, so it's seamless for the users of the service.

Testing, releases, and cutovers

The rolling update feature can work well for a simple blue-green deployment scenario. However, in a real-world blue-green deployment with a stack of multiple applications, there can be a variety of interdependencies that require in-depth testing. The `update-period` command allows us to add a `timeout` flag where some testing can be done, but this will not always be satisfactory for testing purposes.

Similarly, you may want partial changes to persist for a longer time and all the way up to the load balancer or service level. For example, you may wish to run an A/B test on a new user interface feature with a portion of your users. Another example is running a canary release (a replica in this case) of your application on new infrastructure like a newly added cluster node.

Let's take a look at an A/B testing example. For this example, we will need to create a new service that uses `sessionAffinity`. We will set the affinity to `ClientIP`, which will allow us to forward clients to the same backend pod. This is a key if we want a portion of our users to see one version while others see another:

```
apiVersion: v1
kind: Service
metadata:
  name: node-js-scale-ab
  labels:
    service: node-js-scale-ab
spec:
  type: LoadBalancer
  ports:
  - port: 80
  sessionAffinity: ClientIP
  selector:
    service: node-js-scale-ab
```

Listing 4-3: `pod-AB-service.yaml`

Create this service as usual with the `create` command, as follows:

```
$ kubectl create -f pod-AB-service.yaml
```

This will create a service that will point to our pods running both version 0.2 and 0.3 of the application. Next, we will create the two RCs that create two replicas of the application. One set will have version 0.2 of the application, and the other will have version 0.3, as shown here:

```
apiVersion: v1
kind: ReplicationController
metadata:
  name: node-js-scale-a
  labels:
    name: node-js-scale-a
    version: "0.2"
    service: node-js-scale-ab
spec:
  replicas: 2
  selector:
```

```
          name: node-js-scale-a
          version: "0.2"
          service: node-js-scale-ab
      template:
        metadata:
          labels:
            name: node-js-scale-a
            version: "0.2"
            service: node-js-scale-ab
        spec:
          containers:
          - name: node-js-scale
            image: jonbaier/pod-scaling:0.2
            ports:
            - containerPort: 80
            livenessProbe:
              # An HTTP health check
              httpGet:
                path: /
                port: 80
              initialDelaySeconds: 30
              timeoutSeconds: 5
            readinessProbe:
              # An HTTP health check
              httpGet:
                path: /
                port: 80
              initialDelaySeconds: 30
              timeoutSeconds: 1
```

Listing 4-4: `pod-A-controller.yaml`

```
apiVersion: v1
kind: ReplicationController
metadata:
  name: node-js-scale-b
  labels:
    name: node-js-scale-b
    version: "0.3"
    service: node-js-scale-ab
spec:
  replicas: 2
  selector:
    name: node-js-scale-b
    version: "0.3"
    service: node-js-scale-ab
  template:
    metadata:
```

```
    labels:
      name: node-js-scale-b
      version: "0.3"
      service: node-js-scale-ab
  spec:
    containers:
    - name: node-js-scale
      image: jonbaier/pod-scaling:0.3
      ports:
      - containerPort: 80
      livenessProbe:
        # An HTTP health check
        httpGet:
          path: /
          port: 80
        initialDelaySeconds: 30
        timeoutSeconds: 5
      readinessProbe:
        # An HTTP health check
        httpGet:
          path: /
          port: 80
        initialDelaySeconds: 30
        timeoutSeconds: 1
```

Listing 4-5: `pod-B-controller.yaml`

Note that we have the same service label, so these replicas will also be added to the service pool based on this selector. We also have `livenessProbe` and `readinessProbe` defined to make sure that our new version is working as expected. Again, use the `create` command to spin up the controller:

```
$ kubectl create -f pod-A-controller.yaml
$ kubectl create -f pod-B-controller.yaml
```

Now we have a service balancing to both versions of our app. In a true A/B test, we would now want to start collecting metrics on the visit to each version. Again, we have `sessionAffinity` set to `ClientIP`, so all requests will go to the same pod. Some users will see v0.2, and some will see v0.3.

 Because we have `sessionAffinity` turned on, your test will likely show the same version every time. This is expected, and you would need to attempt a connection from multiple IP addresses to see both user experiences with each version.

Since the versions are each on their own pod, one can easily separate logging and even add a logging container to the pod definition for a sidecar logging pattern. For brevity, we will not cover that setup in this book, but we will look at some of the logging tools in Chapter 8, *Monitoring and Logging*.

We can start to see how this process will be useful for a canary release or a manual blue-green deployment. We can also see how easy it is to launch a new version and slowly transition over to the new release.

Let's look at a basic transition quickly. It's really as simple as a few scale commands, which are as follows:

```
$ kubectl scale --replicas=3 rc/node-js-scale-b
$ kubectl scale --replicas=1 rc/node-js-scale-a
$ kubectl scale --replicas=4 rc/node-js-scale-b
$ kubectl scale --replicas=0 rc/node-js-scale-a
```

Use the get pods command combined with the -l filter in between the scale commands to watch the transition as it happens.

Now, we have fully transitioned over to version 0.3 (node-js-scale-b). All users will now see the version 0.3 of the site. We have four replicas of version 0.3 and none of 0.2. If you run a get rc command, you will notice that we still have an RC for 0.2 (node-js-scale-a). As a final cleanup, we can remove that controller completely, as follows:

```
$ kubectl delete rc/node-js-scale-a
```

Application autoscaling

A recent feature addition to Kubernetes is that of the **Horizontal Pod Autoscaler**. This resource type is really useful as it gives us a way to automatically set thresholds for scaling our application. Currently, that support is only for CPU, but there is alpha support for custom application metrics as well.

Let's use the node-js-scale Replication Controller from the beginning of the chapter and add an autoscaling component. Before we start, let's make sure we are scaled back down to one replica using the following command:

```
$ kubectl scale --replicas=1 rc/node-js-scale
```

Now we can create a Horizontal Pod Autoscaler with the following `hpa` definition:

```
apiVersion: autoscaling/v1
kind: HorizontalPodAutoscaler
metadata:
  name: node-js-scale
spec:
  minReplicas: 1
  maxReplicas: 3
  scaleTargetRef:
    apiVersion: v1
    kind: ReplicationController
    name: node-js-scale
  targetCPUUtilizationPercentage: 20
```

Listing 4-6. `node-js-scale-hpa.yaml`

Go ahead and create this with the `kubectl create -f` command. Now we can list the hpas and get a description as well:

```
$ kubectl get hpa
```

We can also create autoscaling in the command line with the `kubectl autoscale` command. The preceding YAML will look like the following:
`$ kubectl autoscale rc/node-js-scale --min=1 --max=3 --cpu-percent=20`

This will show us an autoscaler on the `node-js-scale` Replication Controller with a Target CPU of 30%. Additionally, you will see that the minimum pods is set to 1 and maximum is 3:

NAME	REFERENCE		TARGET	CURRENT
MINPODS	MAXPODS	AGE		
node-js-scale	ReplicationController/node-js-scale		30%	0%
1	3	2d		

Horizontal Pod Autoscaler with no load

Let's also query our pods to see how many are running right now:

```
$ kubectl get pods -l name=node-js-scale
```

We should see only one `node-js-scale` pod because our HPA is showing 0% utilization, so we will need to generate some load. We will use the popular `boom` application common in many container demos. The following listing will help us create continuous load until we can hit the CPU threshold for autoscaler:

```
apiVersion: v1
kind: ReplicationController
metadata:
  name: boomload
spec:
  replicas: 1
  selector:
    app: loadgenerator
  template:
    metadata:
      labels:
        app: loadgenerator
    spec:
      containers:
      - image: williamyeh/boom
        name: boom
        command: ["/bin/sh","-c"]
        args: ["while true ; do boom http://node-js-scale/ -c 10 -n 100
        ; sleep 1 ; done"]
```

Listing 4-7. `boomload.yaml`

Use the `kubectl create -f` command with this listing and then be ready to start monitoring the `hpa`. We can do this with the `kubectl get hpa` command we used earlier.

It may take a few moments, but we should start to see the current CPU utilization increase. Once it goes above the 20% threshold we set the autoscaler will kick in:

Horizontal Pod Autoscaler after load starts

Once we see this, we can run `kubectl get pod` again and see there are now several `node-js-scale` pods:

```
$ kubectl get pods -l name=node-js-scale
```

We can clean up now by killing our load generation pod:

```
$ kubectl delete rc/boomload
```

Now if we watch the `hpa`, we should start to see the CPU usage drop. It may take a few minutes, but, eventually, we will go back down to 0% CPU load.

Scaling a cluster

All these techniques are great for the scaling of the application, but what about the cluster itself. At some point, you will pack the nodes full and need more resources to schedule new pods for your workloads.

Autoscaling

When you create your cluster, you can customize the starting number of nodes (minions) with the `NUM_MINIONS` environment variable. By default, it is set to **4**.

Additionally, the Kubernetes team has started to build autoscaling capability into the cluster itself. Currently, this is the only support on GCE and GKE, but work is being done on other providers. This capability utilizes the `KUBE_AUTOSCALER_MIN_NODES`, `KUBE_AUTOSCALER_MAX_NODES`, and `KUBE_ENABLE_CLUSTER_AUTOSCALER` environment variables.

The following example shows how to set the environment variables for autoscaling before running `kube-up.sh`:

```
$ export NUM_MINIONS=5
$ export KUBE_AUTOSCALER_MIN_NODES=2
$ export KUBE_AUTOSCALER_MAX_NODES=5
$ export KUBE_ENABLE_CLUSTER_AUTOSCALER=true
```

Also, bear in mind that changing this after the cluster is started will have no effect. You would need to tear down the cluster and create it once again. Thus, this section will show you how to add nodes to an existing cluster without rebuilding it.

Once you start a cluster with these settings, your cluster will automatically scale up and down with the minimum and maximum limits based on compute resource usage in the cluster.

GKE clusters also support autoscaling when launched, when using the alpha features. The preceding example will use a flag such as `--enable-autoscaling --min-nodes=2 --max-nodes=5` in a command-line launch.

Scaling up the cluster on GCE

If you wish to scale out an existing cluster, we can do it with a few steps. Manually scaling up your cluster on GCE is actually quite easy. The existing plumbing uses managed instance groups in GCE, which allow you to easily add more machines of a standard configuration to the group via an instance template.

You can see this template easily in the GCE console. First, open the console; by default, this should open your default project console. If you are using another project for your Kubernetes cluster, simply select it from the project dropdown at the top of the page.

On the side panel, see under **Compute** and then **Compute Engine**, and select **Instance templates**. You should see a template titled **kubernetes-minion-template**. Note that the name could vary slightly if you've customized your cluster naming settings. Click on that template to see the details. Refer to the following screenshot:

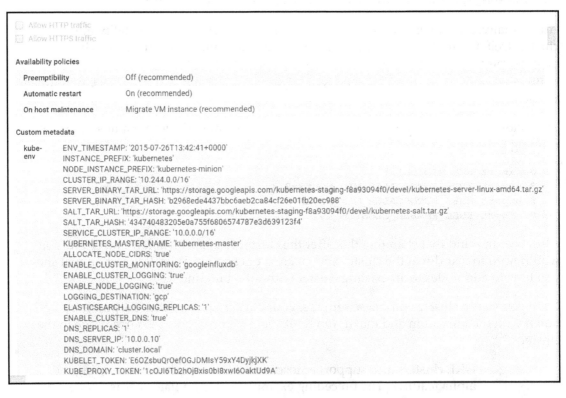

The GCE Instance template for minions

You'll see a number of settings, but the meat of the template is under the **Custom** metadata. Here, you will see a number of environment variables and also a startup script that is run after a new machine instance is created. These are the core components that allow us to create new machines and have them automatically added to the available cluster nodes.

Because the template for new machines is already created, it is very simple to scale out our cluster in GCE. Once in the Compute section of the console, simply go to **Instance groups** located right above the **Instance templates** link on the side panel. Again, you should see a group titled **kubernetes-minion-group** or something similar. Click on that group to see the details, as shown in the following screenshot:

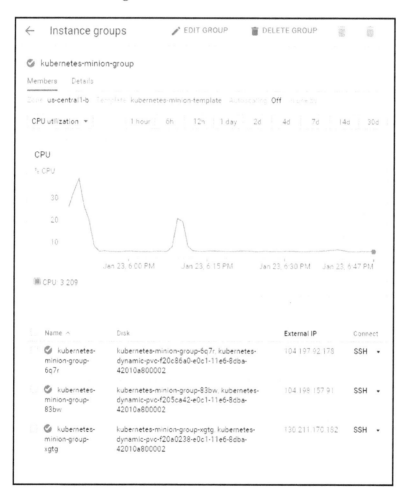

The GCE Instance group for minions

You'll see a page with a CPU metrics graph and three instances listed here. By default, the cluster creates three nodes. We can modify this group by clicking on the **EDIT GROUP** button at the top of the page:

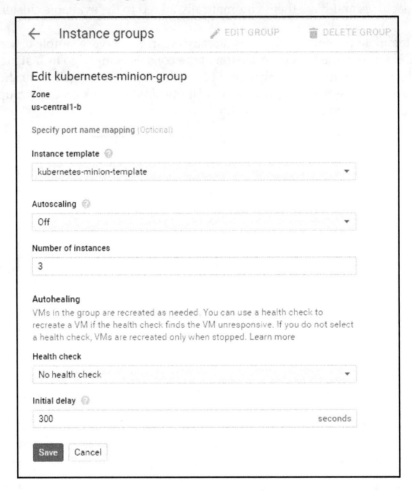

The GCE Instance group edit page

You should see **kubernetes-minion-template** selected in **Instance template** that we reviewed a moment ago. You'll also see an **Autoscaling** setting, which is **Off** by default and an instance count of 3. Simply, increment this to 4 and click on **Save**. You'll be taken back to the group details page and you'll see a pop-up dialog showing the pending changes.

 You'll also see some auto healing properties on the `Instance Group` edit page. This recreates failed instances and allows you to set health checks as well as an initial delay period before an action is taken.

In a few minutes, you'll have a new instance listed on the details page. We can test that this is ready using the `get nodes` command from the command line:

```
$ kubectl get nodes
```

 A word of caution on autoscaling and scale down in general
First, if we repeat the earlier process and decrease the countdown to four, GCE will remove one node. However, it will not necessarily be the node you just added. The good news is that pods will be rescheduled on the remaining nodes. However, it can only reschedule where resources are available. If you are close to full capacity and shut down a node, there is a good chance that some pods will not have a place to be rescheduled. In addition, this is not a live migration, so any application state will be lost in the transition. The bottom line is that you should carefully consider the implications before scaling down or implementing an autoscaling scheme.

 For more information on general autoscaling in GCE, refer to the `https://cloud.google.com/compute/docs/autoscaler/?hl=en_US#sc aling_based_on_cpu_utilization` link.

Scaling up the cluster on AWS

The AWS provider code also makes it very easy to scale up your cluster. Similar to GCE, the AWS setup uses autoscaling groups to create the default four minion nodes. In the future, the autoscaling groups will hopefully be integrated into the Kubernetes cluster autoscaling functionality. For now, we will walk though a manual setup.

This can also be easily modified using the CLI or the web console. In the console, from the EC2 page, simply go to the **Auto Scaling Groups** section at the bottom of the menu on the left. You should see a name similar to **kubernetes-minion-group**. Select this group and you will see details as shown in the following screenshot:

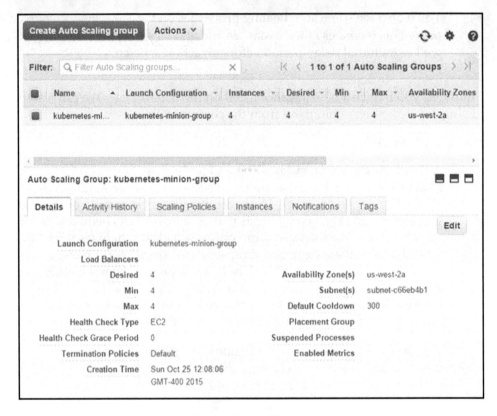

Kubernetes minion autoscaling details

We can scale this group up easily by clicking on **Edit**. Then, change the **Desired**, **Min**, and **Max** values to 5 and click on **Save**. In a few minutes, you'll have the fifth node available. You can once again check this using the get nodes command.

Scaling down is the same process, but remember that we discussed the same considerations in the previous *Scaling up the cluster on GCE* section. Workloads could get abandoned or, at the very least, unexpectedly restarted.

Scaling manually

For other providers, creating new minions may not be an automated process. Depending on your provider, you'll need to perform various manual steps. It can be helpful to look at the provider-specific scripts in the `cluster` directory.

Summary

We should now be a bit more comfortable with the basics of application scaling in Kubernetes. We also looked at the built-in functions in order to roll updates as well as a manual process for testing and slowly integrating updates. We took a look at how to scale the nodes of our underlying cluster and increase the overall capacity for our Kubernetes resources. Finally, we explored some of the new auto scaling concepts for both the cluster and our applications themselves.

In the next chapter, we will look at the latest techniques for scaling and updating applications with the new **deployments** resource type, as well as some of the other types of workloads we can run on Kubernetes.

5
Deployments, Jobs, and DaemonSets

This chapter will cover the various types of workloads that Kubernetes supports. We will cover **Deployments** for applications that are regularly updated and long running. We will also revisit the topics of application updates and gradual rollouts using Deployments. In addition, we will look at **Jobs** used for short-running tasks. Finally, we will look at **DaemonSets**, which allow programs to be run on every node in our Kubernetes cluster.

This chapter will discuss the following:

- Deployments
- Application scaling with deployments
- Application updates with deployments
- Jobs
- DaemonSets

Deployments

In the previous chapter, we explored some of the core concepts for application updates using the old rolling-update method. Starting with version 1.2, Kubernetes added the Deployment construct, which improves on the basic mechanisms of rolling-update and Replication Controllers. As the name suggests, it gives us a finer control of the code deployment itself. Deployments allow us to pause and resume application rollouts. Additionally, it keeps a history of past deployments and allows the user to easily rollback to previous versions.

In the following, *listing 5-1*, we can see that the definition is very similar to a Replication Controller. The main difference is that we now have an ability to make changes and updates to the deployment objects and let Kubernetes manage updating the underlying pods and replicas for us:

```
apiVersion: extensions/v1beta1
kind: Deployment
metadata:
  name: node-js-deploy
labels:
    name: node-js-deploy
spec:
    replicas: 1
  template:
    metadata:
      labels:
        name: node-js-deploy
    spec:
      containers:
      - name: node-js-deploy
        image: jonbaier/pod-scaling:0.1
        ports:
        - containerPort: 80
```

Listing 5-1: `node-js-deploy.yaml`

We can run the familiar `create` command with the optional `--record` flag so that the creation of the deployment is recorded in the rollout history. Otherwise, we will only see subsequent changes in the rollout history:

```
$ kubectl create -f node-js-deploy.yaml --record
```

You may need to add `--validate=false` if this beta type is not enabled on your cluster.

We should see a message about the deployment being successfully created. After a few moments, it will finish creating our pod, which we can check for ourselves with a `get pods` command. We add the `-l` flag to only see the pods relevant to this deployment:

```
$ kubectl get pods -l name=node-js-deploy
```

We create a service just as we did with Replication Controllers. The following is a `Service` definition for the deployment we just created. We'll notice that it is almost identical to the Services we created in the past:

```
apiVersion: v1
kind: Service
metadata:
  name: node-js-deploy
  labels:
    name: node-js-deploy
spec:
  type: LoadBalancer
  ports:
  - port: 80
  sessionAffinity: ClientIP
  selector:
    name: node-js-deploy
```

Listing 5-2. `node-js-deploy-service.yaml`

Once this service is created using `kubectl`, you'll be able to access the deployment pods through the service IP or the service name if you are inside a pod on this namespace.

Scaling

The `scale` command works the same way as it did in our Replication Controller. To scale up, we simply use the deployment name and specify the new number of replicas, as shown here:

```
$ kubectl scale deployment node-js-deploy --replicas 3
```

If all goes well, we'll simply see a message about the deployment being **scaled** on the output of our terminal window. We can check the number of running pods using the `get pods` command from earlier, once more.

Updates and rollouts

Deployments allow for updating in a few different ways. First, there is the `kubectl set` command, which allows us to change the deployment configuration without redeploying manually. Currently, it only allows for updating the image, but as new versions of our application or container image are processed, we will need to do this quite often.

Let's take a look using our deployment from the previous section. We should have three replicas running right now. Verify this by running the `get pods` command with a filter for our deployment:

```
$ kubectl get pods -l name=node-js-deploy
```

We should see three pods similar to those listed in the following screenshot:

NAME	READY	STATUS	RESTARTS	AGE
node-js-deploy-1713031517-itnwi	1/1	Running	0	6m
node-js-deploy-1713031517-nx8vs	1/1	Running	0	6m
node-js-deploy-1713031517-uge5y	1/1	Running	0	6m

Deployment Pod Listing

Take one of the pods listed on our setup, replace it in the following command where it says `{POD_NAME_FROM_YOUR_LISTING}`, and run the command:

```
$ kubectl describe pod/{POD_NAME_FROM_YOUR_LISTING} | grep Image:
```

We should see an output like the following image with the current image version of `0.1`:

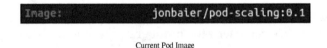

Current Pod Image

Now that we know what our current deployment is running, let's try to update to the next version. This can be achieved easily using the `kubectl set` command and specifying the new version, as shown here:

```
$ kubectl set image deployment/node-js-deploy node-js-deploy=jonbaier/pod-scaling:0.2
```

If all goes well, we should see the text that says `deployment "node-js-deploy" image updated` displayed on the screen.

We can double–check the status using the following `rollout status` command:

```
$ kubectl rollout status deployment/node-js-deploy
```

We should see some text about the deployment successfully rolled out. If you see any text about waiting for the rollout to finish, you may need to wait a moment for it to finish or alternatively check the logs for issues.

Once it's finished, run the `get pods` command as earlier, once more. This time we will see new pods listed:

```
NAME                             READY    STATUS    RESTARTS   AGE
node-js-deploy-1794296158-5wivi  1/1      Running   0          5m
node-js-deploy-1794296158-b2any  1/1      Running   0          5m
node-js-deploy-1794296158-y2tx3  1/1      Running   0          5m
```

Deployment Pod Listing After Update

Once again plug one of your pod names into the `describe` command we ran earlier. This time we should see the image has been updated to 0.2.

What happened behind the scenes is that Kubernetes has *rolled out* a new version for us. It basically creates a new replica set with the new version. Once this pod is online and healthy it kills one of the older versions. It continues this behavior, scaling out the new version and scaling down the old versions, until only the new pods are left.

The following figure describes the workflow for your reference:

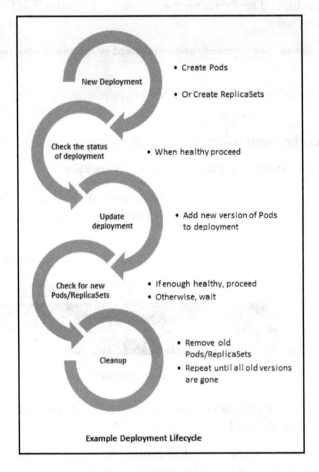

Deployment Lifecycle

It's worth noting that the rollback definition allows us to control the pod replace method in our deployment definition. There is a `strategy.type` field that defaults to `RollingUpdate` and the preceding behavior. Optionally, we can also specify `Recreate` as the replacement strategy and it will kill all the old pods first before creating the new versions.

History and rollbacks

One of the useful features of the rollout api is the ability to track the deployment history. Let's do one more update before we check the history. Run the `kubectl set` command once more and specify version `0.3`:

```
$ kubectl set image deployment/node-js-deploy node-js-deploy=jonbaier/pod-scaling:0.3
```

Once again we'll see text that says `deployment "node-js-deploy" image updated` displayed on the screen. Now run the `get pods` command once more:

```
$ kubectl get pods -l name=node-js-deploy
```

Let's also take a look at our deployment history. Run the `rollout history` command:

```
$ kubectl rollout history deployment/node-js-deploy
```

We should see an output similar to the following:

```
REVISION        CHANGE-CAUSE
1               kubectl scale deployment node-js-deploy --replicas 3
2               kubectl set image deployment/node-js-deploy node-js-
deploy=jonbaier/pod-scaling:0.2
3               kubectl set image deployment/node-js-deploy node-js-
deploy=jonbaier/pod-scaling:0.3
```

Rollout History

As we can see, the history shows us the initial deployment creation, our first update to `0.2`, and then our final update to `0.3`. In addition to status and history, the `rollout` command also supports the `pause`, `resume`, and `undo` sub-commands. The `rollout pause` command allows us to pause a command while the rollout is still in progress. This can be useful for troubleshooting and also helpful for canary type launches, where we wish to do final testing of the new version before rolling out to the entire user base. When we are ready to continue the rollout, we can simply use the `rollout resume` command.

But what if something goes wrong? That is where the `rollout undo` command and the rollout history itself is really handy. Let's simulate this by trying to update to a version of our pod that is not yet available. We will set the image to version `42.0`, which does not exist:

```
$ kubectl set image deployment/node-js-deploy node-js-deploy=jonbaier/pod-scaling:42.0
```

We should still see the text that says `deployment "node-js-deploy" image updated` displayed on the screen. But if we check the status, we will see that it is still waiting:

```
$ kubectl rollout status deployment/node-js-deploy
```

We can press *Ctrl + C* to kill the `status` command and then run the `get pods` command once more:

```
$ kubectl get pods -l name=node-js-deploy
```

We should now see an `ErrImagePull`, as in the following screenshot:

```
NAME                              READY    STATUS         RESTARTS   AGE
node-js-deploy-1875560799-ehi0o   1/1      Running        0          40m
node-js-deploy-1875560799-tqset   1/1      Running        0          40m
node-js-deploy-1907673490-cadw2   0/1      ErrImagePull   0          1m
node-js-deploy-1907673490-qvc9w   0/1      ErrImagePull   0          1m
```

Image Pull Error

As we expected, it can't pull the 42.0 version of the image because it doesn't exist. We may also have issues with deployments if we run out of resources on the cluster or hit limits that are set for our namespace. Additionally, the deployment can fail for a number of application-related causes, such as health check failure, permission issues, and application bugs, of course.

Whenever a failure to rollout happens, we can easily rollback to a previous version using the `rollout undo` command. This command will take our deployment back to the previous version:

```
$ kubectl rollout undo deployment/node-js-deploy
```

After that, we can run a `rollout status` command once more and we should see everything rolled out successfully. Run the `rollout history` command again and we'll see both our attempt to rollout version `42.0` and the revert to `0.3`:

```
REVISION     CHANGE-CAUSE
1            kubectl scale deployment node-js-deploy --replicas 3
2            kubectl set image deployment/node-js-deploy node-js-de
ploy=jonbaier/pod-scaling:0.2
4            kubectl set image deployment/node-js-deploy node-js-de
ploy=jonbaier/pod-scaling:42.0
5            kubectl set image deployment/node-js-deploy node-js-de
ploy=jonbaier/pod-scaling:0.3
```

Rollout History After Rollback

We can also specify the `--to-revision` flag when running an undo to rollback to a specific version. This can be handy for times when our rollout succeeds, but we discover logical errors down the road.

Autoscaling

As you can see, Deployments are a great improvement over Replication Controllers allowing us to seamlessly update our applications, while integrating with the other resources of Kubernetes in much the same way.

Another area that we saw in the previous chapter, and also supported for Deployments, is **Horizontal Pod Autoscalers** (**HPAs**). As you may have guessed, this also integrates perfectly with Deployments. We will walk through a quick remake of the HPAs from the previous chapter, this time using the Deployments we have created so far:

```
apiVersion: autoscaling/v1
kind: HorizontalPodAutoscaler
metadata:
  name: node-js-deploy
spec:
  minReplicas: 3
  maxReplicas: 6
  scaleTargetRef:
    apiVersion: v1
    kind: Deployment
    name: node-js-deploy
  targetCPUUtilizationPercentage: 10
```

Listing 5-3. `node-js-deploy-hpa.yaml`

We have lowered the CPU threshold to 10% and changed our minimum and maximum pods to 3 and 6, respectively. Create the preceding HPA with our trusty `kubectl create -f` command. After this is completed, we can check that it's available with the `kubectl get hpa` command:

NAME	REFERENCE	TARGET	CURRENT	MIN
PODS	MAXPODS	AGE		
node-js-deploy	Deployment/node-js-deploy	10%	0%	3
	6	3h		
node-js-scale	ReplicationController/node-js-scale	30%	0%	1
	3	10d		

Horizontal Pod Autoscaler

We can also check that we have only 3 pods running with the `kubectl get deploy` command. Now let's add some load to trigger the autoscaler:

```
apiVersion: extensions/v1beta1
kind: Deployment
metadata:
  name: boomload-deploy
spec:
  replicas: 1
  template:
    metadata:
      labels:
        app: loadgenerator-deploy
    spec:
      containers:
      - image: williamyeh/boom
        name: boom-deploy
        command: ["/bin/sh","-c"]
        args: ["while true ; do boom http://node-js-deploy/ -c 10 -n
        100 ; sleep 1 ;
        done"]
```

Listing 5-4. `boomload-deploy.yaml`

Create *listing 5-4* as usual. Now monitor the HPA with the alternating `kubectl get hpa` and `kubectl get deploy` commands. After a few moments, we should see the load jump above `10%`. After a few more moments, we should also see the number of pods increase all the way up to `6` replicas:

```
$ kubectl get hpa
NAME                     REFERENCE                                TARGET     CURRENT     MIN
PODS     MAXPODS     AGE
node-js-deploy           Deployment/node-js-deploy                10%        20%         3
         6               8m
node-js-scale            ReplicationController/node-js-scale      30%        0%          1
         3               9d
$ kubectl get deploy
NAME                DESIRED     CURRENT     UP-TO-DATE     AVAILABLE     AGE
boomload-deploy     1           1           1              1             4m
node-js-deploy      6           6           6              6             10d
```

HPA Increase and Pod Scale Up

Again, we can clean this up by removing our load generation pod and waiting a few moments:

```
$ kubectl delete deploy boomload-deploy
```

Again, if we watch the HPA, we'll start to see the CPU usage drop. After a few minutes, we will go back down to 0% CPU load and then the Deployment will scale back to 3 replicas.

Jobs

Deployments and Replication Controllers are a great way to ensure long running applications are always up and able to tolerate a wide array of infrastructure failures. However, there are some use cases this does not address—specifically short running, *run once*, tasks as well as regularly scheduled tasks. In both cases, we need the tasks to run until completion, but then terminate and start again at the next scheduled interval.

To address this type of workload, Kubernetes has added a **Batch API**, which includes the **Job** type. This type will create 1 to n pods and ensure that they all run to completion with a successful exit. Based on restartPolicy, we can either allow pods to simply fail without retry (restartPolicy: Never) or retry when a pods exits without successful completion (restartPolicy: OnFailure). In this example, we will use the latter technique:

```
apiVersion: batch/v1
kind: Job
metadata:
  name: long-task
spec:
  template:
    metadata:
      name: long-task
    spec:
      containers:
      - name: long-task
        image: docker/whalesay
        command: ["cowsay", "Finishing that task in a jiffy"]
      restartPolicy: OnFailure
```

Listing 5-5: longtask.yaml

Let's go ahead and run this with the following command:

```
$ kubectl create -f longtask.yaml
```

If all goes well, you'll see `job "long-task" created` printed on the screen.

This tells us the job was created, but doesn't tell us if it completed successfully. To check that, we need to query the job status with the following command:

```
$ kubectl describe jobs/long-task
```

```
Name:           long-task
Namespace:      default
Image(s):       docker/whalesay
Selector:       controller-uid=eff2fcd2-d5e1-11e6-90ee-42010a800002
Parallelism:    1
Completions:    1
Start Time:     Sun, 08 Jan 2017 15:35:05 -0500
Labels:         <none>
Pods Statuses:  0 Running / 1 Succeeded / 0 Failed
No volumes.
Events:
  FirstSeen     LastSeen        Count   From                    SubobjectPath   Type
Reason                          Message
  ---------     --------        -----   ----                                    ----------
  -----                         -------
  4m            4m              1       {job-controller }                       Normal
SuccessfulCreate                Created pod: long-task-a6i9v
```

Job Status

You should see that we had 1 task that succeeded and in the `Events` logs, a SuccessfulCreate message. If we use `kubectl get pods` command, we won't see our **long-task** pods in the list, but we may notice the message at the bottom if the listing states that there are completed jobs that are not shown. We will need to run the command again with the `-a` or `--show-all` flag to see the **long-task** pod and the completed Job status.

Let's dig a little deeper to prove to ourselves the work was completed successfully. We could use the `logs` command to look at the pods logs. However, we can also use the UI for this task. Open a browser and go to the following UI URL: `https://<your master ip>/ui/`

Click on **Jobs** and then **long-task** from the list, so we can see the details. Then, in the **Pods** section, click on the pod listed there. This will give us the **Pod details** page. At the bottom of the details, click on **View Logs** and we will see the log output:

```
Logs from long-task          ▼  in long-task-a6i9v               A   Tт

2017-01-08T20:35:19.747705449Z   ----------------------------------
2017-01-08T20:35:19.747740036Z  < Finishing that task in a jiffy >
2017-01-08T20:35:19.747747931Z   ----------------------------------
2017-01-08T20:35:19.747752786Z      \
2017-01-08T20:35:19.747756904Z       \
2017-01-08T20:35:19.747761135Z        \
2017-01-08T20:35:19.747765442Z                      ##        .
2017-01-08T20:35:19.747770620Z                ## ## ##       ==
2017-01-08T20:35:19.747775118Z             ## ## ## ##      ===
2017-01-08T20:35:19.747779445Z         /""""""""""""""""___/ ===
2017-01-08T20:35:19.747784865Z    ~~~ {~~ ~~~~ ~~~ ~~~~ ~~ ~ /  ===- ~~~
2017-01-08T20:35:19.747789250Z         _____ o          __/
2017-01-08T20:35:19.747793504Z          \    \        __/
2017-01-08T20:35:19.747797946Z           _____/

Logs from 1/8/17 3:35 PM to 1/8/17 3:35 PM              |<  <   >   >|
```

Job Log

As you can see in the preceding image, the whalesay container is complete with the ASCII art and our custom message from the runtime parameters in the example.

Other types of jobs

While this example provides a basic introduction to short running jobs, it only addresses the use case of once and done tasks. In reality, batch work is often done in **Parallel** or as part of a regularly occurring task.

Parallel jobs

Using **Parallel** jobs, we may be grabbing tasks from an ongoing queue or simply running a set number of tasks that are not dependent on each other. In the case of jobs pulling from a queue, our application must be aware of the dependencies and have the logic to decide how tasks are processed and what to work on next. Kubernetes is simply scheduling the jobs.

You can learn more about parallel jobs from the Kubernetes documentation and batch API reference (you can refer to more details about this in point 1 in the *References* section at the end of the chapter).

Scheduled jobs

For tasks that need to run periodically, Kubernetes has also released a `CronJob` type in alpha. As we might expect, this type of job uses the underlying cron formatting to specify a schedule for the task we wish to run. By default, our cluster will not have the alpha batch features enabled, but we can look at an example `CronJob` listing to learn how these types of workloads will work going forward:

```
apiVersion: batch/v2alpha1
kind: CronJob
metadata:
  name: long-task-cron
spec:
  schedule: "15 10 * * 6"
  jobTemplate:
    spec:
      template:
        spec:
          containers:
          - name: long-task-cron
            image: docker/whalesay
            command: ["cowsay", "Developers! Developers! Developers!
          \n\n Saturday task
            complete!"]
          restartPolicy: OnFailure
```

Listing 5-6. `longtask-cron.yaml`

As you can see, the schedule portion reflects a crontab with the following format:

minute hour day-of-month month day-of-week

In this example, `15 10 * * 6` creates a task that will run every `Saturday` at 10:15 am.

DaemonSets

While Replication Controllers and Deployments are great at making sure that a specific number of application instances are running, they do so in the context of the best fit. This means that the scheduler looks for nodes that meet resource requirements (available CPU, particular storage volumes, and so on) and tries to spread across the nodes and zones.

This works well for creating highly available and fault tolerant applications, but what about cases where we need an agent to run on every single node in the cluster? While the default spread does attempt to use different nodes, it does not guarantee that every node will have a replica and, indeed, will only fill a number of nodes equivalent to the quantity specified in the RC or Deployment specification.

To ease this burden, Kubernetes introduced `DaemonSet`, which simply defines a pod to run on every single node in the cluster or a defined subset of those nodes. This can be very useful for a number of production-related activities, such as monitoring and logging agents, security agents, and file system daemons.

In fact, Kubernetes already uses this capability for some of its core system components. If we recall from Chapter 1, *Introduction to Kubernetes*, we saw a `node-problem-detector` running on the nodes. This pod is actually running on every node in the cluster as `DaemonSet`. We can see this by querying DaemonSets in the `kube-system` namespace:

```
$ kubectl get ds --namespace=kube-system
```

```
NAME                         DESIRED   CURRENT   NODE-SELECTOR   AGE
node-problem-detector-v0.1   4         4         <none>          13d
```

kube-system DaemonSets

You can find more information about `node-problem-detector` as well as `yaml` in the following listing at: `http://kubernetes.io/docs/admin/node-problem/#node-problem-detector`:

```
apiVersion: extensions/v1beta1
kind: DaemonSet
metadata:
  name: node-problem-detector-v0.1
  namespace: kube-system
  labels:
    k8s-app: node-problem-detector
    version: v0.1
    kubernetes.io/cluster-service: "true"
```

```
spec:
  template:
    metadata:
      labels:
        k8s-app: node-problem-detector
        version: v0.1
        kubernetes.io/cluster-service: "true"
    spec:
      hostNetwork: true
      containers:
      - name: node-problem-detector
        image: gcr.io/google_containers/node-problem-detector:v0.1
        securityContext:
          privileged: true
        resources:
          limits:
            cpu: "200m"
            memory: "100Mi"
          requests:
            cpu: "20m"
            memory: "20Mi"
        volumeMounts:
        - name: log
          mountPath: /log
          readOnly: true
      volumes:
      - name: log
        hostPath:
          path: /var/log/
```

Listing 5-7. node-problem-detector definition

Node selection

As mentioned previously, we can schedule DaemonSets to run on a subset of nodes as well. This can be achieved using something called **nodeSelectors**. These allow us to constrain the nodes a pods runs on, by looking for specific labels and metadata. They simply match key-value pairs on the labels for each node. We can add our own labels or use those that are assigned by default.

The default labels are listed in the following table:

Default Node Labels	Description
kubernetes.io/hostname	This shows the hostname of the underlying instance or machine
beta.kubernetes.io/os	This shows the underlying operating system as a report through the Go Language
beta.kubernetes.io/arch	This shows the underlying processor architecture as a report through the Go Language
beta.kubernetes.io/instance-type	(**Cloud-Only**) This is the instance type of the underlying cloud provider
failure-domain.beta.kubernetes.io/region	(**Cloud-Only**) This is the region of the underlying cloud provider
failure-domain.beta.kubernetes.io/zone	(**Cloud-Only**) This is the fault-tolerance zone of the underlying cloud provider

Table 5.1 - Kubernetes Default Node Labels

We are not limited to DaemonSets, as nodeSelectors actually work with Pod definitions as well and are not limited to DaemonSets. Let's take a closer look at a job example (a slight modification of our preceding long-task example).

First, we can see these on the nodes themselves. Let's get the names of our nodes:

```
$ kubectl get nodes
```

Use a name from the output of the previous command and plug it into this one:

```
$ kubectl describe node <node-name>
```

```
Name:                    kubernetes-minion-group-1l6g
Labels:                  beta.kubernetes.io/arch=amd64
                         beta.kubernetes.io/instance-type=n1-standard-2
                         beta.kubernetes.io/os=linux
                         failure-domain.beta.kubernetes.io/region=us-central1
                         failure-domain.beta.kubernetes.io/zone=us-central1-b
                         kubernetes.io/hostname=kubernetes-minion-group-1l6g
Taints:                  <none>
CreationTimestamp:       Wed, 11 Jan 2017 07:48:16 -0500
Phase:
Conditions:
```

Excerpt from node describe

Let's now add a nickname label to this node:

```
$ kubectl label nodes <node-name> nodenickname=trusty-steve
```

If we run the `kubectl describe node` command again, we will see this label listed next to the defaults. Now we can schedule workloads and specify this specific node. Here is a modification of our earlier long-running task with `nodeSelector` added:

```
apiVersion: batch/v1
kind: Job
metadata:
  name: long-task-ns
spec:
  template:
    metadata:
      name: long-task-ns
    spec:
      containers:
      - name: long-task-ns
        image: docker/whalesay
        command: ["cowsay", "Finishing that task in a jiffy"]
      restartPolicy: OnFailure
      nodeSelector:
        nodenickname: trusty-steve
```

Listing 5-8. `longtask-nodeselector.yaml`

Create the job from this listing with `kubectl create -f`.

Once that succeeds, it will create a pod based on the preceding specification. Since we have defined `nodeSelector`, it will try to run the pod on nodes that have matching labels and fail if it finds no candidates. We can find the pod by specifying the job name in our query, as follows:

```
$ kubectl get pods -a -l job-name=long-task-ns
```

We use the `-a` flag to show all pods. Jobs are short lived and once they enter the completed state, they will not show up in a basic `kubectl get pods` query. We also use the `-l` flag to specify pods with the `job-name=long-task-ns` label. This will give us the pod name which we can push into the following command:

```
$ kubectl describe pod <Pod-Name-For-Job> | grep Node:
```

The result should show the name of the node this pod was run on. If all has gone well, it should match the node we labeled a few steps earlier with the `trusty-steve` label.

Summary

Now you should have a good foundation of the core constructs in Kubernetes. We explored the new Deployment abstraction and how it improves on the basic Replication Controller, allowing for smooth updates and solid integration with services and autoscaling. We also looked at other types of workload in jobs and DaemonSets. You learned how to run short-running or batch tasks as well as how to run agents on every node in our cluster. Finally, we took a brief look at node selection and how that can be used to filter the nodes in the cluster used for our workloads.

We will build on what you learned in this chapter and look at the **Stateful** applications in the next chapter, exploring both critical application components and the data itself.

References

1. https://kubernetes.io/docs/user-guide/jobs/#parallel-jobs

6
Storage and Running Stateful Applications

In this chapter, we will discuss how to attach persistent volumes and create storage for stateful applications and data. We will walk through storage concerns and how we can persist data across pods and the container life cycle. We will explore the **PersistentVolumes** types as well as **PersistentVolumeClaim**. Finally, we will take a look at the new **StatefulSets** release in version 1.5.

This chapter will discuss the following topics:

- Persistent storage
- PersistentVolumes
- PersistentVolumeClaims
- StorageClasses
- StatefulSets

Persistent storage

So far, we only worked with workloads that we could start and stop at will, with no issue. However, real-world applications often carry state and record data that we prefer (even insist) not to lose. The transient nature of containers themselves can be a big challenge. If you recall our discussion of layered file systems in `Chapter 1`, *Introduction to Kubernetes*, the top layer is writable. (It's also frosting, which is delicious.) However, when the container dies, the data goes with it. The same is true for crashed containers that Kubernetes restarts.

This is where **volumes** or disks come into play. A volume that exists outside the container allows us to save our important data across containers outages. Further, if we have a volume at the pod level, data can be shared between containers in the same application stack and within the same pod.

Docker itself has some support for volumes, but Kubernetes gives us persistent storage that lasts beyond the lifetime of a single container. The volumes are tied to pods and live and die with those pods. Additionally, a pod can have multiple volumes from a variety of sources. Let's take a look at some of these sources.

Temporary disks

One of the easiest ways to achieve improved persistence amid container crashes and data sharing within a pod is to use the `emptydir` volume. This volume type can be used with either the storage volumes of the node machine itself or an optional RAM disk for higher performance.

Again, we improve our persistence beyond a single container, but when a pod is removed, the data will be lost. Machine reboot will also clear any data from RAM-type disks. There may be times when we just need some shared temporary space or have containers that process data and hand it off to another container before they die. Whatever the case, here is a quick example of using this temporary disk with the RAM-backed option.

Open your favorite editor and create a file like the one in the following *Listing 6-1*:

```
apiVersion: v1
kind: Pod
metadata:
  name: memory-pd
spec:
  containers:
  - image: nginx:latest
    ports:
    - containerPort: 80
    name: memory-pd
    volumeMounts:
    - mountPath: /memory-pd
      name: memory-volume
  volumes:
  - name: memory-volume
    emptyDir:
      medium: Memory
```

Listing 6-1: `storage-memory.yaml`

The preceding example is probably of second nature by now, but we will once again issue a `create` command followed by an `exec` command to see the folders in the container:

```
$ kubectl create -f storage-memory.yaml
$ kubectl exec memory-pd -- ls -lh | grep memory-pd
```

This will give us a bash shell in the container itself. The `ls` command shows us a `memory-pd` folder at the top level. We use `grep` to filter the output, but you can run the command without `| grep memory-pd` to see all folders:

```
/home/k8s/nodejs# kubectl.sh exec memory-pd -- ls -lh | grep memory
drwxrwxrwt  2 root  root    40 Oct 24 15:21 memory-pd
```

Temporary storage inside a container

Again, this folder is quite temporary as everything is stored in the node's (minion's) RAM. When the node gets restarted, all the files will be erased. We will look at a more permanent example next.

Cloud volumes

Many companies will already have significant infrastructure running in the public cloud. Luckily, Kubernetes has native support for the durable storage provided by two of the most popular providers.

GCE persistent disks

We have the following from the GCE website:

Google Persistent Disk is durable and high performance block storage for the Google Cloud Platform. Persistent Disk provide SSD and HDD storage which can be attached to instances running in either Google Compute Engine or Google Container Engine. Storage volumes can be transparently resized, quickly backed up, and offer the ability to support simultaneous readers. (you can refer to more details about this in point 1 in the *References* section at the end of the chapter)

Let's create a new **GCE persistent disk**.

1. From the console, in **Compute Engine**, go to **Disks**. On this new screen, click on the **Create Disk** button. We'll be presented with a screen similar to the following **GCE new persistent disk** image.

2. Choose a name for this volume and give it a brief description. Make sure that **Zone** is the same as the nodes in your cluster. GCE PDs can only be attached to machines in the same zone.

3. Enter `mysite-volume-1` in the **Name** field. Choose the zone matching at least one node in your cluster. Choose **None (blank disk)** for **Source type** and give `10` (10 GB) as value in **Size (GB)**. Finally, click on **Create**:

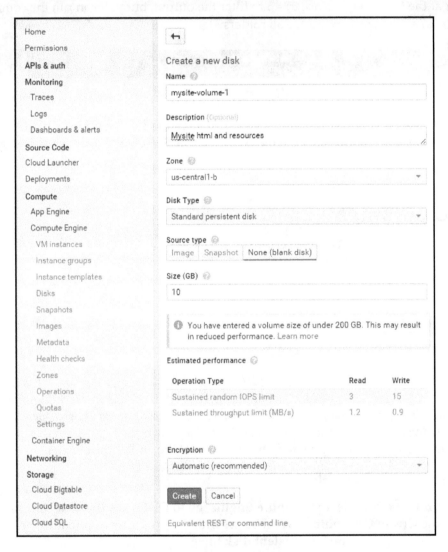

GCE new persistent disk

The nice thing about PDs on GCE is that they allow for mounting to multiple machines (nodes in our case). However, when mounting to multiple machines, the volume must be in read-only mode. So, let's first mount this to a single pod, so we can create some files. Use *Listing 6-2*: `storage-gce.yaml` as follows to create a pod that will mount the disk in read/write mode:

```
apiVersion: v1
kind: Pod
metadata:
  name: test-gce
spec:
  containers:
  - image: nginx:latest
    ports:
    - containerPort: 80
    name: test-gce
    volumeMounts:
    - mountPath: /usr/share/nginx/html
      name: gce-pd
  volumes:
  - name: gce-pd
    gcePersistentDisk:
      pdName: mysite-volume-1
      fsType: ext4
```

Listing 6-2: `storage-gce.yaml`

First, let's issue a `create` command followed by a `describe` command to find out which node it is running on:

```
$ kubectl create -f storage-gce.yaml
$ kubectl describe pod/test-gce
```

Note the node and save the pod IP address for later. Then, open an SSH session into that node:

```
Name:           test-gce
Namespace:      default
Node:           kubernetes-minion-group-zwpm/10.128.0.4
Start Time:     Sun, 15 Jan 2017 16:51:02 -0500
Labels:         <none>
Status:         Running
IP:             10.244.4.5
Controllers:    <none>
Containers:
  test-gce:
    Container ID:   docker://15871d81eb72557cc230df70a5c724617289d710a550da66e4dfaf7083
    Image:          nginx:latest
    Image ID:       docker://sha256:01f818af747d88b4ebca7cdabd0c581e406e0e790be72678d25
    Port:           80/TCP
    Requests:
      cpu:          100m
    State:          Running
      Started:      Sun, 15 Jan 2017 16:53:00 -0500
    Ready:          True
    Restart Count:  0
    Volume Mounts:
      /usr/share/nginx/html from gce-pd (rw)
      /var/run/secrets/kubernetes.io/serviceaccount from default-token-728d1 (ro)
    Environment Variables:      <none>
Conditions:
  Type          Status
  Initialized   True
  Ready         True
  PodScheduled  True
Volumes:
  gce-pd:
    Type:       GCEPersistentDisk (a Persistent Disk resource in Google Compute Engine)
    PDName:     mysite-volume-1
    FSType:     ext4
    Partition:  0
    ReadOnly:   false
  default-token-728d1:
    Type:       Secret (a volume populated by a Secret)
    SecretName: default-token-728d1
QoS Class:      Burstable
Tolerations:    <none>
```

Pod describe with persistent disk

Type the following command:

```
$ gcloud compute --project "<Your project ID>" ssh --zone "<your gce zone>"
"<Node running test-gce pod>"
```

Since we've already looked at the volume from inside the running container, let's access it directly from the node (minion) itself this time. We will run a `df` command to see where it is mounted, but we will need to switch to root first:

```
$ sudo su -
$ df -h | grep mysite-volume-1
```

As you can see, the GCE volume is mounted directly to the node itself. We can use the mount path listed in the output of the earlier `df` command. Use `cd` to change to the folder now. Then, create a new file named `index.html` with your favorite editor:

```
$ cd /var/lib/kubelet/plugins/kubernetes.io/gce-pd/mounts/mysite-volume-1
$ vi index.html
```

Enter a quaint message such as `Hello from my GCE PD!`. Now save the file and exit the editor. If you recall from *Listing 6-2*, the PD is mounted directly to the Nginx HTML directory. So, let's test this out while we still have the SSH session open on the node. Do a simple `curl` command to the pod IP we wrote down earlier:

```
$ curl <Pod IP from Describe>
```

You should see **Hello from my GCE PD!** or whatever message you saved in the `index.html` file. In a real-world scenario, we can use the volume for an entire website or any other central storage. Let's take a look at running a set of load balanced web servers all pointing to the same volume.

First, leave the SSH session with two `exit` commands. Before we proceed, we will need to remove our `test-gce` pod so that the volume can be mounted read-only across a number of nodes:

```
$ kubectl delete pod/test-gce
```

Now we can create a RC that will run three web servers all mounting the same persistent disk, as follows:

```
apiVersion: v1
kind: ReplicationController
metadata:
  name: http-pd
  labels:
    name: http-pd
spec:
  replicas: 3
  selector:
    name: http-pd
  template:
    metadata:
      name: http-pd
      labels:
        name: http-pd
    spec:
      containers:
        - image: nginx:latest
```

```
          ports:
          - containerPort: 80
          name: http-pd
          volumeMounts:
          - mountPath: /usr/share/nginx/html
            name: gce-pd
       volumes:
       - name: gce-pd
         gcePersistentDisk:
           pdName: mysite-volume-1
           fsType: ext4
           readOnly: true
```

Listing 6-3: `http-pd-controller.yaml`

Let's also create an external service, so we can see it from outside the cluster:

```
apiVersion: v1
kind: Service
metadata:
  name: http-pd
  labels:
    name: http-pd
spec:
  type: LoadBalancer
  ports:
  - name: http
    protocol: TCP
    port: 80
  selector:
    name: http-pd
```

Listing 6-4: `http-pd-service.yaml`

Go ahead and create these two resources now. Wait a few moments for the external IP to get assigned. After this, a `describe` command will give us the IP we can use in a browser:

```
$ kubectl describe service/http-pd
```

The following screenshot is the result of the preceding command:

```
Name:                   http-pd
Namespace:              default
Labels:                 name=http-pd
Selector:               name=http-pd
Type:                   LoadBalancer
IP:                     10.0.118.195
LoadBalancer Ingress:   130.211.186.84
Port:                   http     80/TCP
NodePort:               http     32429/TCP
Endpoints:              10.244.2.15:80,10.244.2.16:80,10.244.3.5:80
Session Affinity:       None
No events.
```

K8s service with GCE PD shared across three pods

If you don't see the **LoadBalancer Ingress** field yet, it probably needs more time to get assigned. Type the IP address from **LoadBalancer Ingress** into a browser, and you should see your familiar `index.html` file show up with the text we entered previously!

AWS Elastic Block Store

K8s also supports AWS **Elastic Block Store** (**EBS**) volumes. Like the GCE PDs, EBS volumes are required to be attached to an instance running in the same availability zone. A further limitation is that EBS can only be mounted to a single instance at one time.

For brevity, we will not walk through an AWS example, but a sample YAML file is included to get you started. Again, remember to create the EBS volume before your pod:

```
apiVersion: v1
kind: Pod
metadata:
  name: test-aws
spec:
  containers:
  - image: nginx:latest
    ports:
    - containerPort: 80
    name: test-aws
    volumeMounts:
    - mountPath: /usr/share/nginx/html
      name: aws-pd
  volumes:
  - name: aws-pd
    awsElasticBlockStore:
```

```
volumeID: aws://<availability-zone>/<volume-id>
fsType: ext4
```

Listing 6-5: `storage-aws.yaml`

Other storage options

Kubernetes supports a variety of other types of storage volumes. A full list can be found here: `http://kubernetes.io/v1.0/docs/user-guide/volumes.html#types-of-volumes`.

Here are a few that may be of particular interest:

- `nfs`: This type allows us to mount a **Network File Share** (**NFS**), which can be very useful for both persisting the data and sharing it across the infrastructure
- `gitrepo`: As you might have guessed, this option clones a Git repo into a new and empty folder

PersistentVolumes and StorageClasses

Thus far, we've seen examples of directly provisioning the storage within our pod definitions. This works quite well if you have full control over your cluster and infrastructure, but at larger scales, application owners will want to use storage that is managed separately. Typically, a central IT team or the cloud provider itself will take care of the details behind provisioning storage and leave the application owners to worry about their primary concern, the application itself.

In order to accommodate this, we need some way for the application to specify and request storage without being concerned with how that storage is provided. This is where `PersistentVolumes` and `PersistentVolumeClaims` come into play. `PersistentVolumes` are similar to `volumes` we created earlier, but they are provided by the cluster administer and are not dependent on a particular pod. This volume can then be claimed by pods using `PersistentVolumeClaims`.

`PersistentVolumeClaims` allows us to specify the details of the storage needed. We can defined the amount of storage as well as the access type such as `ReadWriteOnce` (read and write by one node), `ReadOnlyMany` (read-only by multiple nodes), and `ReadWriteMany` (read and write by many nodes). Of course, which modes are supported is dependent on the backing storage provider. For example, we saw in the AWS EBS example that mounting to multiple nodes was not an option.

Additionally, Kubernetes provides two other methods for specifying certain groupings or types of storage volumes. The first is the use of selectors as we have seen previously for pod selection. Here, labels can be applied to storage volumes and then claims can reference these labels to further filter the volume they are provided. Second, Kubernetes has a concept of StorageClass which allows us specify a storage provisioner and parameters for the type of volumes it provisions.

We will dive into StorageClasses in the next section, but here is a quick example of a `PersistentVolumeClaims` for illustration purposes. You can see in the annotations that we request `1Gi` of storage in `ReadWriteOnce` mode with a StorageClass of `solidstate` and label of `aws-storage`.

```
kind: PersistentVolumeClaim
apiVersion: v1
metadata:
  name: demo-claim
  annotations:
    volume.beta.kubernetes.io/storage-class: "solidstate"
spec:
  accessModes:
  - ReadWriteOnce
  resources:
    requests:
      storage: 1Gi
  selector:
    matchLabels:
      release: "aws-storage"
```

Listing 6-6: `pvc-example.yaml`

StatefulSets

The purpose of **StatefulSets** is to provide some consistency and predictability to application deployments with stateful data. Thus far, we have deployed applications to the cluster defining loose requirements around needed resources such as computer and storage. The cluster has scheduled our workload on any node that can meet these requirements. While we can use some of these constraints to deploy in a more predictable manner, it will be helpful if we had a construct built to help us provide this consistency.

 StatefulSets were set to GA in 1.6 as we went to press. There were previously beta in version 1.5 and were known as PetSets prior to that (alpha in 1.3 and 1.4).

This is where StatefulSets come in. StatefulSets provide us first with numbered and reliable naming for both network access and storage claims. The pods themselves are names with the following convention, where N is from 0 to the number of replicas:

```
"Name of Set"-N
```

This means that a Statefulset called db with 3 replicas will create the following pods:

```
db-0
db-1
db-2
```

This gives Kubernetes a way to associate network names and PersistentVolumes with specific pods. Additionally, it also serves to order creation and termination of pods. Pod will be started from 0 to N and terminated from N to 0.

A stateful example

Let's take a look at an example of a stateful application. First, we will want to create and use a StorageClass as we discussed earlier. This will allow us to hook into the Google Cloud Persistent Disk provisioner. The Kubernetes community is building provisioners for a variety of StorageClasses including GCP and AWS. Each provisioner has its own set of parameters available. Both GCP and AWS providers let you choose the type of disk (solid-state, standard, and so on) as well as the fault zone which is needed to match the pod attaching to it. AWS additionally allows you to specify encryption parameters as well as IOPs for Provisioned IOPs volumes. There are a number of other provisioners in the works including Azure and a variety of non-cloud options:

```
kind: StorageClass
apiVersion: storage.k8s.io/v1beta1
metadata:
  name: solidstate
provisioner: kubernetes.io/gce-pd
parameters:
  type: pd-ssd
  zone: us-central1-b
```

Listing 6-7: solidstate-sc.yaml

Use the following command with the preceding listing to create a `StorageClass` kind of SSD drives in `us-central1-b`:

```
$ kubectl create -f solidstate.yaml
```

Next, we will create a `StatefulSet` kind with our trusty `httpwhalesay` demo (you can refer to more details about this in point 2 in the *References* section at the end of the chapter). While this application does include any real state, we can see the storage claims and explore the communication path:

```
apiVersion: apps/v1beta1
kind: StatefulSet
metadata:
  name: whaleset
spec:
  serviceName: sayhey-svc
  replicas: 3
  template:
    metadata:
      labels:
        app: sayhey
    spec:
      terminationGracePeriodSeconds: 10
      containers:
      - name: sayhey
        image: jonbaier/httpwhalesay:0.2
        command: ["node", "index.js", "Whale it up!."]
        ports:
        - containerPort: 80
          name: web
        volumeMounts:
        - name: www
          mountPath: /usr/share/nginx/html
  volumeClaimTemplates:
  - metadata:
      name: www
      annotations:
        volume.beta.kubernetes.io/storage-class: solidstate
    spec:
      accessModes: [ "ReadWriteOnce" ]
      resources:
        requests:
          storage: 1Gi
```

Listing 6-8: `sayhey-statefulset.yaml`

Use the following command to get to start the creation of this StatefulSet. If you observe pod creation closely, you will see it create **whaleset-0**, **whaleset-1**, and **whaleset-2** in succession:

```
$ kubectl create -f sayhey-statefulset.yaml
```

Immediately after this, we can see our StatefulSet and the corresponding pods using the familiar get subcommand:

```
$ kubectl get statefulsets
$ kubectl get pods
```

These pods should create an output similar to the following images:

```
NAME          DESIRED     CURRENT      AGE
whaleset      3           3            46s
```

StatefulSet listing

The get pods output will show the following:

```
NAME          READY       STATUS                   RESTARTS     AGE
whaleset-0    1/1         Running                  0            54s
whaleset-1    1/1         Running                  0            29s
whaleset-2    0/1         ContainerCreating        0            11s
```

Pods created by StatefulSet

Depending on your timing, the pods may still be creating. As you can see in the preceding image, the third container is still being spun up.

We can also see the volumes the set has created and claim for each pod. First PersistentVolumes themselves:

```
$ kubectl get pv
```

The preceding command should show the three PersistentVolumes named www-whaleset-N. We notice the size is 1Gi and the access mode is set to **ReadWriteOnce (RWO)** just as we defined in our StorageClass:

NAME	STATUS	VOLUME	CAPACITY	ACCESSMODES
AGE				
www-whaleset-0	Bound	pvc-43346a3d-e024-11e6-af6d-42010a800002	1Gi	RWO
4m				
www-whaleset-1	Bound	pvc-43381dc9-e024-11e6-af6d-42010a800002	1Gi	RWO
4m				
www-whaleset-2	Bound	pvc-433a3864-e024-11e6-af6d-42010a800002	1Gi	RWO
4m				

The PersistentVolumes listing

Next we can look at the PersistentVolumeClaims that reserve the volumes for each pod:

```
$ kubectl get pvc
```

Following is the output of the preceding command:

NAME			CAPACITY	ACCESSMODES	RECLAIMPOLICY	STATUS
CLAIM	REASON	AGE				
pvc-43346a3d-e024-11e6-af6d-42010a800002			1Gi	RWO	Delete	Bound
default/www-whaleset-0		4m				
pvc-43381dc9-e024-11e6-af6d-42010a800002			1Gi	RWO	Delete	Bound
default/www-whaleset-1		4m				
pvc-433a3864-e024-11e6-af6d-42010a800002			1Gi	RWO	Delete	Bound
default/www-whaleset-2		4m				

The PersistentVolumeClaims listing

You'll notice much of the same settings here as with the PVs themselves. You might also notice the end of the claim name (or PV name in the previous listing) looks like www-whaleset-N. www is the mount name we specified in the preceding YAML definition. This is then appended to the pod name to create the actual PV and PVC name. One more area we can ensure that the proper disk is linked with it is matching pod.

Another area where this alignment is important is in the network communication. StatefulSets also provide consistent naming here. Before we can do this, let's create a service endpoint so we have a common entry point for incoming requests:

```
apiVersion: v1
kind: Service
metadata:
  name: sayhey-svc
  labels:
    app: sayhey
spec:
  ports:
  - port: 80
```

```
    name: web
  clusterIP: None
  selector:
    app: sayhey
```

Listing 6-9: `sayhey-svc.yaml`

```
$ kubectl create -f sayhey-svc.yaml
```

Now let's open a shell in one of the pods and see if we can communicate with another in the set:

```
$ kubectl exec whaleset-0 -i -t bash
```

The preceding command gives us a bash shell in the first whaleset pod. We can now use the `Service` name to make a simple HTTP request. We can use both the short name, `sayhey-svc`, and the fully qualified name, `sayhey-svc.default.svc.cluster.local`:

```
$ curl sayhey-svc
$ curl sayhey-svc.default.svc.cluster.local
```

You'll see an output similar to the following image. The service endpoint acts as a common communication point for all three pods:

```
<html>
    <head>
        <title>HTTP Whalesay</title>
    </head>
    <body>
        <pre>
            <code>
------------------------------------------------
| Whale it up!. --Sent from whaleset-0 |
------------------------------------------------
            \
             \
              \
                                                   ##        .
                                            ## ## ##       ==
                                         ## ## ## ##      ===
                                     /""""""""""""""""___/ ===
                                ~~~ {~~ ~~~~ ~~~ ~~~~ ~~ ~ /  ===- ~~~
                                     _____ o          __/
                                      \    \        __/
                                       _____/
            </code>
        </pre>
        <body/>
</html>
```

HTTP Whalesay curl output (whalesay-0 Pod)

Now let's see if we can communicate with a specific pod in the StatefulSet. As we noticed earlier, the StatefulSet named the pod in an orderly manner. It also gives them hostnames in a similar fashion so that there is a specific DNS entry for each pod in the set. Again, we will see the convention of "Name of Set"-N and then add the fully qualified service URL. The following example shows this for `whaleset-1`, which is the second Pod in our set:

```
$ curl whaleset-1.sayhey-svc.default.svc.cluster.local
```

Running this command from our existing Bash shell in **whaleset-0** will show us the output from `whaleset-1`:

HTTP Whalesay curl output (whalesay-1 Pod)

You can exit out of this shell now with `exit`.

> For learning purposes, it can also be instructive to describe some of the items from this section in more detail. For example, `kubectl describe svc sayhey-svc` will show us all three pod IP address in the service endpoints.

Summary

In this chapter, we explored a variety of persistent storage options and how to implement them with our pods. We looked at PersistentVolumes and also PersistentVolumeClaims, which allow us to separate storage provisioning and application storage requests. Additionally, we looked at StorageClasses for provisioning groups of storage according to a specification.

We also explored the new StatefulSets abstraction and learned how we can deploy stateful applications in a consistent and ordered manner. In the next chapter, we will look at how to integrate Kubernetes with Continuous Integration and Delivery pipelines.

References

1. `https://cloud.google.com/persistent-disk/`
2. HTTP Whalesay is an adaptation of Docker whalesaym which is in-turn an adaptation of Linux cowsay (circa 1999, Tony Monroe) - `https://hub.docker.com/r/docker/whalesay/`

7
Continuous Delivery

This chapter will show the reader how to integrate their build pipeline and deployments with a Kubernetes cluster. It will cover the concept of using Gulp.js and Jenkins in conjunction with your Kubernetes cluster.

This chapter will discuss the following topics:

- Integrating with continuous deployment pipeline
- Using Gulp.js with Kubernetes
- Integrating Jenkins with Kubernetes

Integrating with continuous delivery pipeline

Continuous integration and delivery are key components to modern development shops. *Speed to market* or *mean-time-to-revenue* are crucial for any company that is creating their own software. We'll see how Kubernetes can help you.

CI/CD (short for **Continuous Integration / Continuous Delivery**) often requires ephemeral build and test servers to be available whenever changes are pushed to the code repository. Docker and Kubernetes are well suited for this task, as it's easy to create containers in a few seconds and just as easy to remove them after builds are run. In addition, if you already have a large portion of infrastructure available on your cluster, it can make sense to utilize the idle capacity for builds and testing.

In this article, we will explore two popular tools used in building and deploying software:

- **Gulp.js**: This is a simple task runner used to automate the build process using **JavaScript** and **Node.js**
- **Jenkins**: This is a fully-fledged continuous integration server

Gulp.js

Gulp.js gives us the framework to do *Build as code*. Similar to *Infrastructure as code*, this allows us to programmatically define our build process. We will walk through a short example to demonstrate how you can create a complete workflow from a Docker image build to the final Kubernetes service.

Prerequisites

For this section of the article, you will need a **NodeJS** environment installed and ready including the **node package manager** (**npm**). If you do not already have these packages installed, you can find instructions for installing them at `https://docs.npmjs.com/getting-started/installing-node`.

You can check whether NodeJS is installed correctly with a `node -v` command.

You'll also need **Docker CE** and a **DockerHub** account to push a new image. You can find instructions to install Docker CE at `https://docs.docker.com/installation/`.

You can easily create a DockerHub account at `https://hub.docker.com/`.

After you have your credentials, you can log in with the CLI using `$ docker login` command.

Gulp build example

Let's start by creating a project directory named `node-gulp`:

```
$ mkdir node-gulp
$ cd node-gulp
```

Next, we will install the `gulp` package and check whether it's ready by running the `npm` command with the version flag, as follows:

```
$ npm install -g gulp
```

You may need to open a new terminal window to make sure that `gulp` is on your path. Also, make sure to navigate back to your `node-gulp` directory:

```
$ gulp -v
```

Next, we will install `gulp` locally in our project folder as well as the `gulp-git` and `gulp-shell` plugins, as follows:

```
$ npm install --save-dev gulp
$ npm install gulp-git -save
$ npm install --save-dev gulp-shell
```

Finally, we need to create a Kubernetes controller and service definition file, as well as a `gulpfile.js` file, to run all our tasks. Again, these files are available in the book file bundle, if you wish to copy them instead. Refer to the following code:

```
apiVersion: v1
kind: ReplicationController
metadata:
  name: node-gulp
  labels:
    name: node-gulp
spec:
  replicas: 1
  selector:
    name: node-gulp
  template:
    metadata:
      labels:
        name: node-gulp
    spec:
      containers:
      - name: node-gulp
        image: <your username>/node-gulp:latest
        imagePullPolicy: Always
        ports:
        - containerPort: 80
```

Listing 7-1: `node-gulp-controller.yaml`

As you can see, we have a basic controller. You will need to replace **\<your username\>**/node-gulp:latest with your Docker Hub username:

```
apiVersion: v1
kind: Service
metadata:
  name: node-gulp
  labels:
    name: node-gulp
spec:
  type: LoadBalancer
  ports:
  - name: http
    protocol: TCP
    port: 80
  selector:
    name: node-gulp
```

Listing 7-2: node-gulp-service.yaml

Next, we have a simple service that selects the pods from our controller and creates an external load balancer for access, as earlier:

```
var gulp = require('gulp');
var git = require('gulp-git');
var shell = require('gulp-shell');

// Clone a remote repo
gulp.task('clone', function(){
  return
git.clone('https://github.com/jonbaierCTP/getting-started-with-kubernetes-s
e.git', function (err) {
    if (err) throw err;
  });

});

// Update codebase
gulp.task('pull', function(){
  return git.pull('origin', 'master', {cwd: './getting-started-with-
kubernetes-se'}, function (err) {
    if (err) throw err;
  });
});

//Build Docker Image
gulp.task('docker-build', shell.task([
  'docker build -t <your username>/node-gulp ./getting-started-with-
```

```
kubernetes-se/docker-image-source/container-info/',
  'docker push <your username>/node-gulp'
]));

//Run New Pod
gulp.task('create-kube-pod', shell.task([
  'kubectl create -f node-gulp-controller.yaml',
  'kubectl create -f node-gulp-service.yaml'
]));

//Update Pod
gulp.task('update-kube-pod', shell.task([
  'kubectl delete -f node-gulp-controller.yaml',
  'kubectl create -f node-gulp-controller.yaml'
]));
```

Listing 7-3: `gulpfile.js`

Finally, we have the `gulpfile.js` file. This is where all our build tasks are defined. Again, fill in your Docker Hub username in both the **<your username>**/node-gulp sections.

Looking through the file, first, the clone task downloads our image source code from GitHub. The pull tasks execute a `git` pull on the cloned repository. Next, the `docker-build` command builds an image from the `container-info` subfolder and pushes it to DockerHub. Finally, we have the `create-kube-pod` and `update-kube-pod` commands. As you can guess, the `create-kube-pod` command creates our controller and service for the first time, whereas the `update-kube-pod` command simply replaces the controller.

Let's go ahead and run these commands and see our end-to-end workflow:

```
$ gulp clone
$ gulp docker-build
```

The first time through, you can run the `create-kube-pod` command, as follows:

```
$ gulp create-kube-pod
```

This is all there is to it. If we run a quick `kubectl` describe command for the `node-gulp` service, we can get the external IP for our new service. Browse to that IP and you'll see the familiar `container-info` application running. Note that the host starts with `node-gulp`, just as we named it in the previously mentioned pod definition:

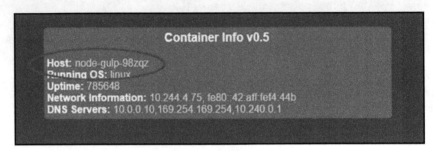

Service launched by Gulp build

On subsequent updates, run the `pull` and `update-kube-pod` commands, as shown here:

```
$ gulp pull
$ gulp docker-build
$ gulp update-kube-pod
```

This is a very simple example, but you can begin to see how easy it is to coordinate your build and deployment end to end with a few simple lines of code. Next, we will look at how to use Kubernetes to actually run builds using Jenkins.

Kubernetes plugin for Jenkins

One way we can use Kubernetes for our CI/CD pipeline is to run our Jenkins build slaves in a containerized environment. Luckily, there is already a plugin, written by Carlos Sanchez, which allows you to run Jenkins slaves in Kubernetes' pods.

Prerequisites

You'll need a Jenkins server handy for this next example. If you don't have one you can use, there is a Docker image available at `https://hub.docker.com/_/jenkins/`.

Running it from the Docker CLI is as simple as this:

```
docker run --name myjenkins -p 8080:8080 -v /var/jenkins_home jenkins
```

Installing plugins

Log in to your Jenkins server, and from your home dashboard, click on **Manage Jenkins**. Then, select **Manage Plugins** from the list.

A note for those installing a new Jenkins server: When you first log in to the Jenkins server, it asks you to install plugins. Choose the default ones or no plugins will be installed:

Jenkins main dashboard

The credentials plugin is required, but should be installed by default. We can check the **Installed** tab if in doubt, as shown in the following screenshot:

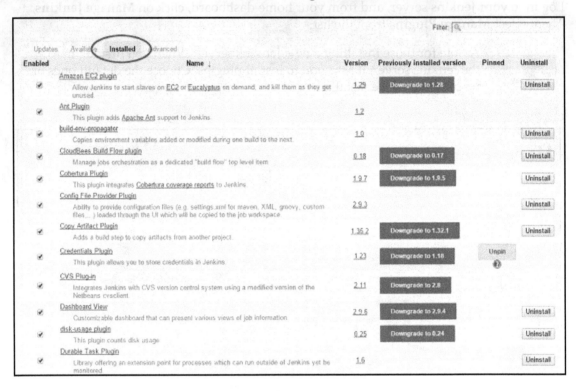

Jenkins installed plugins

Next, we can click on the **Available** tab. The Kubernetes plugin should be located under **Cluster Management and Distributed Build** or **Misc (cloud)**. There are many plugins, so you can alternatively search for Kubernetes on the page. Check the box for **Kubernetes Plugin** and click on **Install without restart**.

This will install the**Kubernetes Plugin** and the **Durable Task Plugin**:

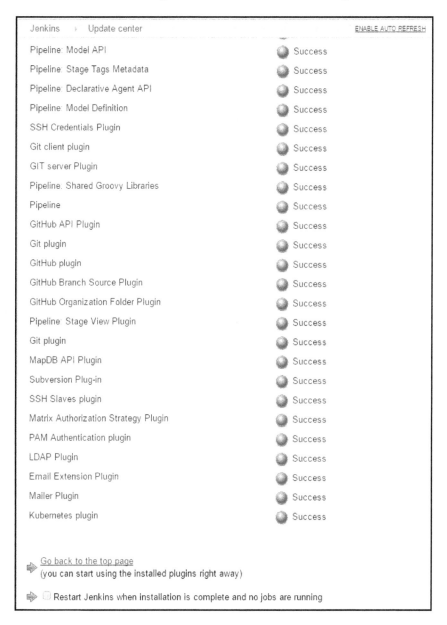

Plugin installation

If you wish to install a nonstandard version or just like to tinker, you can optionally download the plugins. The latest **Kubernetes** and **Durable Task** plugins can be found here:

Kubernetes plugin:

`https://wiki.jenkins-ci.org/display/JENKINS/Kubernetes+Plugin`

Durable Task plugin:

`https://wiki.jenkins-ci.org/display/JENKINS/Durable+Task+Plugin`

Next, we can click on the **Advanced** tab and scroll down to **Upload Plugin**. Navigate to the `durable-task.hpi` file and click on **Upload**. You should see a screen that shows an installing progress bar. After a minute or two, it will update to **Success**.

Finally, install the main Kubernetes plugin. On the left-hand side, click on **Manage Plugins** and then the **Advanced** tab once again. This time, upload the `kubernetes.hpi` file and click on **Upload**. After a few minutes, the installation should be complete.

Configuring the Kubernetes plugin

Click on **Back to Dashboard** or the **Jenkins** link in the top-left corner. From the main dashboard page, click on the **Credentials** link. Choose a domain from the list; in my case, I just used the default **Global** credentials domain. Click on **Add Credentials**:

Add credentials screen

Leave **Kind** as **Username with password** and **Scope** as **Global**. Add your Kubernetes admin credentials. Remember that you can find these by running the `config` command:

```
$ kubectl config view
```

You can leave **ID** blank, give it a sensible description, and click on the **OK** button.

Now that we have our credentials saved, we can add our Kubernetes server. Click on the **Jenkins** link in the top-left corner and then **Manage Jenkins**. From there, select **Configure System** and scroll all the way down to the **Cloud** section. Select **Kubernetes** from the **Add a new cloud** dropdown and a **Kubernetes** section will appear, as follows:

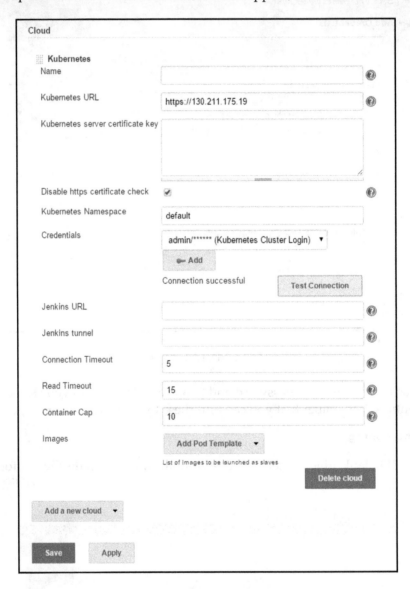

New Kubernetes cloud settings

You'll need to specify the URL for your master in the form of `https://<Master IP>/`.

Next, choose the credentials we added from the drop-down list. Since Kubernetes use a self-signed certificate by default, you'll also need to check the **Disable https certificate check** checkbox.

Click on **Test Connection** and if all goes well, you should see **Connection** successful appearing next to the button.

 If you are using an older version of the plugin, you may not see the **Disable https certificate check** checkbox. If this is the case, you will need to install the self-signed certificate directly on the **Jenkins Master**.

Finally, we will add a pod template by choosing **Kubernetes Pod Template** from the **Add Pod Template** dropdown next to **Images**.

This will create another new section. Use `jenkins-slave` for the **Name** and **Labels** section. Click on **Add** next to **Containers** and again use `jenkins-slave` for the **Name**. Use `csanchez/jenkins-slave` for the **Docker Image** and leave `/home/jenkins` for the **Working Directory**.

 Labels can be used later on in the build settings to force the build to use the Kubernetes cluster:

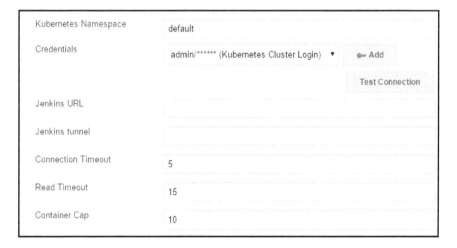

Kubernetes cluster addition

Here is the Pod Template that expands below the cluster addition:

Kubernetes pod template

Click on **Save** and you are all set. Now, new builds created in Jenkins can use the slaves in the Kubernetes pod we just created.

 Here is another note about firewalls. The Jenkins Master will need to be reachable by all the machines in your Kubernetes cluster, as the pod could land anywhere. You can find out your port settings in Jenkins under **Manage Jenkins** and **Configure Global Security**.

Bonus fun

Fabric8 bills itself as an integration platform. It includes a variety of logging, monitoring, and continuous delivery tools. It also has a nice console, an API registry, and a 3D game that lets you shoot at your pods. It's a very cool project, and it actually runs on Kubernetes. Refer to `http://fabric8.io/`.

It's an easy single command to set up on your Kubernetes cluster, so refer to `http://fabric8.io/guide/getStarted/gke.html`.

Summary

We looked at two continuous integration tools that can be used with Kubernetes. We did a brief walk-through of deploying the Gulp.js task on our cluster. We also looked at a new plugin used to integrate Jenkins build slaves into your Kubernetes cluster. You should now have a better sense of how Kubernetes can integrate with your own CI/CD pipeline.

8

Monitoring and Logging

This chapter will cover the usage and customization of both built-in and third-party monitoring tools on our Kubernetes cluster. We will cover how to use the tools to monitor the health and performance of our cluster. In addition, we will look at built-in logging, the **Google Cloud Logging** service, and **Sysdig**.

This chapter will discuss the following topics:

- How Kuberentes uses cAdvisor, Heapster, InfluxDB, and Grafana
- Customizing the default Grafana dashboard
- Using FluentD and Grafana
- Installing and using logging tools
- Working with popular third-party tools, such as StackDriver and Sysdig, to extend our monitoring capabilities

Monitoring operations

Real-world monitoring goes far beyond checking whether a system is up and running. Although health checks, like those you learned in `Chapter 2`, *Pods, Services, Replication Controllers, and Labels*, in the *Health checks* section, can help us isolate problem applications. Operation teams can best serve the business when they can anticipate the issues and mitigate them before a system goes offline.

Best practices in monitoring are to measure the performance and usage of core resources and watch for trends that stray from the normal baseline. Containers are not different here, and a key component to managing our Kubernetes cluster is having a clear view into performance and availability of the OS, network, system (CPU and memory), and storage resources across all nodes.

In this chapter, we will examine several options to monitor and measure the performance and availability of all our cluster resources. In addition, we will look at a few options for alerting and notifications when irregular trends start to emerge.

Built-in monitoring

If you recall from Chapter 1, *Introduction to Kubernetes*, we noted that our nodes were already running a number of monitoring services. We can see these once again by running the get pods command with the kube-system namespace specified as follows:

```
$ kubectl get pods --namespace=kube-system
```

The following screenshot is the result of the preceding command:

NAME	READY	STATUS	RESTARTS	AGE
etcd-empty-dir-cleanup-kubernetes-master	1/1	Running	2	2d
etcd-server-events-kubernetes-master	1/1	Running	2	2d
etcd-server-kubernetes-master	1/1	Running	2	2d
fluentd-cloud-logging-kubernetes-master	1/1	Running	2	2d
fluentd-cloud-logging-kubernetes-minion-group-rh7t	1/1	Running	0	3m
fluentd-cloud-logging-kubernetes-minion-group-s345	1/1	Running	0	3m
fluentd-cloud-logging-kubernetes-minion-group-tp2h	1/1	Running	0	3m
heapster-v1.2.0-2805816975-80mjc	4/4	Running	0	20h
kube-addon-manager-kubernetes-master	1/1	Running	2	2d
kube-apiserver-kubernetes-master	1/1	Running	4	2d
kube-controller-manager-kubernetes-master	1/1	Running	2	2d
kube-dns-4101612645-bwsd4	4/4	Running	0	20h
kube-dns-autoscaler-2715466192-gt3r7	1/1	Running	0	20h
kube-proxy-kubernetes-minion-group-rh7t	1/1	Running	0	4m
kube-proxy-kubernetes-minion-group-s345	1/1	Running	0	4m
kube-proxy-kubernetes-minion-group-tp2h	1/1	Running	0	3m
kube-scheduler-kubernetes-master	1/1	Running	2	2d
kubernetes-dashboard-3543765157-65g1m	1/1	Running	0	20h
l7-default-backend-2234341178-g4wct	1/1	Running	0	20h
l7-lb-controller-v0.8.0-kubernetes-master	1/1	Running	2	2d
monitoring-influxdb-grafana-v4-7x0n0	2/2	Running	0	20h
node-problem-detector-v0.1-1zfml	1/1	Running	0	4m
node-problem-detector-v0.1-cjrtz	1/1	Running	0	4m
node-problem-detector-v0.1-f87pp	1/1	Running	2	2d
node-problem-detector-v0.1-vj001	1/1	Running	0	4m
rescheduler-v0.2.1-kubernetes-master	1/1	Running	2	2d

System pod listing

Again, we see a variety of services, but how does this all fit together? If you recall the *Node (formerly minions)* section from `Chapter 2`, *Pods, Services, Replication Controllers, and Labels*, each node is running a kublet. The kublet is the main interface for nodes to interact and update the API server. One such update is the **metrics** of the node resources. The actual reporting of the resource usage is performed by a program named **cAdvisor**.

cAdvisor is another open-source project from Google, which provides various metrics on container resource use. Metrics include CPU, memory, and network statistics. There is no need to tell cAdvisor about individual containers; it collects the metrics for all containers on a node and reports this back to the kublet, which in turn reports to Heapster.

> **Google's open-source projects**
> Google has a variety of open-source projects related to Kubernetes. Check them out, use them, and even contribute your own code!
>
> cAdvisor and Heapster are mentioned in the following section:
>
> - **cAdvisor**: `https://github.com/google/cadvisor`
> - **Heapster**: `https://github.com/kubernetes/heapster`
>
> **Contrib** is a catch-all for a variety of components that are not part of core Kubernetes. It is found at:
>
> `https://github.com/kubernetes/contrib`.
>
> **LevelDB** is a key store library that was used in the creation of InfluxDB. It is found at:
>
> `https://github.com/google/leveldb`.

Heapster is yet another open-source project from Google; you may start to see a theme emerging here (see the preceding information box). Heapster runs in a container on one of the minion nodes and aggregates the data from kublet. A simple REST interface is provided to query the data.

When using the GCE setup, a few additional packages are set up for us, which saves us time and gives us a complete package to monitor our container workloads. As we can see from the preceding *System pod listing* screenshot, there is another pod with `influx-grafana` in the title.

InfluxDB is described on its official website as follows (you can refer to more details about this in point 1 in the *References* section at the end of the chapter):

An open-source distributed time series database with no external dependencies.

InfluxDB is based on a key store package (refer to the previous *Google's open-source projects* information box) and is perfect to store and query event—or time-based statistics such as those provided by Heapster.

Finally, we have **Grafana**, which provides a dashboard and graphing interface for the data stored in InfluxDB. Using Grafana, users can create a custom monitoring dashboard and get immediate visibility into the health of their Kubernetes cluster and therefore their entire container infrastructure.

Exploring Heapster

Let's quickly look at the REST interface by running SSH to the node with the Heapster pod. First, we can list the pods to find the one running Heapster, as follows:

```
$ kubectl get pods --namespace=kube-system
```

The name of the pod should start with `monitoring-heapster`. Run a `describe` command to see which node it is running on, as follows:

```
$ kubectl describe pods/<Heapster monitoring Pod> --namespace=kube-system
```

From the output in the following screenshot, we can see that the pod is running in `kubernetes-minion-merd`. Also note the IP for the pod, a few lines down, as we will need that in a moment:

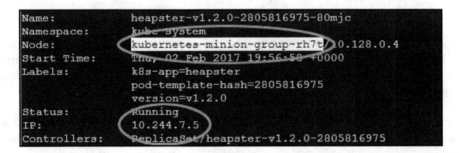

Heapster pod details

Next, we can SSH to this box with the familiar `gcloud ssh` command, as follows:

```
$ gcloud compute --project "<Your project ID>" ssh --zone "<your gce zone>"
"<kubernetes minion from describe>"
```

From here, we can access the Heapster REST API directly using the pod's IP address. Remember that pod IPs are routable not only in the containers but also on the nodes themselves. The `Heapster` API is listening on port `8082`, and we can get a full list of metrics at `/api/v1/metric-export-schema/`.

Let's see the list now by issuing a `curl` command to the pod IP address we saved from the `describe` command, as follows:

```
$ curl -G <Heapster IP from describe>:8082/api/v1/metric-export-schema/
```

We will see a listing that is quite long. The first section shows all the metrics available. The last two sections list fields by which we can filter and group. For your convenience, I've added the following tables that are a little bit easier to read:

Metric	Description	Unit	Type
uptime	The number of milliseconds since the container was started	ms	cumulative
cpu/usage	The cumulative CPU usage on all cores	ns	cumulative
cpu/limit	The CPU limit in millicores	-	gauge
memory/usage	Total memory usage	bytes	gauge
memory/working_set	Total working set usage; the working set is the memory being used and not easily dropped by the kernel	bytes	gauge
memory/limit	The memory limit	bytes	gauge
memory/page_faults	The number of page faults	-	cumulative
memory/major_page_faults	The number of major page faults	-	cumulative
network/rx	The cumulative number of bytes received over the network	bytes	cumulative
network/rx_errors	The cumulative number of errors while receiving over the network	-	cumulative
network/tx	The cumulative number of bytes sent over the network	bytes	cumulative

network/tx_errors	The cumulative number of errors while sending over the network	-	cumulative
filesystem/usage	The total number of bytes consumed on a filesystem	bytes	gauge
filesystem/limit	The total size of filesystem in bytes	bytes	gauge
filesystem/available	The number of available bytes remaining in a the filesystem	bytes	gauge

Table 6.1. Available Heapster metrics

Field	Description	Label type
nodename	The nodename where the container ran	Common
hostname	The hostname where the container ran	Common
host_id	An identifier specific to a host, which is set by the cloud provider or user	Common
container_base_image	The user-defined image name that is run inside the container	Common
container_name	The user-provided name of the container or full container name for system containers	Common
pod_name	The name of the pod	Pod
pod_id	The unique ID of the pod	Pod
pod_namespace	The namespace of the pod	Pod
namespace_id	The unique ID of the namespace of the pod	Pod
labels	A comma-separated list of user-provided labels	Pod

Table 6.2. Available Heapster fields

Customizing our dashboards

Now that we have the fields, we can have some fun. Recall the Grafana page we looked at in `Chapter 1`, *Introduction to Kubernetes*. Let's pull that up again by going to our cluster's monitoring URL. Note that you may need to log in with your cluster credentials. Refer to the following format of the link you need to use:

```
https://<your master IP>/api/v1/proxy/namespaces/kube-
system/services/monitoring-grafana
```

We'll see the default **Home** dashboard. Click on the down arrow next to **Home** and select **Cluster**. This shows the Kubernetes cluster dashboard, and now we can add our own statistics to the board. Scroll all the way to the bottom and click on **Add a Row**. This should create a space for a new row and present a green tab on the left-hand side of the screen.

Let's start by adding a view into the filesystem usage for each node (minion). Click on the *green* tab to expand and then select **Add Panel** and then **graph**. An empty graph should appear on the screen along with a query panel for our custom graph.

The first field in this panel should show a query that starts with '**SELECT mean("value") FROM ...**'. Click on the **A** character next to this field to expand it. Leave the first field next to **FROM** as **default** and then click on the next field with the **select measurement** value. A dropdown menu will appear with the Heapster metrics we saw in the previous tables. Select `filesystem/usage_bytes_gauge`. Now in the **SELECT** row, click on **mean()** and then on the **x** symbol to remove it. Next, click on the + symbol on the end of the row and add **selectors** -> **max**. Then, you'll see a **GROUP BY** row with **time($interval)** and **fill(none)**. Carefully click on **fill** and not on the **(none)** portion and again on **x** to remove it. Then, click on the + symbol at the end of the row and select **tag(hostname)**.

Finally, at the bottom of the screen we should see a **Group by time interval.** Enter 5s there and you should have something similar to the following screenshot:

Heapster pod details

Next, let's click on the **Axes** tab, so that we can set the units and legend. Under **Left Y Axis**, click on the field next to **Unit** and set it to **data -> bytes** and **Label** to **Disk Space Used**. Under **Right Y Axis**, set **Unit** to **none -> none**. Next, on the **Legend** tab, make sure to check **Show** in **Options** and **Max** in **Values**.

Now, let's quickly go to the **General** tab and choose a title. In my case, I named mine `Filesystem Disk Usage by Node (max)`.

We don't want to lose this nice new graph we've created, so let's click on the save icon in the top right corner. It looks like a *floppy disk* (you can do a Google image search if you don't know what this is).

After we click on the save icon, we will see a green dialog box that verifies the dashboard was saved. We can now click the **x** symbol above the graph details panel and below the graph itself.

This will return us to the dashboard page. If we scroll all the way down, we will see our new graph. Let's add another panel to this row. Again use the *green* tab and then select **Add Panel -> singlestat**. Once again, an empty panel will appear with a setting form below it.

Let's say, we want to watch a particular node and monitor network usage. We can easily do this by first going to the **Metrics** tab. Then expand the query field and set the second value in the **FROM** field to **network/rx**. Now we can specify the **WHERE** clause by clicking the + symbol at the end of the row and choosing **hostname** from the dropdown. After **hostname =** click on **select tag value** and choose one of the minion nodes from the list.

Finally, leave **mean()** for the second **SELECT** field:

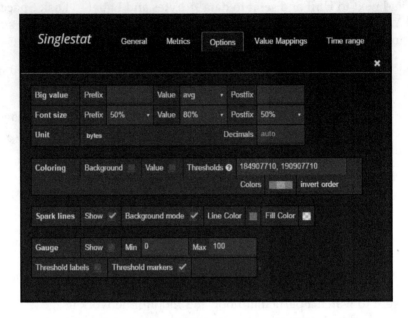

Singlestat options

In the **Options** tab, make sure that **Unit format** is set to **data -> bytes** and check the **Show** box next to **Spark lines**. The **sparkline** gives us a quick history view of the recent variation in the value. We can use **Background mode** to take up the entire background; by default, it uses the area below the value.

> In **Coloring**, we can optionally check the **Value** or **Background** box and choose **Thresholds** and **Colors.** This will allow us to choose different colors for the value based on the threshold tier we specify. Note that an unformatted version of the number must be used for threshold values.

Now, let's go back to the **General** tab and set the title as `Network bytes received`
`(Node35ao)`. Use the identifier for your minion node. Once again, let's save our work and
return to the dashboard. We should now have a row that looks like the following
screenshot:

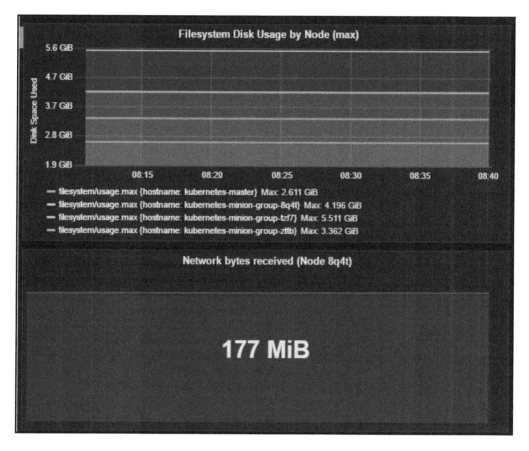

Custom dashboard panels

Grafana has a number of other panel types you can play with such as **Dashboard list**,
Plugin list, **Table**, and **Text**.

As we can see, it is pretty easy to build a custom dashboard and monitor the health of our
cluster at a glance.

FluentD and Google Cloud Logging

Looking back at the *System pod listing* screenshot at the beginning of the chapter, you may have noted a number of pods starting with the words `fluentd-cloud-logging-kubernetes....`. These pods appear when using the GCE provider for your K8s cluster. A pod like this exists on every node in our cluster and its sole purpose is to handle the processing of Kubernetes logs.

If we log in to our Google Cloud Platform account, we can see some of the logs processed there. Simply use the left side, under **Stackdriver** select **Logging**. This will take us to a log listing page with a number of drop-down menus on the top. If this is your first time visiting the page, the first dropdown will likely be set to **Cloud HTTP Load Balancer**.

In this drop-down menu, we'll see a number of GCE types of entries. Select GCE VM Instances and then the Kubernetes master or one of the nodes. In the second dropdown, we can choose various log groups, including **kublet.** We can also filter by the event log level and date. Additionally, we can use the *play* button to watch events stream in live:

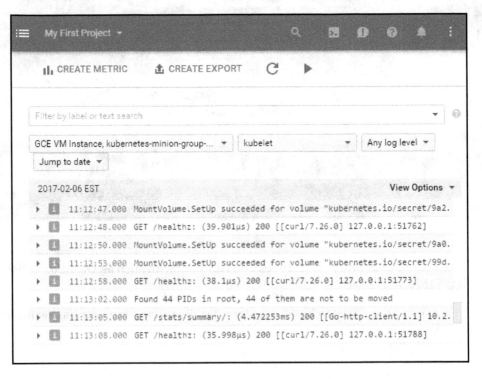

The Google Cloud Logging filter

FluentD

Now we know that the `fluentd-cloud-logging-kubernetes` pods are sending the data to the Google Cloud, but why do we need FluentD? Simply put, **FluentD** is a collector. It can be configured to have multiple sources to collect and tag logs, which are then sent to various output points for analysis, alerting, or archiving. We can even transform data using plugins before it is passed on to its destination.

Not all provider setups have FluentD installed by default, but it is one of the recommended approaches to give us greater flexibility for future monitoring operations. The AWS Kubernetes setup also uses FluentD, but instead forwards events to **Elasticsearch**.

Exploring FluentD

If you are curious about the inner workings of the FluentD setup or just want to customize the log collection, we can explore quite easily using the `kubectl exec` command and one of the pod names from the command we ran earlier in the chapter.
First, let's see if we can find the FluentD `config` file:

```
$ kubectl exec fluentd-cloud-logging-kubernetes-minion-
group-r4qt --namespace=kube-system -- ls /etc/td-agent
```

We will look in the `etc` folder and then `td-agent`, which is the `fluent` subfolder. While searching in this directory, we should see a `td-agent.conf` file. We can view that file with a simple `cat` command, as follows:

```
$ kubectl exec fluentd-cloud-logging-kubernetes-minion-
group-r4qt --namespace=kube-system -- cat /etc/td-
agent/td-agent.conf
```

We should see a number of sources including the various Kubernetes components, Docker, and some GCP elements.
While we can make changes here, remember that it is a running container and our changes won't be saved if the pod dies or is restarted. If we really want to customize, it's best to use this container as a base and build a new container which we can push to a repository for later use.

Maturing our monitoring operations

While Grafana gives us a great start to monitor our container operations, it is still a work in progress. In the real world of operations, having a complete dashboard view is great once we know there is a problem. However, in everyday scenarios, we'd prefer to be proactive and actually receive notifications when issues arise. This kind of alerting capability is a must to keep the operations team ahead of the curve and out of *reactive mode*.

There are many solutions available in this space, and we will take a look at two in particular—GCE monitoring (StackDriver) and Sysdig.

GCE (StackDriver)

StackDriver is a great place to start for infrastructure in the public cloud. It is actually owned by Google, so it's integrated as the Google Cloud Platform monitoring service. Before your lock-in alarm bells start ringing, StackDriver also has solid integration with AWS. In addition, StackDriver has alerting capability with support for notification to a variety of platforms and webhooks for anything else.

Sign-up for GCE monitoring

In the GCE console, in the **Stackdriver** section click on **Monitoring.** This will open a new window, where we can sign up for a free trial of Stackdriver. We can then add our GCP project and optionally an AWS account as well. This requires a few more steps, but instructions are included on the page. Finally, we'll be given instructions on how to install the agents on our cluster nodes. We can skip this for now, but will come back to it in a minute.

Click on **Continue**, set up your daily alerts, and click on **Continue** again.

Click on **Launch Monitoring** to proceed. We'll be taken to the main dashboard page, where we will see some basic statistics on our node in the cluster. If we select **Resources** from the side menu and then **Instances**, we'll be taken to a page with all our nodes listed. By clicking on the individual node, we can again see some basic information even without an agent installed.

> Stackdriver also offers monitoring and logging agents that can be installed on the nodes. However, it currently does not support the container OS that is used by default in the GCE kube-up script. You can still see the basic metrics for any nodes in GCE or AWS, but will need to use another OS if you want the detailed agent install.

Alerts

Next, we can look at the alerting policies available as part of the monitoring service. From the instance details page, click on the **Create Alerting Policy** button in the **Incidents** section at the top of the page.

We will click on **Add Condition** and select a M**etric Threshold**. In the **Target** section, set **RESOURCE TYPE** to **Instance (GCE)**. Then, set **APPLIES TO** to **Group** and **kubernetes**. Leave **CONDITION TRIGGERS IF** set to **Any Member Violates**.

In the **Configuration** section, leave **IF METRIC** as **CPU Usage (GCE Monitoring)** and **CONDITION** as **above**. Now set **THRESHOLD** to 80 and set the time in **FOR** to **5 minutes**.

Click on **Save Condition**:

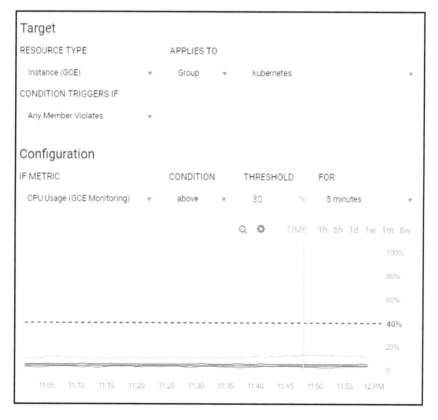

Google Cloud Monitoring alert policy

Next, we will add a notification. In the **Notification** section, leave **Method** as **Email** and enter your e-mail address.

We can skip the **Documentation** section, but this is where we can add text and formatting to alert messages.

Finally, name the policy as `Excessive CPU Load` and click on **Save Policy.**

Now whenever the CPU from one of our instances goes above 80 percent, we will receive an e-mail notification. If we ever need to review our policies, we can find them in the **Alerting** dropdown and then in **Policies Overview** at the menu on the left-hand side of the screen.

Beyond system monitoring with Sysdig

Monitoring our cloud systems is a great start, but what about visibility to the containers themselves? Although there are a variety of cloud monitoring and visibility tools, Sysdig stands out for its ability to dive deep not only into system operations but specifically containers.

Sysdig is open source and is billed as *a universal system visibility tool with native support for containers* (you can refer to more details about this in point 2 in the *References* section at the end of the chapter). It is a command-line tool, which provides insight into the areas we've looked at earlier, such as storage, network, and system processes. What sets it apart is the level of detail and visibility it offers for these process and system activities. Furthermore, it has native support for containers, which gives us a full picture of our container operations. This is a highly recommended tool for your container operations arsenal. The main website of Sysdig is `http://www.sysdig.org/`.

Sysdig Cloud

We will take a look at the Sysdig tool and some of the useful command-line-based UIs in a moment. However, the team at Sysdig has also built a commercial product, named **Sysdig Cloud**, which provides the advanced dashboard, alerting, and notification services we discussed earlier in the chapter. Also, the differentiator here has high visibility into containers, including some nice visualizations of our application topology.

If you'd rather skip the *Sysdig Cloud* section and just try out the command-line tool, simply skip to the *Sysdig command line* section later in this chapter.

If you have not done so already, sign up for Sysdig Cloud at `http://www.sysdigcloud.com`.

After activating and logging in for the first time, we'll be taken to a welcome page. Clicking on **Next**, we are shown a page with various options to install the `sysdig` agents. For our example environment, we will use the Kubernetes setup. Selecting Kubernetes will give you a page with your API key and a link to instructions. The instructions will walk you through how to create a Sysdig agent DaemonSet on your cluster. Don't forget to add the API Key from the install page.

We will not be able to continue on the install page until the agents connect. After creating the DaemonSet and waiting a moment, the page should continue to the AWS integration page. You can fill this out if you like, but for this walk-through we will click on **Skip**. Then, click on **Let's Get Started**.

 As of this writing, Sysdig and Sysdig Cloud were not fully compatible with the latest container OS deployed by default in the GCE `kube-up` script, Container-Optimized OS from Google: `https://cloud.google.com/container-optimized-os/docs`.

We'll be taken to the main **sysdig cloud** dashboard screen. We should see at least two minion nodes appear under the **Explore** tab. We should see something similar to the following screenshot with our minion nodes:

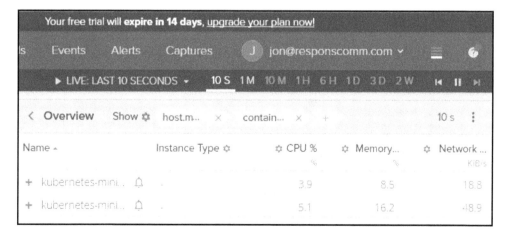

Sysdig Cloud Explore page

This page shows us a table view, and the links on the left let us explore some key metrics for CPU, memory, networking, and so on. Although this is a great start, the detailed views will give us a much deeper look at each node.

Detailed views

Let's take a look at these views. Select one of the minion nodes and then scroll down to the detail section that appears below. By default, we should see the **System: Overview by Process** view (if it's not selected, just click on it from the list on the left-hand side). If the chart is hard to read, simply use the maximize icon in the top-left corner of each graph for a larger view.

There are a variety of interesting views to explore. Just to call out a few others, **Services | HTTP Overview** and **Hosts & Containers | Overview by Container** give us some great charts for inspection. In the later view, we can see stats for CPU, memory, network, and file usage by container.

Topology views

In addition, there are three topology views at the bottom. These views are perfect for helping us understand how our application is communicating. Click on **Topology | Network Traffic** and wait a few seconds for the view to fully populate. It should look similar to the following screenshot:

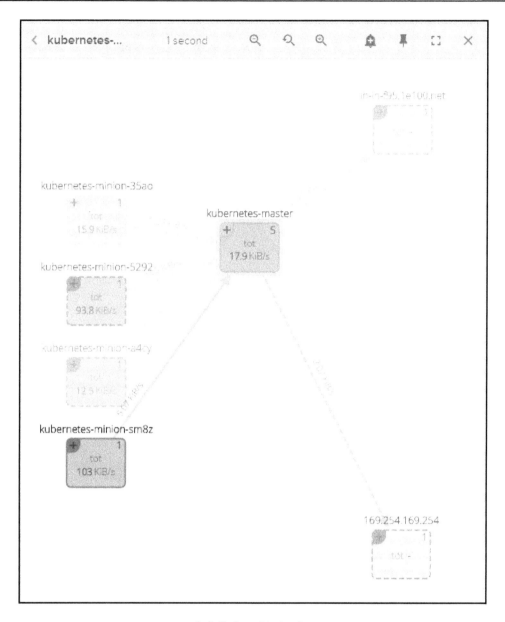

Sysdig Cloud network topology view

We note the view maps out the flow of communication between the minion nodes and the master in the cluster. You may also note a + symbol in the top corner of the node boxes. Click on that in one of the minion nodes and use the zoom tools at the top of the view area to zoom into the details, as you see in the following screenshot:

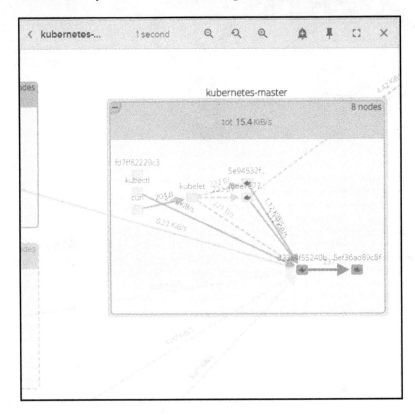

The Sysdig Cloud network topology detailed view

Note that we can now see all the components of Kubernetes running inside the master. We can see how the various components work together. We will see `kube-proxy` and the `kublet` process running, as well as a number of boxes with the Docker whale, which indicate that they are containers. If we zoom in and use the plus icon, we will see that these are the containers for our pods and core Kubernetes processes, as we saw in the services running on the master section in `Chapter 1`, *Introduction to Kubernetes*.

Also, if you have the master included in your monitored nodes, we can watch `kublet` initiate communication from a minion and follow it all the way through the `kube-apiserver` container in the master.

We can even sometimes see the instance communication with GCE infrastructure to update metadata. This view is great in order to get a mental picture of how our infrastructure and underlying containers are talking to one another.

Metrics

Next, let's switch over to the **Metrics** tab in the left-hand menu next to **Views**. Here, there are also a variety of helpful views.

Let's look at **capacity.estimated.request.total.count** in **System**. This view shows us an estimate of how many requests a node is capable of handling when fully loaded. This can be really useful for infrastructure planning:

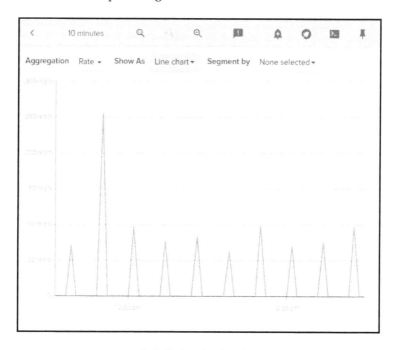

Sysdig Cloud capacity estimate view

Alerting

Now that we have all this great information, let's create some notifications. Scroll back up to the top of the page and find the bell icon next to one of your minion entries. This will open a **Create Alert** dialog. Here, we can set manual alerts similar to what we did earlier in the chapter. However, there is also the option to use **BASELINE** and **HOST COMPARISON**.

Using the BASELINE option is extremely helpful as Sysdig will watch the historical patterns of the node and alert us whenever one of the metrics strays outside the expected metric thresholds. No manual settings are required, so this can really save time for the notification setup and help our operations team to be proactive before issues arise. Refer to the following image:

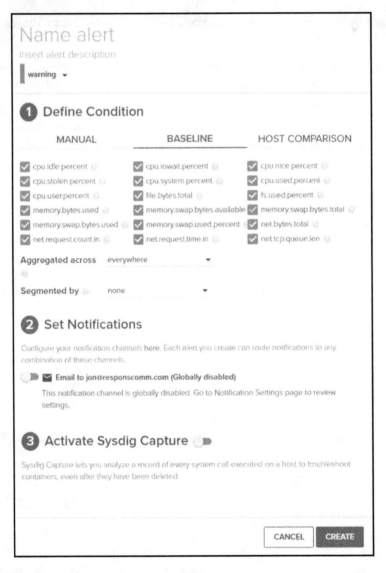

Sysdig Cloud new alert

The **HOST COMPARISON** option is also a great help as it allows us to compare metrics with other hosts and alert whenever one host has a metric that differs significantly from the group. A great use case for this is monitoring resource usage across minion nodes to ensure that our scheduling constraints are not creating a bottleneck somewhere in the cluster.

You can choose whichever option you like and give it a name and warning level. Enable the notification method. Sysdig supports e-mail, **SNS** (short for **Simple Notification Service**), and **PagerDuty** as notification methods. You can optionally enable **Sysdig Capture** to gain deeper insight into issues. Once you have everything set, just click on **Create** and you will start to receive alerts as issues come up.

The sysdig command line

Whether you only use the open-source tool or you are trying out the full Sysdig Cloud package, the command-line utility is a great companion to have to track down issues or get a deeper understanding of your system.

In the core tool, there is the main `sysdig` utility and also a command-line style UI named `csysdig`. Let's take a look at a few useful commands.

Find the relevant install instructions for your OS here:

`http://www.sysdig.org/install/`

Once installed, let's first look at the process with the most network activity by issuing the following command:

```
$ sudo sysdig -pc -c topprocs_net
```

The following screenshot is the result of the preceding command:

Bytes	Process	Host_pid	Container_pid	container.name
79.06KB	kube-apise	5152	15	host
58.10KB	etcd	5211	10	host
6.29KB	dragent	19284	19292	host
4.52KB	kube-contr	5164	11	host
4.11KB	etcd	5211	11	host
1.95KB	kube-sched	5227	13	host
1.72KB	sshd	18963	18963	host

A Sysdig top process by network activity

This is an interactive view that will show us a top process in terms of network activity. Also, there are a plethora of commands to use with `sysdig`. A few other useful commands to try out include the following:

```
$ sudo sysdig -pc -c topprocs_cpu
$ sudo sysdig -pc -c topprocs_file
$ sudo sysdig -pc -c topprocs_cpu container.name=<Container Name NOT ID>
```

More examples can be found at
`http://www.sysdig.org/wiki/sysdig-examples/`.

The csysdig command-line UI

Because we are in a shell on one of our nodes doesn't mean we can't have a UI. Csysdig is a customizable UI to explore all the metrics and insight that Sysdig provides. Simply type `csysdig` at the prompt:

```
$ csysdig
```

After entering csysdig, we see a real-time listing of all processes on the machine. At the bottom of the screen, you'll note a menu with various options. Click on **Views** or press *F2* if you love to use your keyboard. On the left-hand menu, there are a variety of options, but we'll look at threads. Double-click to select **Threads**.

On some operating systems and with some SSH clients, you may have issues with the Function keys. Check the settings on your terminal and make sure the function keys are using the VT100+ sequences.

We can see all the threads currently running on the system and some information about the resource usage. By default, we see a big list that is updating often. If we click on the **Filter**, *F4* for the mouse challenged, we can slim down the list.

Type `kube-apiserver`, if you are on the master, or `kube-proxy`, if you are on a node (minion), in the filter box and press *Enter*. The view now filters for only the threads in that command:

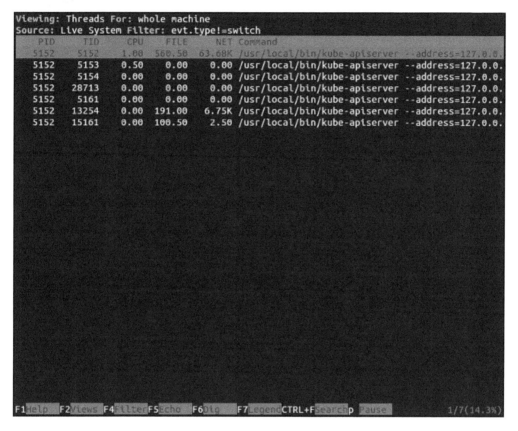

Csysdig threads

If we want to inspect a little further, we can simply select one of the threads in the list and click on **Dig** or press *F6*. Now we see a detailed listing of system calls from the command in real time. This can be a really useful tool to gain deep insight into the containers and processing running on our cluster.

Click on **Back** or press the *Backspace* key to go back to the previous screen. Then, go to **Views** once more. This time, we will look at the **Containers** view. Once again, we can filter and also use the **Dig** view to get more in-depth visibility into what is happening at a system call level.

Another menu item you might note here is **Actions**, which is available in the newest release. These features allow us to go from process monitoring to action and response. It gives us the ability to perform a variety of actions from the various process views in csysdig. For example, the container view has actions to drop into a bash shell, kill containers, inspect logs, and more. It's worth getting to know the various actions and hotkeys and even add your own custom hotkeys for common operations.

Prometheus

A newcomer to the monitoring scene is an open-source tool called **Prometheus**. Prometheus is an open-source monitoring tool that was built by a team at SoundCloud. You can find more about the project from `https://prometheus.io`.

Their website offers the following features (you can refer to more details about this in point 3 in the *References* section at the end of the chapter):

- A multi-dimensional `data model` (time series identified by metric name and key/value pairs)
- A `flexible query language` to leverage this dimensionality
- No reliance on distributed storage; single server nodes are autonomous
- Time series collection happens via a pull model over HTTP
- `pushing time series` is supported via an intermediary gateway
- Targets are discovered via service discovery or static configuration
- Multiple modes of graphing and dashboard support

CoreOS has a nice blog post on setting up Prometheus with Kubernetes here:

`https://coreos.com/blog/monitoring-kubernetes-with-prometheus.html`

Summary

We took a quick look at monitoring and logging with Kubernetes. You should now be familiar with how Kubernetes uses cAdvisor and Heapster to collect metrics on all the resources in a given cluster. Furthermore, we saw how Kubernetes saves us time by providing InfluxDB and Grafana set up and configured out of the box. Dashboards are easily customizable for our everyday operational needs.

In addition, we looked at the built-in logging capabilities with FluentD and the Google Cloud Logging service. Also, Kubernetes gives us great time savings by setting up the basics for us.

Finally, you learned about the various third-party options available to monitor our containers and clusters. Using these tools will allow us to gain even more insight into the health and status of our applications. All these tools combine to give us a solid toolset to manage day-to-day operations.

In the next chapter, we will explore the new cluster federation capabilities. Still mostly in beta, this functionality will allow us to run multiple clusters in different datacenters and even clouds, but manage and distribute applications from a single control plane.

References

1. `http://stackdriver.com/`
2. `http://www.sysdig.org/wiki/`
3. `https://prometheus.io/docs/introduction/overview/`

9
Cluster Federation

This chapter will discuss the new federation capabilities and how to use them to manage multiple clusters across cloud providers. We will also cover the federated version of the core constructs. We will walk you through federated Deployments, ReplicaSets, ConfigMaps, and Events.

This chapter will discuss the following topics:

- Federating clusters
- Federating multiple clusters
- Inspecting and controlling resources across multiple clusters
- Launching resources across multiple clusters

Introduction to federation

While **federation** is still very new in Kubernetes, it lays the ground work for the highly sought cross-cloud provider solution. Using federation, we can run multiple Kubernetes clusters on-premise and in one or more public cloud providers and manage applications utilizing the entire set of all our organizational resources.

This begins to create a path for avoiding cloud provider lock-in and highly available deployment that can place application servers in multiple clusters and allow for communication to other services located in single points among our federated clusters. We can improve isolation on outages at a particular provider or geographic location while providing greater flexibility for scaling and utilizing total infrastructure.

Currently, the federation plane supports these resources (ConfigMap, DaemonSets, Deployment, Events, Ingress, Namespaces, ReplicaSets, Secrets, and Services). Note that federation and its components are in alpha and beta phases of release, so functionality may still be a bit temperamental.

Setting up federation

While we can use the cluster we had running for the rest of the examples, I would highly recommend that you start fresh. The default naming of the clusters and contexts can be problematic for the federation system. Note that the `--cluster-context` and `--secret-name` flags are there to help you work around the default naming, but for first-time federation, it can still be confusing and less than straightforward.

Hence, starting fresh is how we will walk through the examples in this chapter. Either use new and separate cloud provider (AWS and/or GCE) accounts or tear down the current cluster and reset your Kubernetes control environment by running the following commands:

```
$ kubectl config unset contexts
$ kubectl config unset clusters
```

Double-check that nothing is listed using the following commands:

```
$ kubectl config get-contexts
$ kubectl config get-clusters
```

Next, we will want to get the `kubefed` command on our path and make it executable. Navigate back to the folder where you have the Kubernetes download extracted. The `kubefed` command is located in the `/kubernetes/client/bin` folder. Run the following commands to get in the bin folder and change the execution permissions:

```
$ sudo cp kubernetes/client/bin/kubefed /usr/local/bin
$ sudo chmod +x /usr/local/bin/kubefed
```

Contexts

Contexts are used by the Kubernetes control plane to keep authentication and cluster configuration stored for multiple clusters. This allow us to access and manage multiple clusters accessible from the same `kubectl`. You can always see the contexts available with the `get-contexts` command that we used earlier.

New clusters for federation

Again, make sure you navigate to wherever Kubernetes was downloaded and move into the `cluster` sub-folder:

```
$ cd kubernetes/cluster/
```

 Before we proceed, make sure you have the GCE command line and the AWS command line installed, authenticated, and configured. Refer to `Chapter 1`, *Introduction to Kubernetes*, if you need assistance doing so on a new box.

First, we will create the AWS cluster. Note that we are adding an environment variable named `OVERRIDE_CONTEXT` that will allow us to set the context name to something that complies with the DNS naming standards. DNS is a critical component for federation as it allows us to do cross-cluster discovery and service communication. This is important in a federated world where clusters may be in different data centers and even providers.

Run these commands to create your AWS cluster:

```
$ export KUBERNETES_PROVIDER=aws
$ export OVERRIDE_CONTEXT=awsk8s
$ ./kube-up.sh
```

Next, we will create a GCE cluster, once again using the `OVERRIDE_CONTEXT` environment variable:

```
$ export KUBERNETES_PROVIDER=gce
$ export OVERRIDE_CONTEXT=gcek8s
$ ./kube-up.sh
```

If we take a look at our contexts now, we will notice both the `awsk8s` and the `gcek8s` that we just created. The star in front of `gcek8s` denotes that it's where `kubectl` is currently pointing and executing against:

```
$ kubectl config get-contexts
```

The preceding command should produce something like the following:

CURRENT	NAME	CLUSTER	AUTHINFO	NAMESPACE
	awsk8s	awsk8s	awsk8s	
*	gcek8s	gcek8s	gcek8s	

Context Listing

Initializing the federation control plane

Now that we have two clusters, let's set up the federation control plane in the GCE cluster. First, we'll need to make sure that we are in the GCE context, and then we will initialize the federation control plane:

```
$ kubectl config use-context gcek8s
$ kubefed init master-control --host-cluster-context=gcek8s --dns-zone-name="mydomain.com"
```

The preceding command creates a new context just for federation called `master-control`. It uses the `gcek8s` cluster/context to host the federation components (such as API server and controller). It assumes GCE DNS as the federations DNS service. You'll need to update `dns-zone-name` with a domain suffix you manage.

> By default, the DNS provider is GCE. You can use `--dns-provider="aws-route53"` to set it to AWS `route53`; however, out of the box implementation still has issues for many users.

If we check our contexts once again we will now see three contexts:

```
$ kubectl config get-contexts
```

The preceding command should produce something like the following:

CURRENT	NAME	CLUSTER	AUTHINFO	NAMESPACE
	awsk8s	awsk8s	awsk8s	
*	gcek8s	gcek8s	gcek8s	
	master-control	master-control	master-control	

Context Listing #2

Let's make sure we have all the federation components running before we proceed. The federation control plane uses the `federation-system` namespace. Use the `kubectl get pods` command with the namespace specified to monitor the progress. Once you see two API server pods and one controller pod you should be set:

```
$ kubectl get pods --namespace=federation-system
```

```
NAME                                                READY      STATUS
RESTARTS     AGE
master-control-apiserver-3595964982-s61x9           2/2        Running
0            8m
master-control-controller-manager-516854663-r8m37   1/1        Running
0            8m
```

Federation pod listing #

Now that we have the federation components set up and running, let's switch to that context for the next steps:

```
$ kubectl config use-context master-control
```

Adding clusters to the federation system

Now that we have our federation control plane we can add the clusters to the federation system. First, we will join the GCE cluster and then the AWS cluster:

```
$ kubefed join gcek8s --host-cluster-context=gcek8s --secret-name=fed-
secret-gce
$ kubefed join awsk8s --host-cluster-context=gcek8s --secret-name=fed-
secret-aws
```

Federated resources

Federated resources allow us to deploy across multiple clusters and/or regions. Currently, version 1.5 of Kubernetes support a number of core resource types in the federation API, including ConfigMap, DaemonSets, Deployment, Events, Ingress, Namespaces, ReplicaSets, Secrets, and Services.

Let's take a look at a **Federated Deployment** that will allow us to schedule pods across both AWS and GCE:

```
apiVersion: extensions/v1beta1
kind: Deployment
metadata:
  name: node-js-deploy
  labels:
    name: node-js-deploy
spec:
  replicas: 3
  template:
    metadata:
      labels:
        name: node-js-deploy
    spec:
      containers:
      - name: node-js-deploy
        image: jonbaier/pod-scaling:latest
        ports:
        - containerPort: 80
```

Listing 9-1. `node-js-deploy-fed.yaml`

Create this deployment with the following command:

```
$ kubectl create -f node-js-deploy-fed.yaml
```

Now let's try listing the pods from this deployment:

```
$ kubectl get pods
```

```
the server doesn't have a resource type "pods"
```

No pods in federation context

We should see a message like the preceding one depicted. This is because we are still using the `master-control` or federation context, which does not itself run pods. We will, however, see the deployment in the federation plane and if we inspect the events we will see that the deployment was in fact created on both our federated clusters:

```
$ kubectl get deployments
$ kubectl describe deployments node-js-deploy
```

We should see something like the following. Notice that the `Events:` section shows deployments in both our GCE and AWS contexts:

```
Name:                   node-js-deploy
Namespace:              default
CreationTimestamp:      Fri, 10 Mar 2017 22:15:11 +0000
Labels:                 name=node-js-deploy
Selector:               name=node-js-deploy
Replicas:               0 updated | 3 total | 3 available | 0 unavailable
StrategyType:           RollingUpdate
MinReadySeconds:        0
RollingUpdateStrategy:  1 max unavailable, 1 max surge
Events:
   FirstSeen       LastSeen            Count      From
SubObjectPath       Type                Reason           Message
---------       ---------           -----      ----
-------------       ---------           ------           -------
   4m              4m                  1          {federated-deployment-controller }
Normal          CreateInCluster Creating deployment in cluster gcek8s
   4m              4m                  1          {federated-deployment-controller }
Normal          CreateInCluster Creating deployment in cluster awsk8s
```

Federated pod Deployment

We can also see the federated events using the following command:

```
$ kubectl get events
```

```
LASTSEEN    FIRSTSEEN    COUNT    NAME                KIND          SUBOBJECT    TYPE
   REASON               SOURCE                                    MESSAGE
10m         10m          1        node-js-deploy    Deployment                   Normal
   CreateInCluster      {federated-deployment-controller }    Creating deployment in
cluster gcek8s
10m         10m          1        node-js-deploy    Deployment                   Normal
   CreateInCluster      {federated-deployment-controller }    Creating deployment in
cluster awsk8s
```

Federated events

It may take a moment for all three pods to run. Once that happens, we can switch to each cluster context and see some of the pods on each. Note that we can now use `get pods` since we are on the individual clusters and not on the control plane:

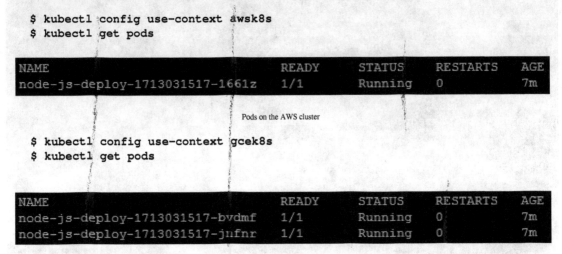

```
$ kubectl config use-context awsk8s
$ kubectl get pods
```

NAME	READY	STATUS	RESTARTS	AGE
node-js-deploy-1713031517-1661z	1/1	Running	0	7m

Pods on the AWS cluster

```
$ kubectl config use-context gcek8s
$ kubectl get pods
```

NAME	READY	STATUS	RESTARTS	AGE
node-js-deploy-1713031517-bvdmf	1/1	Running	0	7m
node-js-deploy-1713031517-jnfnr	1/1	Running	0	7m

Pods on the GCE cluster

We should see the three pods spread across the clusters with two on one and a third on the other. Kubernetes has spread it across the cluster without any manual intervention. Any pods that fail will be restarted, but now we have the added redundancy of two cloud providers.

Federated configurations

In modern software development, it is common to separate configuration variables from the application code itself. In this way it is easier to make updates to service URLs, credentials, common paths, and so on. Having these values in external configuration files means we can easily update configuration without rebuilding the entire application.

This separation solves the initial problem, but true portability comes when you can remove the dependency from the application completely. Kubernetes offers a configuration store for exactly this purpose. **ConfigMaps** are simple constructs that store key-value pairs.

Kubernetes also supports **Secrets** for more sensitive configuration data. This will be covered in more detail in `Chapter 10`, *Container Security*. You can use the example there in both single clusters or on the federation control plane as we are demonstrating with ConfigMaps here.

Let's take a look at an example that will allow us to store some configuration and then consume it in various pods. The following listings will work for both federated and single clusters, but we will continue using a federated setup for this example.

The ConfigMap kind can be created using literal values, flat files and directories, and finally YAML definition files. The following listing is a YAML definition file:

```
apiVersion: v1
kind: ConfigMap
metadata:
  name: my-application-config
  namespace: default
data:
  backend-service.url: my-backend-service
```

Listing 9-2: configmap-fed.yaml

Let's first switch back to our federation plane:

```
$ kubectl config use-context master-control
```

Now, create this listing with the following command:

```
$ kubectl create -f configmap-fed.yaml
```

Let's display the configmap object that we just created. The -o yaml flag helps us display the full information:

```
$ kubectl get configmap my-application-config -o yaml
```

```
apiVersion: v1
data:
  backend-service.url: my-backend-service
kind: ConfigMap
metadata:
  creationTimestamp: 2017-03-10T22:28:38Z
  name: my-application-config
  namespace: default
  resourceVersion: "1959"
  selfLink: /api/v1/namespaces/default/configmaps/my-application-config
  uid: e85a0028-05e0-11e7-bdf8-42010a800002
```

Federated ConfigMap description

Now that we have a `ConfigMap` object, let's start up a federated `ReplicaSet` that can use the `ConfigMap`. This will create replicas of pods across our cluster that can access the `ConfigMap` object. ConfigMaps can be accessed via environment variables or mount volumes. This example will use a mount volume that provides a folder hierarchy and the files for each key with the contents representing the values:

```
apiVersion: extensions/v1beta1
kind: ReplicaSet
metadata:
  name: node-js-rs
spec:
  replicas: 3
  selector:
    matchLabels:
      name: node-js-configmap-rs
  template:
    metadata:
      labels:
        name: node-js-configmap-rs
    spec:
      containers:
      - name: configmap-pod
        image: jonbaier/node-express-info:latest
        ports:
        - containerPort: 80
          name: web
        volumeMounts:
        - name: configmap-volume
          mountPath: /etc/config
      volumes:
      - name: configmap-volume
        configMap:
          name: my-application-config
```

Listing 9-3: `configmap-rs-fed.yaml`

Create this pod with `kubectl create -f configmap-rs-fed.yaml`. After creation, we will need to switch contexts to one of the clusters where the pods are running. You can choose either, but we will use the GCE context here:

```
$ kubectl config use-context gcek8s
```

Now that we are on the GCE cluster specifically, let's check the `configmaps` here:

```
$ kubectl get configmaps
```

As you can see, the `ConfigMap` is propagated locally to each cluster. Next, let's find a pod from our federated `ReplicaSet`:

```
$ kubectl get pods
```

```
NAME                                READY   STATUS    RESTARTS   AGE
node-js-deploy-1713031517-cmd7q     1/1     Running   0          39m
node-js-deploy-1713031517-zncxr     1/1     Running   0          39m
node-js-rs-6g7nj                    1/1     Running   0          9m
node-js-rs-f4w7b                    1/1     Running   0          9m
```

Pods on the GCE cluster

Let's take one of the `node-js-rs` pod names from the listing and run a bash shell with `kubectl exec`:

```
$ kubectl exec -it node-js-rs-6g7nj bash
```

Then change directories to the `/etc/config` folder that we set up in the pod definition. Listing this directory reveals a single file with the name of the `ConfigMap` we defined earlier:

```
$ cd /etc/config
$ ls
```

If we then display the contents of the files with the following command, we should see the value we entered earlier: `my-backend-service`:

```
$ echo $(cat backend-service.url)
```

If we were to look in any of the pods across our federated cluster we would see the same values. This is a great way to decouple configuration from an application and distribute it across our fleet of clusters.

Other federated resources

So far we saw federated Deployments, ReplicaSets, Events, and ConfigMaps in action. DaemonSets, Ingress, Namespaces, Secrets, and Services are also supported. Your specific setup will vary and you may have a set of clusters that differ from our example here. As mentioned earlier, these resources are still in beta, so it's worth spending some time to experiment with the various resource types and understand how well the federation constructs are supported for your particular mix of infrastructure.

True multi-cloud

This is an exciting space to watch. As it grows it gives us a really good start to doing multi-cloud implementations and providing redundancy across regions, data centers, and even cloud providers.

While Kubernetes does provide an easy and exciting path to multi-cloud infrastructure, it's important to note that production multi-cloud requires much more than distributed deployments. A full set of capabilities from logging and monitoring to compliance and host-hardening, there is much to manage in a multi-provider setup.

True multi-cloud adoption will require a well-planned architecture, and Kubernetes takes a big step forward in pursuing this goal.

Summary

In this chapter, we looked at the new federation capabilities in Kubernetes. We saw how we can deploy clusters to multiple cloud providers and manage them from a single control plane. We also deployed an application across clusters in both AWS and GCE. While these features are new and still mainly in alpha and beta, we should now have the skills to utilize them as they evolve and become part of the standard Kubernetes operating model.

In the next chapter, we will take a look at another advanced topic, security. We will cover the basics for secure containers and also how to secure your Kubernetes cluster. We will also look at the Secrets construct, which gives us the capability to store sensitive configuration data similar to our preceding `ConfigMap` example.

10
Container Security

This chapter will discuss the basics of container security from the container runtime level to the host itself. We will discuss how to apply these concepts to workloads running in a Kubernetes cluster and some of the security concerns and practices that relate specifically to running your Kubernetes cluster.

This chapter will discuss the following topics:

- Basic container security
- Container image security and continuous vulnerability scanning
- Kubernetes cluster security
- Kubernetes secrets

Basics of container security

Container security is a deep subject area and in itself can fill its own book. Having said this, we will cover some of the high-level concerns and give a starting point to think about this area.

In the *A brief overview of containers* section of `Chapter 1`, *Introduction to Kubernetes*, we looked at some of the core isolation features in the Linux kernel that enable container technology. Understanding the details of how containers work is the key to grasping the various security concerns in managing them.

A good paper to dive deeper is *NCC's Whitepaper, Understanding and Hardening Linux Containers* (you can refer to more details about this in point 1 in the *References* section at the end of the chapter). In *section 7*, the paper explores the various attack vectors of concern for container deployments, which I will summarize (you can refer to more details about this in point 1 in the *References* section at the end of the chapter).

Keeping containers contained

One of the most obvious features discussed in the paper is that of escaping the isolation/virtualization of the container construct. Modern container implementations guard against this using namespaces to isolate processes as well as allowing control of the Linux capabilities available to a container. Additionally, there is an increased move towards secure default configurations of the out-of-the-box container environment. For example, Docker by default only enables a small set of capabilities (you can refer to more details about this in point 2 in the *References* section at the end of the chapter). Networking is another avenue of escape and it can be challenging since there are a variety of network options that plug in to most modern container setups.

The next area discussed in the paper is that of attacks between two containers. The *User* namespace model gives us added protection here by mapping the root user within the container to a lower level user on the host machine. Networking is of course still an issue and something that requires proper diligence and attention when selecting and implementing your container networking solution.

Attacks within the container itself are another vector and as with previous concerns, namespaces and networking are key to protection here. Another aspect that is vital in this scenario is the application security itself. The code still needs to follow secure coding practices and the software should be kept up-to-date and patched regularly. Finally, the efficiency of container images has an added benefit of shrinking the attack surface. The images should be built with only the packages and software necessary.

Resource exhaustion and orchestration security

Similar to the Denial of Service attacks, we've seen in various other areas of computing that resource exhaustion is very much a pertinent concern in the container world. While cgroups provide some limitations on resource usage for things such as CPU, memory, and disk usage, there are still valid attack avenues for resource exhaustion. Tools such as Docker offer some starting defaults to the cgroups limitations, and Kubernetes also offers additional limits that can be placed on groups of containers running in the cluster. It's important to understand these defaults and adjust for your deployments.

While the Linux kernel and the features that enable containers give us some form of isolation, they are fairly new to the Linux operating system. As such, they still contain their own bugs and vulnerabilities. The built-in mechanisms for capabilities and namespaces can and do have issues and it is important to track these as part of your secure container operations.

The final area covered in the NCC paper is the attack of the container management layer itself. The Docker engine, image repositories, and orchestration tools are all significant vectors of attack and should be considered when developing your strategy. We'll look more in depth at how we can address the repositories and Kubernetes as an orchestration layer in the next sections.

> If you're interested in knowing more about the specific security features of Docker's implementation, take a look here:
> `https://docs.docker.com/engine/security/security/`.

Image repositories

Vulnerability management is a critical component of any modern day IT operation. Zero-day vulnerabilities are on the rise and even those vulnerabilities with patches can be cumbersome to remediate. First, application owners must be made aware of their vulnerabilities and potential patches. Then these patches must be integrated into systems and code and often this requires additional deployments or maintenance windows. Even when there is visibility to vulnerabilities, there is often a lag in remediation, often taking large organizations several months to patch.

While containers greatly improve the process of updating applications and minimizing downtime, there still remains a challenge inherent in vulnerability management. Especially since an attacker only needs to expose one such vulnerability; making anything less than 100% of systems patched is a risk for compromise.

What's needed is a faster feedback loop in addressing vulnerabilities. Continuous scanning and tying into the software deployment life cycle is key to speeding the information and remediation of vulnerabilities. Luckily, this is exactly the approach being built into the latest container management and security tooling.

Continuous vulnerability scanning

One such open-source project that has emerged in this space is **Clair**. We get to know this from the *Clair* GitHub page: *Clair is an open source project for the static analysis of vulnerabilities in* `appc` *and* `docker` *containers.*

You can visit Clair at the following link: `https://github.com/coreos/clair`.

Clair scans your code against **Common Vulnerabilities and Exploits (CVEs)**. It can be integrated into your CI/CD pipeline and run as a response to new builds. If vulnerabilities are found, they can be taken as feedback into the pipeline, even stop deployment, and fail the build. This forces developers to be aware of and remediate vulnerabilities during their normal release process.

Clair can be integrated with a number of container image repositories and CI/CD pipelines.

Clair can even be deployed on Kubernetes: `https://github.com/coreos/clair#kubernetes`.

Clair is also used as the scanning mechanism in CoreOS's Quay image repository. Quay offers a number of enterprise features including continuous vulnerability scanning:

`https://quay.io/`

Both Docker Hub and Docker Cloud support security scanning. Again, containers that are pushed to the repository are automatically scanned against CVEs and notifications of vulnerabilities are sent as a result of any findings. Additionally, binary analysis of the code is performed to match the signature of the components with that of known versions.

There are a variety of other scanning tools that can be used as well for scanning your image repositories including **OpenSCAP** as well as **Twistlock** and **AquaSec**, which we will cover in `Chapter 12`, *Towards Production Ready*.

Image signing and verification

Whether you are using a private image repository in-house or a public repo such as Docker Hub, it's important to know that you are running only the code that your developers have written. The potential for malicious code or man-in-the-middle attacks on downloads is an important factor in protecting your container images.

As such, both rkt and Docker support the ability to sign images and verify that the contents have not changed. Publishers can use keys to sign the images when they are pushed to the repositories and users can verify the signature on the client-side when downloading for use:

From the rkt documentation:

"Before executing a remotely fetched ACI, rkt will verify it based on attached signatures generated by the ACI creator."

- `https://coreos.com/rkt/docs/latest/subcommands/trust.html`
- `https://coreos.com/rkt/docs/latest/signing-and-verification-guide.html`

From the Docker documentation:

"Content trust gives you the ability to verify both the integrity and the publisher of all the data received from a registry over any channel."
`https://docs.docker.com/engine/security/trust/content_trust/`

From the Docker Notary GitHub page:

"The Notary project comprises a server and a client for running and interacting with trusted collections."
`https://github.com/docker/notary`

Kubernetes cluster security

Kubernetes has continued to add a number of security features in their latest releases and has a well-rounded set of control points that can be used in your cluster; everything from secure node communication to pod security and even storage of sensitive configuration data.

Secure API calls

During every API call, Kubernetes applies a number of security controls. This security life cycle is depicted here:

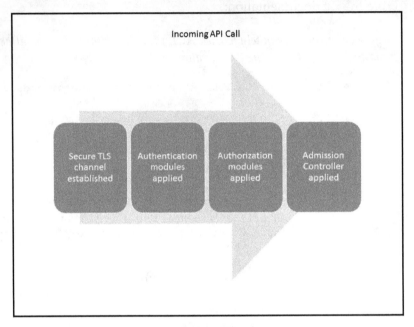

API call life cycle

After secure TLS communication is established, the API server runs through **Authorization** and **Authentication**. Finally, an **Admission Controller** loop is applied to the request before it reaches the API server.

Secure node communication

Kubernetes supports the use of secure communication channels between the API server and any client including the nodes themselves. Whether it's a GUI or command-line utility such as kubectl, we can use certificates to communicate with the API server. Hence, the API server is the central interaction point for any changes to the cluster and is a critical component to secure.

In deployments such as GCE, the kubelet on each node is deployed for secure communication by default. This setup uses the TLS bootstrapping and the new certificates' API to establish a secure connection with the API server using TLS client certificates and a **Certificate Authority (CA)** cluster.

Authorization and authentication plugins

The plugin mechanisms for authentication and authorization in Kubernetes are in their infancy. However, these features also continue to develop in the next few releases. There are also third-party providers that integrate with the features here.

Authentication is currently supported in the form of tokens, passwords, and certificates with plans to add the plugin capability at a later stage. OpenID Connect tokens are supported and several third-party implementations, such as Dex from CoreOS and aser account and authentication from Cloud Foundry, are available.

Authorization already supports three modes. The full **RBAC** (short for **Role-Based Access Control**)mode is still a work in progress and will eventually bring a mature role-based authentication from Kubernetes itself. **Attribute-Based Access Control** (**ABAC**) is already supported and lets a user define privileges via attributes in a file. Finally, a webhook mechanism is supported, which allows for integration with third-party authorization via REST web service calls.

Learn more about each area here:

- http://kubernetes.io/docs/admin/authorization/
- http://kubernetes.io/docs/admin/authentication/

Admission controllers

Kubernetes also provides a mechanism for integrating with additional verification as a final step. This could be in the form of image scanning, signature checks, or anything that is able to respond in the specified fashion. When an API call is made, the hook is called and that server can run its verification. Admission controllers can also be used to transform requests and add or alter the original request. Once the operations are run, a response is then sent back with a status that instructs Kubernetes to allow or deny the call.

This can be especially helpful for verifying or testing images as we mentioned in the last section. The ImagePolicyWebhook plugin provides an admission controller that allows for integration with additional image inspection.

For more information, visit the **Using Admission Controller** page in the following documentation:
`https://kubernetes.io/docs/admin/admission-controllers/`.

Pod security policies and context

One of the latest additions to the Kubernetes' security arsenal is that of **Pod security policies and contexts**. These allow users to control users and groups for container processes and attached volumes, limit the use of host networks or namespaces, and even set the root filesystem to read-only. Additionally, we can limit the capabilities available and also set SELinux options for the labels that are applied to the containers in each pod.

In addition to SELinux, Kubernetes also added support for using AppArmor with your pods using annotations. For more information, refer to the following documentation page:
`https://kubernetes.io/docs/admin/apparmor/`.

We'll walk through an example of using a pod security context to add some constraints to our pods. Since the functionality is still in beta, we'll need to enable the beta extensions API and also add `PodSecurityPolicy` to the list of admission controllers in use.

Enabling beta APIs

First, you'll need to SSH into your master node, switch to a **root** user, and then edit the `/etc/kubernetes/manifests/kube-apiserver.manifest` file in your preferred editor. Again, we can SSH via the Google Cloud CLI or use the Google Cloud Console, which has a built-in SSH client on the VM instances page.

The best practice is not to SSH onto the nodes themselves. However, we have done so at several points in this book for illustrative purposes. It's important to understand how things are running on the nodes themselves and can sometimes be necessary both for learning and troubleshooting. Having said this, use the tools such as `kubectl exec` when you simply need to run a command from within the cluster or a pod.

Scroll down to the command section and we should see something like the following listing:

```
"bin/sh",
"-c",
"/usr/local/bin/kube-apiserver --v=2 --cloud-config=/etc/gce.conf --
address=127.0.0.1 --allow-
privileged=true --authorization-policy-file=/etc/srv/kubernetes/abac-authz-
policy.jsonl --basic-auth-file=/etc/srv/kubernetes/basic_auth.csv --cloud-
provider=gce --client-ca-file=/etc/srv/kubernetes/ca.crt
--etcd-servers=http://127.0.0.1:2379 --etcd-servers-
overrides=/events#http://127.0.0.1:4002 --secure-port=443 --tls-cert-
file=/etc
/srv/kubernetes/server.cert --tls-private-key-
file=/etc/srv/kubernetes/server.key --token-auth-
file=/etc/srv/kubernetes/known_tokens.csv --storage-backend=etcd2 --target-
ram-mb=180 --service-cluster-ip-range=10.0.0.0/16 --etcd-quorum-read=false
--admission-
control=NamespaceLifecycle,LimitRanger,ServiceAccount,PersistentVolumeLabel
,DefaultStorageClass,ResourceQuota
--authorization-mode=ABAC --allow-privileged=true 1>>/var/log/kube-
apiserver.log 2>&1"
```

Your listing may vary, so just add the parameters highlighted in bold as follows. Also, copy the original listing as a backup so you can restore it if needed later on:

```
"bin/sh",
"-c",
"/usr/local/bin/kube-apiserver --v=2 --cloud-config=/etc/gce.conf --
address=127.0.0.1
--allow-privileged=true --authorization-policy-
file=/etc/srv/kubernetes/abac-authz-policy.jsonl --basic-auth-
file=/etc/srv/kubernetes/basic_auth.csv --cloud-provider=gce --client-ca-
file=/etc/srv/kubernetes/ca.crt --etcd-servers=http://127.0.0.1:2379 --
etcd-servers-overrides=/events#http://127.0.0.1:4002 --secure-port=443 --
tls-cert-file=/etc/srv/kubernetes/server.cert --tls-private-key-
file=/etc/srv/kubernetes/server.key --token-auth-
file=/etc/srv/kubernetes/known_tokens.csv --storage-backend=etcd2 --target-
ram-mb=180 --service-cluster-ip-range=10.0.0.0/16 --etcd-quorum-read=false
--admission-
control=NamespaceLifecycle,LimitRanger,ServiceAccount,PersistentVolumeLabel
,DefaultStorageClass,ResourceQuota,PodSecurityPolicy --authorization-
mode=ABAC --allow-privileged=true --runtime-
config=extensions/v1beta1=true,extensions/v1beta1/podsecuritypolicy=true
1>>/var/log/kube-apiserver.log 2>&1"
```

Save the file and exit `sudo` if you have a root shell. If all goes well, Kubernetes should notice the manifest changes and restart the API Server. This may take a few minutes and during reboot, `kubectl` may become unresponsive. I usually watch this with the following command:

```
$ kubectl get pods --namespace=kube-system
```

Watch the `STATUS` and `AGE` columns. Once the restart is successful, we'll have a `STATUS of Running` and an `AGE` on the order of a few minutes or less.

 If we had any typos with the manifest, we may see errors in `STATUS` or even get a permanently unresponsive `kubectl`. If this happens, we'll need to restore our earlier parameters. If all else fails, you can reboot the instance. The default for GCE setups has a boot script that will replace the manifest with the default settings.

Once your API server is updated and running, we can add a security policy and run a pod with a pod security context defined. The policy runs at the cluster level and enforces the policy for all pods. The pod security context is set in the pod definition and applies only to that pod.

Creating a PodSecurityPolicy

Now that we've added the `PodSecurityPolicy` admission controller, we'll need to add a pod security policy before we can create our example in *listing 10-2* further down. If we try to create that pod now, we will see an error similar to this:

```
Error from server (Forbidden): error when creating "nodejs-pod-nopsc.yaml": pods
"node-js-nopsc" is forbidden: no providers available to validate pod request
```

Pod error without PodSecurityPolicy

Again, the pod security policy applies cluster wide:

```
{
  "kind": "PodSecurityPolicy",
  "apiVersion":"extensions/v1beta1",
  "metadata": {
    "name": "default"
  },
  "spec": {
    "privileged": false,
    "seLinux": {
      "rule": "RunAsAny"
    },
```

```
    "supplementalGroups": {
      "rule": "RunAsAny"
    },
    "runAsUser": {
      "rule": "RunAsAny"
    },
    "fsGroup": {
      "rule": "RunAsAny"
    },
    "volumes": ["*"],
    "readOnlyRootFilesystem": true
  }
}
```

Listing 10-1: `default-security-policy.json`

Create this with the following:

```
$ kubectl create -f default-security-policy.json
```

The preceding default policy does not allow containers to run in privileged mode. It allows any seLinux labels, any supplemental group IDs, any user to run the first process, and any group ID for the filesytems. It also supports all types of volumes.

You can find all possible parameters in the source code, but I've created the following table for convenience. You can find more handy lookups like this on my new site: `https://www.kubesheets.com`

Parameter	Type	Description	Required
Privileged	bool	Allows or disallows running pod as privileged.	No
DefaultAddCapabilities	[]v1.Capaility	This defines a default set of capabilities added to the container. If the pod specifies a capability drop that will override then add it here. Values are strings of POSIX capabilities minus the leading CAP_. For example, CAP_SETUID would be SETUID. http://man7.org/linux/man-pages/man7/capabilities.7.html	No

RequiredDropCapabilities	[]v1.Capaility	This defines a set of capabilities that must be dropped from a container. The pod cannot specify any of these capabilities. Values are strings of POSIX capabilities minus the leading CAP_. For example, CAP_SETUID would be SETUID. http://man7.org/linux/man -pages/man7/capabilities. 7.html	No
AllowedCapabilities	[]v1.Capaility	This defines a set of capabilities that are allowed and can be added to a container. The pod can specify any of these capabilities. Values are strings of POSIX capabilities minus the leading CAP_. For example, CAP_SETUID would be SETUID. http://man7.org/linux/man -pages/man7/capabilities. 7.html	No
Volumes	[]FSType	This list defines which volumes can be used. Leave empty for all types. https://github.com/kubern etes/kubernetes/blob/rele ase-1.5/pkg/apis/extensio ns/v1beta1/types.go#L1127	No
HostNetwork	bool	This allows or disallows the Pod to use the host network.	No
HostPorts	[]HostPortRange	This lets us restrict allowable host ports that can be exposed.	No
HostPID	bool	This allows or disallows the pod to use the host PID.	No
HostIPC	bool	This allows or disallows the pod to use the host IPC.	No
SELinux	SELinuxStrategyOptions	Set it to one of the strategy options as defined here: https://kubernetes.io/doc s/user-guide/pod-security -policy/#strategies	Yes

RunAsUser	RunAsUserStrategyOptions	Set it to one of the strategy options as defined here: https://kubernetes.io/docs/user-guide/pod-security-policy/#strategies	Yes
SupplementalGroups	SupplementalGroupsStrategyOptions	Set it to one of the strategy options as defined here: https://kubernetes.io/docs/user-guide/pod-security-policy/#strategies	Yes
FSGroup	FSGroupStrategyOptions	Set it to one of the strategy options as defined here: https://kubernetes.io/docs/user-guide/pod-security-policy/#strategies	Yes
ReadOnlyRootFilesystem	bool	Setting this to true will either deny the pod or force it to run with a read-only root filesystem.	No

Table 10-1. Pod Security Policy Parameters (you can refer to more details about this in point 3 in the *References* section at the end of the chapter)

Now that we have a basic policy for the cluster, let's create a Pod. First, we will create a Pod with our node-express-info container:

```
apiVersion: v1
kind: Pod
metadata:
    name: node-js-nopsc
spec:
  containers:
  - name: node-js-nopsc
    image: jonbaier/node-express-info:latest
    ports:
    - containerPort: 80
```

Listing 10-2: nodejs-pod-nopsc.yaml

Create the pod with the preceding listing. Then use the kubectl exec command to get a shell inside the pod. Next, we will attempt to create a file using the touch command:

```
$ kubectl exec -it node-js-nopsc bash
root@node-js-nopsc:/src# touch file.txt
```

We should get an error similar to touch: cannot touch 'file.txt': Read-only file system. This is because we set the ReadOnlyFileSystem property to true, so all containers (pod security context defined or not) are now run with read-only root filesystems. Type exit to leave this pod.

Creating a pod with a PodSecurityContext

Now that we have seen the effects of the pod security policy, let's explore the pod security context. Here we can define seLinuxOptions that let us define the label context for the containers in the pod. We can also define runAsUser to specify the UID with which each container will run and the runAsNonRoot flag that will simply prevent starting containers that run as UID 0 or root. We can also specify the Group (GID) for the first process in each container with supplementalGroup. Finally, we can specify the Group (GID) for filesystem ownership and new files with fsGroup.

Listing 10-4 is a version of our previous node-express-info pod with the runAsNonRoot set to true. It's important to understand that root (UID 0) is the default user if none is defined in the Dockerfile. *Listing 10-3* shows the Dockerfile for our node-express-info container. We have not defined the USER directive and therefore it will run as root:

```
FROM node:latest

ADD src/ /src
WORKDIR /src

RUN npm install

ENV PORT=80

CMD ["node", "index.js"]
```

Listing 10-3: node-express-info Dockerfile

```
apiVersion: v1
kind: Pod
metadata:
    name: node-js-pod
spec:
  containers:
  - name: node-js-pod
    image: jonbaier/node-express-info:latest
    ports:
    - containerPort: 80
  securityContext:
    runAsNonRoot: true
```

Listing 10-4: nodejs-pod-psc.yaml

Understanding the relationship between the security context and how the containers are built is important. If we try to create the preceding *Listing 10-4* with `kubectl create -f nodejs-pod-psc.yaml`, we will see that it never starts and gives us `VerifyNonRootError`:

```
NAME                READY    STATUS              RESTARTS    AGE
node-js-4zk2s       1/1      Running             0           1h
node-js-77gq7       1/1      Running             0           1h
node-js-g3pvq       1/1      Running             0           1h
node-js-pod         0/1      VerifyNonRootError  0           36s
node-js-rs-852pj    1/1      Running             0           1h
node-js-rs-9zh42    1/1      Running             0           1h
node-js-rs-cnp7b    1/1      Running             0           1h
```

VerifyNonRootError

Understanding that running containers securely is not a merely a task of administrators adding constraints is important. The work must be done in collaboration with developers who will properly create the images.

Clean up

The policy we have put in place may be too restrictive for learning and development, so you may wish to remove it. You can do so with the following command:

```
$ kubectl delete psp default
```

You'll also need to undo the changes to `/etc/kubernetes/manifests/kube-apiserver.manifest` that we did on the Kubernetes master at the beginning of this section. Specifically, you should remove the `PodSecurityPolicy` from the list of the `admission-control` section.

Additional considerations

In addition to the features we just reviewed, Kubernetes has a number of other constructs that should be considered in your overall cluster hardening process. Earlier in the book, we looked at namespaces that provide a logical separation for multi-tenancy. While the namespaces themselves do not isolate the actual network traffic, some of the network plugins, such as Calico and Canal, provide additional capability for network policies. We also looked at quotas and limits that can be set for each namespace and should be used to prevent a single tenant or project from consuming too many resources within the cluster.

Securing sensitive application data (secrets)

Sometimes, our application needs to hold sensitive information. This can be credentials or tokens to log in to a database or service. Storing this sensitive information in the image itself is something to be avoided. Here, Kubernetes provides us a solution in the construct of secrets.

Secrets give us a way to store sensitive information without including plaintext versions in our resource definition files. Secrets can be mounted to the pods that need them and then accessed within the pod as files with the secret values as content. Alternatively, you can also expose the secrets via environment variables.

We can easily create a secret either with YAML or on the command line. Secrets do need to be base-64 encoded, but if we use the `kubectl` command line, this encoding is done for us.

Let's start with the following Secret:

```
$ kubectl create secret generic secret-phrases --from-literal=quiet-
phrase="Shh! Dont' tell"
```

We can then check for the Secret with this command:

```
$ kubectl get secrets
```

Now that we have successfully created the Secret, let's make a pod that can use the secret. Secrets are consumed in pods by way of attached volumes. In the following *Listing 10-5*, you'll notice that we use `volumeMount` to mount the secret to a folder in our container:

```
apiVersion: v1
kind: Pod
metadata:
  name: secret-pod
spec:
  containers:
  - name: secret-pod
    image: jonbaier/node-express-info:latest
    ports:
    - containerPort: 80
      name: web
    volumeMounts:
      - name: secret-volume
        mountPath: /etc/secret-phrases
  volumes:
  - name: secret-volume
    secret:
      secretName: secret-phrases
```

Listing 10-5: `secret-pod.yaml`

Create this pod with `kubectl create -f secret-pod.yaml`. Once created, we can get a bash shell in the pod with `kubectl exec` and then change directories to the `/etc/secret-phrases` folder that we set up in the pod definition. Listing this directory reveals a single file with the name of the secret that we created earlier:

```
$ kubectl exec -it secret-pod bash
$ cd /etc/secret-phrases
$ ls
```

If we then display those contents, we should see the phrase we encoded previously, `Shh! Dont' tell`:

```
$ cat quiet-phrase
```

Typically, this would be used for a username and password to a database or service, or any sensitive credentials and configuration data.

Bear in mind that secrets are still in their early stages, but they are a vital component for production operations. There are several improvements planned here for future releases. At the moment, secrets are still stored in plaintext in the etcd server. However, the secrets construct does allow us to control which pods can access it and it stores the information on the tmpfs, but does not store it at rest for each pod. You'll likely want more protection in place for a production-ready system.

Summary

We took a look at basic container security and some essential areas of consideration. We also touched on basic image security and continuous vulnerability scanning. Later in this chapter, we looked at the overall security features of Kubernetes including secrets for storing sensitive configuration data, secure API calls, and even setting up security policies and contexts for pods running on our cluster.

You should now have a solid starting point for securing your cluster and moving towards production. To that end, the next chapter will cover an overall strategy for moving towards production and will also look at some third-party vendors that offer tools to fill in the gaps and assist you on the way.

References

1. https://www.nccgroup.trust/globalassets/our-research/us/whitepapers/2016/april/ncc_group_understanding_hardening_linux_containers-10pdf/

2. https://github.com/docker/docker/blob/master/oci/defaults_linux.go#L62-L77

3. https://github.com/kubernetes/kubernetes/blob/release-1.5/pkg/apis/extensions/v1beta1/types.go#L1075

11
Extending Kubernetes with OCP, CoreOS, and Tectonic

The first half of this chapter will cover how open standards encourage a diverse ecosystem of container implementations. We'll look at the **Open Container Initiative** (**OCI**) and its mission to provide an open container specification as well. The second half of this chapter will cover CoreOS and its advantages as a host OS, including performance and support for various container implementations. Also, we'll take a brief look at the Tectonic enterprise offering from CoreOS.

This chapter will discuss the following topics:

- Why standards matter?
- The Open Container Initiative and Cloud Native Computing Foundation
- Container specifications versus implementations
- CoreOS and its advantages
- Tectonic

The importance of standards

Over the past two years, containerization technology has had a tremendous growth in popularity. While Docker has been at the center of this ecosystem, there is an increased number of players in the container space. There is already a number of alternatives to the containerization and Docker implementation itself (**rkt**, **Garden**, and so on). In addition, there is a rich ecosystem of third-party tools that enhance and compliment your container infrastructure. Kubernetes lands squarely on the orchestration side of this ecosystem, but the bottom line is that all these tools form the basis to build cloud-native applications.

As we mentioned at the very beginning of the book, one of the most attractive things about containers is their ability to package our application for deployment across various environment tiers (that is, development, testing, and production) and various infrastructure providers (GCP, AWS, On-premise, and so on).

To truly support this type of deployment agility, we need not only the containers themselves to have a common platform, but also the underlying specifications to follow a common set of ground rules. This will allow for implementations that are both flexible and highly specialized. For example, some workloads may need to be run on a highly secure implementation. To provide this, the implementation will have to make more intentional decisions about some aspects of implementation. In either case, we will have more agility and freedom if our containers are built on some common structures that all implementations agree on and support.

The Open Container Initiative

One of the first initiatives to gain widespread industry engagement is the OCI. Among the 36 industry collaborators are Docker, Red Hat, VMware, IBM, Google, and AWS, and they are listed on the OCI website at:

```
https://www.opencontainers.org/.
```

The purpose of the OCI is to split implementations, such as Docker and rkt, from a standard specification for the format and runtime of containerized workloads. By their own terms, the goal of the OCI specification has three basic tenets(you can refer to more details about this in point 1 in the *References* section at the end of the chapter):

- *Creating a formal specification for container image formats and runtime, which will allow a compliant container to be portable across all major, compliant operating systems and platforms without artificial technical barriers.*

- *Accepting, maintaining, and advancing the projects associated with these standards (the **Projects**). It will look to agree on a standard set of container actions (start, exec, pause,.....) as well as runtime environment associated with container runtime.*

- *Harmonizing the previously-referenced standard with other proposed standards, including the appc specification.*

Cloud Native Computing Foundation

A second initiative that also has a widespread industry acceptance is the **Cloud Native Computing Foundation** (**CNCF**). While still focused on containerized workloads, the CNCF operates a bit higher up the stack at an application design level. The purpose is to provide a standard set of tools and technologies to build, operate, and orchestrate cloud-native application stacks. Cloud has given us access to a variety of new technologies and practices that can improve and evolve our classic software designs. This is also particularly focused at the new paradigm of microservice-oriented development.

As a founding participant in CNCF, Google has donated the Kubernetes open-source project as the first step. The goal will be to increase interoperability in the ecosystem and support better integration with projects. CNCF is already hosting a variety of projects in orchestration, logging, monitoring, tracing, and application resiliency.

For more information on CNCF, refer to `https://cncf.io/`.

Standard container specification

A core result of the OCI effort is the creation and development of the overarching container specification. The specification has five core principles for all containers to follow, which I will briefly paraphrase (you can refer to more details about this in point 2 in the *References* section at the end of the chapter):

- The container must have **standard operations** to create, start, and stop containers across all implementations.
- The container must be **content-agnostic**, which means that type of application inside the container does not alter the standard operations or publishing of the container itself.

- The container must be **infrastructure-agnostic** as well. Portability is paramount; therefore, the containers must be able to operate just as easily in GCE as in your company's datacenter or on a developer's laptop.
- A container must also be **designed for automation**, which allows us to automate across the build, updating, and deployment pipelines. While this rule is a bit vague, the container implementation should not require onerous manual steps for creation and release.
- Finally, the implementation must support **industrial-grade delivery**. Once again, speaking to the build and deployment pipelines and requiring a streamlined efficiency to the portability and transit of the containers between infrastructure and deployment tiers.

The specification also defines core principles for container formats and runtimes. You can read more about the specifications on the GitHub project at

```
https://github.com/opencontainers/specs.
```

While the core specification can be a bit abstract, the **runC** implementation is a concrete example of the OCI specs in the form of a container runtime and image format. Again, you can read more of the technical details on the runC site and GitHub at the following URLs:

- `https://github.com/opencontainers/runc`
- `https://runc.io/`

The backing format and runtime for a variety of popular container tools is runC. It was donated to OCI by Docker and was created from the same plumbing work used in the Docker platform. Since its release, it has had a welcome uptake by numerous projects.

Even the popular open source PaaS, **Cloud Foundry** announced that it will use runC in Garden. Garden provides the containerization plumbing for Deigo, which acts as an orchestration layer similar to Kubernetes.

The rkt implementation was originally based on the **appc** specification. The appc specification was actually an earlier attempt by the folks at CoreOS to form a common specification around containerization. Now that CoreOS is participating in OCI, they are working to help merge the appc specification into OCI; it should result in a higher level of compatibility across the container ecosystem.

CoreOS

While the specifications provide us a common ground, there are also some trends evolving around the choice of OS for our containers. There are several tailor-fit OSes that are being developed specifically to run container workloads. Although implementations vary, they all have similar characteristics. Focus on a slim installation base, atomic OS updating, and signed applications for efficient and secure operations.

One OS that is gaining popularity is **CoreOS**. CoreOS offers major benefits for both security and resource utilization. It provides resource utilization by removing package dependencies completely from the picture. Instead, CoreOS runs all applications and services in containers. By providing only a small set of services required to support running containers and bypassing the need of hypervisor usage, CoreOS lets us use a larger portion of the resource pool to run our containerized applications. This allows users to gain a higher performance from their infrastructure and better container to node (server) usage ratios.

> **More container OSes**
> There are several other container-optimized OSes that have emerged recently.
>
> **Red Hat Enterprise Linux Atomic Host** focuses on security with **SELinux** enabled by default and *Atomic* updates to the OS similar to what we saw with CoreOS. Refer to the following link:
> `https://access.redhat.com/articles/rhel-atomic-getting-started`
>
> **Ubuntu Snappy** also capitalizes on the efficiency and security gains of separating the OS components from the frameworks and applications. Using application images and verification signatures, we get an efficient Ubuntu-based OS for our container workloads at `http://www.ubuntu.com/cloud/tools/snappy`.
>
> **Ubuntu LXD** runs a container hypervisor and provides a path for migrating Linux-based VMs to containers with ease:
> `https://www.ubuntu.com/cloud/lxd`.
>
> **VMware Photon** is another lightweight container OS that is optimized specifically for **vSphere** and the VMware platform. It runs Docker, rkt, and Garden and also has some images that you can run on the popular public cloud providers. Refer to the following link:
> `https://vmware.github.io/photon/`.

Using the isolated nature of containers, we increase reliability and decrease the complexity of updates for each application. Now applications can be updated along with supporting libraries whenever a new container release is ready:

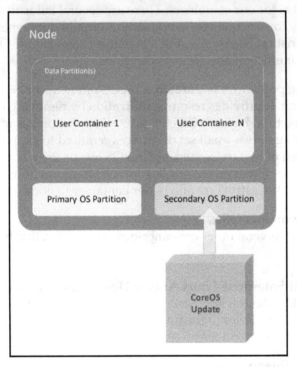

CoreOS updates

Finally, CoreOS has some added advantages in the realm of security. For starters, the OS can be updated as one whole unit instead of via individual packages (refer to the preceding figure). This avoids many issues that arise from partial updates. To achieve this, CoreOS uses two partitions—one as the active OS partition and a secondary one to receive a full update. Once updates are completed successfully, a reboot promotes the secondary partition. If anything goes wrong, the original partition is available for failback.

The system owners can also control when those updates are applied. This gives us the flexibility to prioritize critical updates while working with real-world scheduling for the more common updates. In addition, the entire update is signed and transmitted via SSL for added security across the entire process.

rkt

A central piece of the CoreOS ecosystem is its own container runtime, named rkt. As we mentioned earlier, rkt is another implementation with a specific focus on security. The main advantage of rkt is in running the engine without a daemon as root, the way Docker does today. Initially, rkt also had an advantage in establishing a trust for container images. However, recent updates to Docker have made great strides with the new **Content Trust** feature.

The bottom line is that rkt is still an implementation focused on security to run containers in production. rkt does use an image format named **ACI**, but it also supports running Docker-based images. Over the past year, rkt has undergone significant updates and is now at version 1.24.0. It has gained much momentum as a way to run Docker images securely in production.

In addition, CoreOS is working with **Intel®** to integrate the new **Intel® Virtualization Technology**, which allows containers to run in higher levels of isolation. This hardware-enhanced security allows the containers to be run inside a **Kernel-based Virtual Machine (KVM)** process providing isolation from the kernel similar to what we see with hypervisors today.

etcd

Another central piece in the CoreOS ecosystem worth mentioning is their open-source etcd project. etcd is a distributed and consistent key-value store. A RESTful API is used to interface with etcd, so it's easy to integrate with your project.

If it sounds familiar, it's because we saw this process running in `Chapter 1`, *Introduction to Kubernetes*, in the *Services running on the master* section. Kubernetes actually utilizes etcd to keep track of cluster configuration and current state. K8s uses it for the service discovery capabilities as well. For more details, refer to `https://github.com/coreos/etcd`.

Kubernetes with CoreOS

Now that we understand the benefits, let's take a look at a Kubernetes cluster using CoreOS. The documentation supports a number of platforms, but one of the easiest to spin up is AWS with the CoreOS **CloudFormation** and CLI scripts.

If you are interested in running Kubernetes with CoreOS on other platforms, you can find more details in the CoreOS documentation at
https://coreos.com/kubernetes/docs/latest/.
We can find the latest instructions for AWS at
https://coreos.com/kubernetes/docs/latest/kubernetes-on-aws.ht
ml.

You can follow the instructions mentioned earlier to spin-up Kubernetes on CoreOS. You'll need to create a key pair on AWS and also specify a region, cluster name, cluster size, and DNS to proceed.

In addition, we will need to create a DNS entry and will require a service such as **Route53** or a production DNS service. When following the instructions, you'll want to set the DNS to a domain or sub-domain, where you have permission to set up a record. We will need to update the record after the cluster is up and running and has a dynamic endpoint defined.

There you have it! We now have a cluster running CoreOS. The script creates all the necessary AWS resources, such as **Virtual Private Clouds** (**VPCs**), security groups, and IAM role. Now that the cluster is up and running we can get the endpoint with the `status` command and update our DNS record:

```
$ kube-aws status
```

Copy the entry listed next to `Controller DNS Name` and then edit your DNS records to point the domain or sub-domain you specified earlier to point to this load balancer.

If you forget which domain you specified or need to check on the configuration you can look in the generated `kubeconifg` file with your favorite editor. It will look something like this:

```
apiVersion: v1
kind: Config
clusters:
- cluster:
    certificate-authority: credentials/ca.pem
    server: https://coreos.mydomain.com
  name: kube-aws-my-coreos-cluster-cluster
contexts:
- context:
    cluster: kube-aws-my-coreos-cluster-cluster
    namespace: default
    user: kube-aws-my-coreos-cluster-admin
  name: kube-aws-my-coreos-cluster-context
users:
- name: kube-aws-my-coreos-cluster-admin
```

```
    user:
       client-certificate: credentials/admin.pem
       client-key: credentials/admin-key.pem
    current-context: kube-aws-my-coreos-cluster-context
```

In this case, the `server` line will have your domain name.

> If this is a fresh box, you will need to download `kubectl` separately as it is not bundled with `kube-aws`:
>
> **$ wget**
> **https://storage.googleapis.com/kubernetes-release/release**
> **/v1.0.6/bin/linux/amd64/kubectl**

We can now use `kubectl` to see our new cluster:

```
$ ./kubectl --kubeconfig=kubeconfig get nodes
```

We should see a single node listed with the EC2 internal DNS as the name. Note `kubeconfig`, this tells Kubernetes the path to use the configuration file for the cluster that was just created instead. This is also useful if we want to manage multiple clusters from the same machine.

Tectonic

Running Kubernetes on CoreOS is a great start, but you may find that you want a higher level of support. Enter **Tectonic**, the CoreOS enterprise offering for running Kubernetes with CoreOS. Tectonic uses many of the components we already discussed. CoreOS is the OS and both Docker and rkt runtimes are supported. In addition, Kubernetes, etcd, and flannel are packaged together to give a full stack of cluster orchestration. We discussed flannel briefly in *Chapter 3, Networking, Load Balancers, and Ingress*. It is an overlay network that uses a model similar to the native Kubernetes model, and it uses etcd as a backend.

Offering a support package similar to Red Hat, CoreOS also provides 24x7 support for the open-source software that Tectonic is built on. Tectonic also provides regular cluster updates and a nice dashboard with views for all the components of Kubernetes. **CoreUpdate** allows users to have more control of the automatic updates. In addition, it ships with modules for monitoring, SSO, and other security features.

> You can find more information and the latest instructions to install here:
> `https://coreos.com/tectonic/docs/latest/install/aws/index.html`.

Dashboard highlights

Here are some highlights of the Tectonic dashboard:

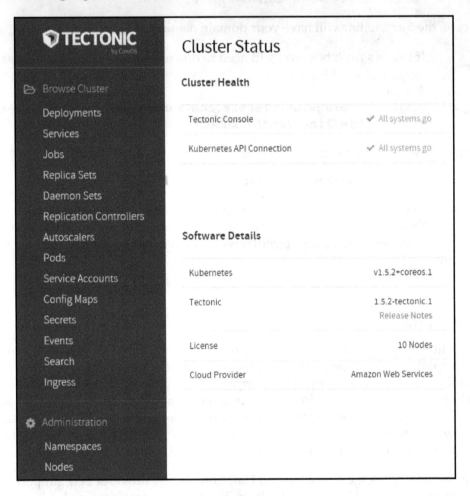

The Tectonic main dashboard

Tectonic is now generally available and the dashboard already has some nice features. As you can see in the following screenshot, we can see a lot of detail about our replication controller and can even use the GUI to scale up and down with the click of a button:

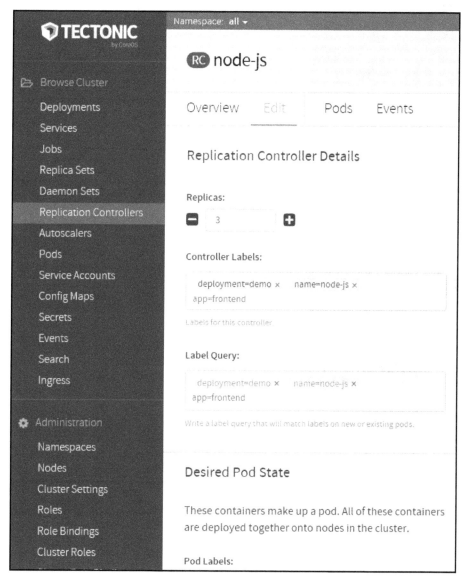

Tectonic replication controller detail

This graphic is quite large, so it's broken across two pages:

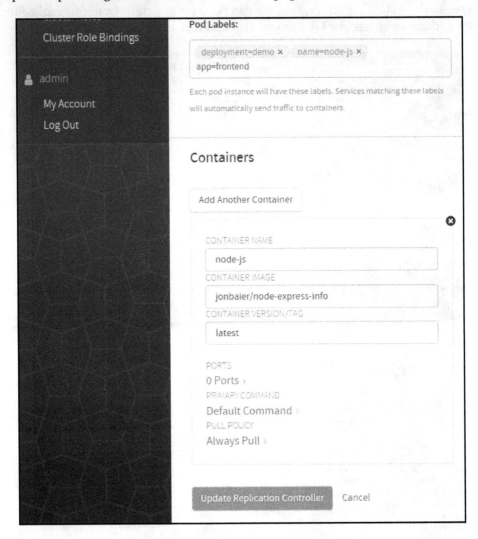

Another nice feature is the **Events** page. Here, we can watch the events live, pause, and filter based on event severity and resource type:

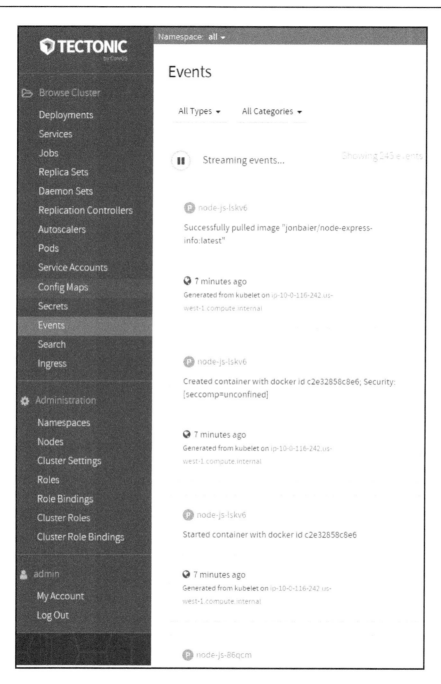

Events stream

A useful feature to browse anywhere in the dashboard system is the **Namespace:** filtering option. Simply click on the dropdown next to the word **Namespace:** at the top of any page that shows resources, and we can filter our views by namespace. This can be helpful if we want to filter out the Kubernetes system pods or just look at a particular collection of resources:

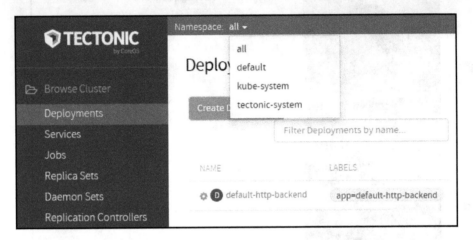

Namespace filtering

Summary

In this chapter, we looked at the emerging standards bodies in the container community and how they are shaping the technology for the better with open specifications. We also took a closer look at CoreOS, a key player in both the container and the Kubernetes community. We explored the technology they are developing to enhance and compliment container orchestration and saw first-hand how to use some of it with Kubernetes. Finally, we looked at the supported enterprise offering of Tectonic and some of the features that are available now.

In the next chapter, which is the last one, we will explore the broader Kubernetes ecosystem and the tools available to move your cluster from development and testing into full blown production.

References

1. `https://www.opencontainers.org/faq/` (Under **How broad is the mission of the OCI?**)
2. `https://github.com/opencontainers/specs/blob/master/principles.md`

12
Towards Production Ready

In this chapter, we'll look at considerations to move to production. We will also show some helpful tools and third-party projects available in the Kubernetes community at large and where you can go to get more help.

This chapter will discuss the following topics:

- Production characteristics
- The Kubernetes ecosystem
- Where to get help?

Ready for production

We walked through a number of typical operations using Kubernetes. As we saw, K8s offers a variety of features and abstractions that ease the burden of day-to-day management for container deployments.

There are many characteristics that define a production ready system for containers. The following diagram provides a high-level view of the major concerns for production ready clusters. This is by no means an exhaustive list, but it's meant to provide some solid ground heading into production operations:

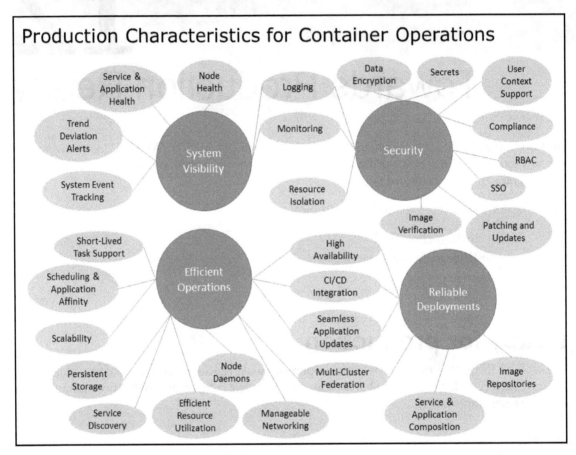

Production characteristics for container operations

We saw how the core concepts and abstractions of Kubernetes address a few of these concerns. The service abstraction has built-in service discovery and health checking at both the service and application level. We also get seamless application updates and scalability from the replication controller and deployment constructs. All the core abstractions of services, replication controllers, replica sets, and pods work with a core scheduling and affinity rulesets and give us easy service and application composition.

There is built-in support for a variety of persistent storage options, and the networking model provides manageable network operations with options to work with other third-party providers. Also, we took a brief look at CI/CD integration with some of the popular tools in the marketplace.

Furthermore, we have built-in system events tracking, and with the major cloud providers, an out-of-the-box setup for monitoring and logging. We also saw how this can be extended to third-party providers such as **StackDriver** and **Sysdig**. These services also address overall node health and proactive trend deviation alerts.

The core constructs also help us address high availability in our application and service layers. The scheduler can be used with autoscaling mechanisms to provide this at a node level. Then there is support for making the Kubernetes master itself highly available. In Chapter 9, *Cluster Federation*, we took a brief look at the new federation capabilities that which promise a multi-cloud and multi-datacenter model for the future.

We finally explored a new breed of operating systems that give us a slim base to build on and secure update mechanisms for patching and updates. The slim base, together with scheduling, can help us with efficient resource utilization. In addition, we looked at some hardened concerns and explored the image trust and verification tools available. Security is a wide topic and capabilities matrix exist for this topic alone.

Ready, set, go

While there are still some gaps, a variety of the remaining security and operation concerns are actively being addressed by third-party companies, as we will see in the following section. Going forward, the Kubernetes project will continue to evolve, and the community of projects and partners around K8s and Docker will also grow. The community is closing the remaining gaps at a phenomenal pace.

Third-party companies

Since the Kubernetes project's initial release, there has been a growing ecosystem of partners. We looked at CoreOS, Sysdig, and many others in the previous chapters, but there are a variety of projects and companies in this space. We will highlight a few that may be useful as you move towards production. This is by no means an exhaustive list and it is merely meant to provide some interesting starting points.

Private registries

In many situations, organizations will not want to place their applications and/or intellectual property in public repositories. For those cases, a private registry solution is helpful in securely integrating deployments end to end.

Google Cloud offers the **Google Container Registry** at `https://cloud.google.com/container-registry/`.

Docker has its own **Trusted Registry** offering at `https://www.docker.com/docker-trusted-registry`.

Quay.io also provides secure private registries, vulnerability scanning, and comes from the CoreOS team at `https://quay.io/`.

Google Container Engine

Google was the main author of the original Kubernetes project and is still a major contributor. Although this book has mostly focused on running Kubernetes on our own, Google is also offering a fully managed container service through the Google Cloud Platform.

Find more information on the **Google Container Engine** (**GKE**) website at `https://cloud.google.com/container-engine/`.

Kubernetes will be installed on GCE and will be managed by Google engineers. They also provide private registries and integration with your existing private networks.

Create your first GKE cluster

From the GCP console, in **Compute**, click on **Container Engine**, and then on **Container Clusters**.
If this is your first time creating a cluster, you'll have an information box in the middle of the page. Click on the **Create a container cluster** button. Choose a name for your cluster and the zone. You'll also be able to choose the machine type (instance size) for your nodes and how many nodes (cluster size) you want in your cluster. You'll also see a choice for node image, which lets you choose the base OS and machine image for the nodes themselves. The master is managed and updated by the Google team themselves. Leave **Stackdriver Logging** and

Stackdriver Monitoring checked. Click on **Create**, and in a few minutes, you'll have a new cluster ready for use.

You'll need `kubectl` that is included with the Google SDK to begin using your GKE cluster. Refer to `Chapter 1`, *Introduction to Kubernetes*, for details on installing the SDK. Once we have the SDK, we can configure `kubectl` and the SDK for our cluster using the steps outlined at `https://cloud.google.com/container-engine/docs/before-you-begin#install_kubectl`.

Azure Container Service

Another cloud-managed offering is Microsoft's **Azure Container Service** (**ACS**). ACS is really nice because it allows you to choose from industry standard tools such as Docker Swarm, Kubernetes, and Mesos. It then creates a managed cluster for you, but uses one of these tool sets as the foundation. The advantage is that you can still use the tool's native API and management tools, but leave the management of the cloud infrastructure to Azure.

Find out more about ACS at `https://azure.microsoft.com/en-us/services/container-service/`.

ClusterHQ

ClusterHQ provides a solution for bringing stateful data into your containerized applications. They provide Flocker, a tool for managing persistent storage volumes with containers, and FlockerHub which provides a storage repository for your data volumes.

Please refer to the ClusterHQ website for more information at `https://clusterhq.com/`.

Portworx

Portworx is another player in the storage space. It provides solutions for bringing persistence storage to your containers. Additionally, it has features for snapshotting, encryption, and even multi-cloud replication.

Please refer to the portworx website for more information at
`https://portworx.com/`.

Shippable

Shippable is a continuous integration, continuous deployment, and release automation platform that has built-in support for a variety of modern container environments. The product touts supporting any language with a uniform support for packaging and test.

Please refer to the Shippable website for more information at
`https://app.shippable.com/`.

Twistlock

Twistlock.io is a vulnerability and hardening tool tailor-made for containers. It provides the ability to enforce policies, hardens according to CIS standards, and scans images in any popular registry for vulnerabilities. It also provides scan integration with popular CI/CD tools and RBAC solutions for many orchestration tools such as Kubernetes.

Please refer to the Twistlock website for more information at
`https://www.twistlock.io/`.

AquaSec

AquaSec is another security tool providing a variety of features. Image scanning with popular registries, policy enforcement, user access control, and container hardening are all covered. Additionally, AquaSec has some interesting functionality in network segmentation.

Please refer to the Aqua's website for more information at
`https://www.aquasec.com/`.

Mesosphere (Kubernetes on Mesos)

Mesosphere itself is building a commercially supported product (**DCOS**) around the open-source Apache Mesos project. **Apac**he Mesos is a cluster management system that offers scheduling and resource sharing a bit like Kubernetes itself, but at a much higher level. The open-source project is used by several well-known companies, such as **Twitter** and **AirBnB**.

Get more information on the Mesos OS project and the Mesosphere offerings at these sites:

- http://mesos.apache.org/
- https://mesosphere.com/

Mesos by its nature is modular and allows the use of different frameworks for a variety of platforms. A Kubernetes framework is now available, so we can take advantage of the cluster managing in Mesos while still maintaining the useful application-level abstractions in K8s. Refer to the following link:

https://github.com/kubernetes-incubator/kube-mesos-framework

Deis

The **Deis** project provides an open-source **Platform as a Service** (**PaaS**) solution based on and around Kubernetes. This allows companies to deploy their own PaaS on-premise or on the public cloud. Deis provides tools for application composition and deployment, package management (at the pod level), and service brokering.

You can refer to the following website for more information on Deis: https://deis.com/.

OpenShift

Another PaaS solution is **OpenShift** from Red Hat. The OpenShift platform uses the Red Hat Atomic platform as a secure and slim OS for running containers. In version 3, Kubernetes has been added as the orchestration layer for all container operations on your PaaS. This is a great combination to manage PaaS installations at a large scale.

More information on OpenShift can be found at
`https://enterprise.openshift.com/`.

Where to learn more?

The Kubernetes project is an open-source effort, so there is a broad community of contributors and enthusiasts. One great resource in order to find more assistance is the Kubernetes **Slack** channel:

`http://slack.kubernetes.io/`

There is also a Kubernetes group on Google groups. You can join it at

`https://groups.google.com/forum/#!forum/kubernetes-users.`

If you enjoyed this book, you can find more of my articles, how-tos, and various musings on my blogs and Twitter page:

- `https://medium.com/@grizzbaier`
- `https://twitter.com/grizzbaier`

Summary

In this final chapter, we left a few breadcrumbs to guide you on your continued journey with Kubernetes. You should have a solid set of production characteristics to get you started. There is a wide community in both the Docker and Kubernetes world. There are also a few additional resources that we provided if you need a friendly face along the way.

By now, we have seen the full spectrum of container operations with Kubernetes. You should be more confident in how Kubernetes can streamline the management of your container deployments and how you can plan to move containers off the developer laptops onto production servers. Now get out there and start shipping your containers!

Index

A

advanced services
  about 82, 84
  cross-node proxy 89
  custom addressing 100
  custom load balancing 86, 87, 88
  custom ports 90, 91
  external services 84, 85
  Ingress 92, 93, 96, 97, 98
  internal services 85, 86
  migrations 98, 99
  multicluster 98, 99
  multiple ports 91
AirBnB 263
Amazon Web Services (AWS) 16
Apache 12
Apache Mesos 263
API call security
  about 228
  Admission Controller loop 228
  admission controllers 229
  authentication 228
  authentication plugin 229
  authorization 228
  authorization plugin 229
  node communication, securing 228
appc specification 244
application scheduling
  about 71
  example 71, 73, 74, 75
applications
  autoscaling 118, 119, 120
  cutovers 117, 118
  releases 115, 118
  scaling up 111
  testing 114

  updates 112, 113, 114
AquaSec
  about 226, 262
  URL 262
architecture, Kubernetes
  about 45, 46
  master 47
  node 47
Attribute-Based Access Control (ABAC) 229
AWS Command Line Interface (CLI)
  reference 33
AWS Elastic Block Store (EBS) 157
Azure Container Service (ACS)
  about 38, 261
  reference 261

B

balanced design, networking 81, 82
Batch API 139
Border Gateway Protocol (BGP) 81
Borg 16
bridged network 79
built-in monitoring
  about 184
  dashboards, customizing 189, 190, 191, 192, 193
  Heapster 186

C

cAdvisor
  about 185
  reference 185
calico project
  URL 41
Canal
  about 81
  URL 81

Certificate Authority (CA) cluster 228
Clair 225
Cloud Foundry 244
Cloud Native Computing Foundation (CNCF)
  about 243
  reference 243
cloud volumes
  about 151
  AWS Elastic Block Store 157
  GCE persistent disks 151
CloudFormation 247
cluster, setup process
  about 38
  cluster, joining 42
  kubeadm, installing 39
  kubelet, installing 39
  master, setting up 40
  networking 41
  nodes, joining 40
cluster
  autoscaling 121
  scaling 121
  scaling manually 127
  scaling up, on AWS 125, 126
  scaling up, on GCE 122, 123, 124, 125
ClusterHQ
  about 261
  URL 261
command line 26
Common Vulnerabilities and Exploits (CVEs) 226
ConfigMaps 218
Container Networking Interface (CNI) 78
container networking
  Canal 81
  Docker 79
  Docker user-defined networks 79
  Flannel 80
  Project Calico 81
  Weave 80
container OSes
  Red Hat Enterprise Linux Atomic Host 245
  Ubuntu LXD 245
  Ubuntu Snappy 245
  VMware Photon 245
container security

basics 223
  containers, keeping contained 224
  orchestration security 224, 225
  resource exhaustion 224
containers
  about 10, 12
  advantages 13
  Continuous Integration/Continuous Deployment,
    advantages 13
  overview 10
  resource utilization 14
Content Trust feature 247
content-agnostic 243
continuous delivery pipeline
  Kubernetes, integrating with 167
Continuous Deployment
  advantages 13
Continuous Integration
  advantages 13
Contrib 185
control groups (cgroups) 10
core constructs
  about 48
  container's afterlife 50
  labels 50
  pods 48
  replica sets 52
  replication controllers (RCs) 52
  services 51
CoreOS
  about 245, 246
  etcd 247
  rkt 247
CoreUpdate 249
CPU-shares 71
cross-node proxy 89
custom addressing 100
custom load balancing 86, 87, 88
custom ports 90, 91

D

DaemonSets 143
Deis
  about 263
  URL 263

denial-of-service attacks 10
Deployments
  about 130
  autoscaling 137, 138, 139
  history 135
  rollouts 132, 133, 134
  scaling 131
  updates 132, 134
development environment
  example, setting up 110
Docker CE
  URL 168
Docker user-defined networks
  bridge driver 79
  Macvlan driver 80
  overlay driver 80
Docker
  about 45
  bridged network 79
  host network 79
  none network 79
DockerHub
  URL 168
Domain Name System (DNS) 47, 101
Durable Task plugin
  URL 175

E

EC2 instances
  reference 39
Elasticsearch 35, 195
external services 84

F

Fabric8
  about 181
  URL 181
federation
  about 211
  clusters, adding 215
  contexts 212
  federated configurations 218, 219, 220, 221
  federated resources 215, 216, 217, 218
  federation control plane, initializing 214
  new clusters 213

  other federated resources 221
  setting up 212
Flannel 80
FluentD 195

G

GCE persistent disks
  about 151
  creating 151, 153, 154, 155, 157
gcloud SDK
  installing 17
Google Cloud Logging 194
Google Cloud Platform (GCP)
  account, configuring 17
Google Compute Engine (GCE) 16
Google Container Engine (GKE) 38
  about 260
  reference 260
Google Container Registry
  reference 260
Grafana 24, 186
Gulp.js
  about 168
  example 168, 169, 170, 172
  prerequisites 168

H

health checks
  about 63
  implementing 63, 65, 66, 67
  life cycle hooks 69
  TCP checks 68
Heapster
  about 26, 185
  exploring 186, 187
  reference 185
Horizontal Pod Autoscaler (HPA) 118, 137

I

image repositories
  about 225
  continuous vulnerability scanning 225, 226
  image signing and verification 226, 227
industrial-grade delivery 244
InfluxDB 26, 186

infrastructure-agnostic 244
Ingress 92, 93, 95, 97
internal services 85, 86
iptables 89

J

Jenkins Master 179
Jenkins
  about 168
  Kubernetes plugin, used for 172
  prerequisites 172
  URL 172
job controllers 52
jobs
  about 139, 140
  parallel jobs 142
  scheduled jobs 142
  types 141

K

Kernel-based Virtual Machine (KVM) process 247
Kibana 35
KOPs
  URL 37
kube-aws
  URL 37
kube-proxy 47, 51, 52, 89
kubeadm
  installing 39
  reference 39
kubelet
  about 47
  installing 39
Kubernetes cluster security
  about 227
  additional considerations 237
  API call, securing 228
  Pod security policies and contexts 230
Kubernetes cluster
  command line 26
  environment, setting up 16, 18
  Grafana 24
  services, executing on minions 30
  services, running on master 27
  tearing down 32

UI, exploring 22, 24
Kubernetes plugin
  configuring 176, 178, 179, 180, 181
  for Jenkins 172
  installing 173, 174, 175
  URL 175
Kubernetes Slack channel
  reference 264
Kubernetes
  application, creating 52, 53, 54, 55, 56, 57, 58
  architecture 45
  history 15
  integrating, with continuous delivery pipeline 167
  reference 16
  with CoreOS 247, 248

L

labels
  about 50, 59
  using 60, 61, 62
LevelDB 185
long-task pods 140

M

master server
  creating 20
master, Kubernetes architecture
  about 47
  scheduler 47
memory limit flags 71
Mesosphere 263
metrics 185
microservices
  about 14
  future challenges 15
migrations 98
minions 21
monitoring operations
  about 183
  GCE (StackDriver) 196
  maturing 196
  system monitoring, with Sysdig 198
  with Prometheus 208
multi-cloud infrastructure 222
multicluster 98

multiple ports 91
multitenancy
  about 102
  limits 103, 105, 106, 107

N

namespaces 10
Network Address Translation (NAT) 78
networking
  about 77
  balanced design 81
  container networking 79
  options 78
Nginx 12
node 21, 26, 47
node package manager (npm)
  about 168
  URL 168
node selection 144
NodeJS 168
nodeSelectors 144, 145, 146, 147

O

Omega 16
Open Container Initiative (OCI) 241, 242
OpenSCAP 226
OpenShift
  about 263
  URL 263
orchestration 14

P

PagerDuty 205
parallel jobs 142
persistent storage
  about 149, 150
  cloud volumes 151
  PersistentVolumes 158
  storage options 158
  StorageClass 159
  temporary disks 150, 151
  volumes 150
PersistentVolumes 158
placeholder 78
Platform as a Service (PaaS) 263

plugins
  URL 41
pod infrastructure container 78
Pod security policies and context
  about 230
  beta APIs, enabling 230, 231, 232
  clean up 237
  pod, creating with PodSecurityContext 236, 237
  PodSecurityPolicy, creating 232
pods
  about 26, 48
  example 48, 50
PodSecurityPolicy
  creating 232, 234, 235
port mapping 79
Portworx
  about 261
  URL 261
private registries 260
production
  characteristics 257, 258, 259
Project Calico 81
project ID
  URL 17
Prometheus
  about 208
  features 208
  reference 208
providers
  cluster, creating with alternative method 37
  cluster, resetting 36
  cluster, setup process 38
  kube-up parameters, modifying 37
  working with 32

Q

Quay.io
  about 226, 260
  reference 226, 260

R

RBAC (Role-Based Access Control) mode 229
Red Hat Linux 12
replica sets 52, 62
replication controllers (RCs) 52

resource usage 107
Route53 248
runC implementation 244

S

scheduled jobs 142
secrets 238
sensitive application data
  securing 238
service discovery 101
services 51
Shippable
  about 262
  URL 262
SNS (Simple Notification Service) 205
Software-defined Networking (SDN) 78
sparkline 192
SSH (Secure Shell) 57
StackDriver
  about 196, 259
  alerts 197, 198
  GCE monitoring, signing up 196
standard container specification 243
standard operations 243
standards
  importance 241
StatefulSets
  about 159, 160
  stateful example 160, 161, 162, 164, 165
StorageClass 159
Sysdig 259
Sysdig Capture 205
Sysdig Cloud
  about 198, 200
  Detailed views 200
  Metrics 203
  reference 199
  Topology views 200, 202
system monitoring, with Sysdig
  about 198
  alerting 203, 204, 205

csysdig command-line UI 206, 207
Sysdig Cloud 198, 199
sysdig command line 205, 206

T

Tectonic
  about 249
  dashboard highlights 250, 251, 252, 254
third-party companies
  about 259
  AquaSec 262
  Azure Container Service (ACS) 261
  ClusterHQ 261
  Deis 263
  Google Container Engine 260
  Mesosphere 263
  OpenShift 263
  Portworx 261
  Shippable 262
  Twistlock.io 262
Trusted Registry
  reference 260
Twistlock.io
  about 262
  URL 262
Twitter 263

U

Ubuntu 12
union filesystems 11

V

Virtual Extensible LAN (VXLAN) 80
virtual IP (VIP) 83
virtual machine (VM) 14
Virtual Private Cloud (VPC) 34
Virtual Private Clouds (VPCs) 248

W

Weave 80

www.ingramcontent.com/pod-product-compliance
Lightning Source LLC
Chambersburg PA
CBHW060523060326
40690CB00017B/3370